Physique and Character

Physique and Character

An Investigation of the Nature of Constitution and of the Theory of Temperament

By

ERNST KRETSCHMER

Professor of Psychiatry and Neurology in the University of Marburg

Second Edition Revised
with an Appendix by

E. MILLER, M.R.C.S., L.R.C.P., D.P.M.

Psychiatrist West End Hospital for Nervous Diseases
Author of " Types of Mind and Body," etc.

COOPER SQUARE PUBLISHERS, INC.
NEW YORK
1970

Translated by
W. J. H. SPROTT, M.A.

Originally Published 1936
Published by Cooper Square Publishers, Inc.
59 Fourth Avenue, New York, N. Y. 10003
Standard Book No. 8154-0332-1
Library of Congress Catalog Card No. 73-119165

Printed in the United States of America

CONTENTS

LIST OF ILLUSTRATIONS

PREFACE TO THE FIRST EDITION

WHOEVER believes in the progress of scientific knowledge, and experiences the swinging backwards and forwards of fundamental beliefs in the course of a century, is prone to picture scientific development as proceeding in a kind of spiral fashion. But those who are less confident only notice the changes of theory, and are pained by the narrow limits of the possibilities of obtaining knowledge, and these, with unwarrantable pessimism, also make use of the analogy of a pendulum, which swings now right, now left, but for them it never reaches a higher and more satisfactory position. Anyone who knows about the great problems in philosophy and psychology realizes that this is the state of affairs; the biologist and pathologist will be aware of it if he reflects on the age of Neovitalism and Antidarwinism; the Psychiatrist stands in the midst of an enormous variety of changes of attitude towards the ultimate relationship between body and soul, brought about by the latest discoveries in all branches of science in so far as they have a bearing on pathological events. Empirical science may with equanimity leave out of account such swingings of the pendulum in the often premature theoretical statement of the problem, but it may be forced to seek advice and methodological assistance from neighbouring fields of inquiry. Thus, after decades of laborious and successful collecting and arranging, clinical investigation has more then ever to call genealogists and biologists to its aid; introspective psychology ventures on a subtle analysis of the intelligibility of what is, *prima facie*, unintelligible, and in the distorted caricature of psychic anomaly it finds the corner-stone for a plausible psychology of healthy and diseased alike, the basis for a characterology which may unite theory and practice. Their study points towards the problems of heredity; and, then again, these problems find their answer in the investigation of morphological processes. And so the subject which is dealt with in a very general manner in this book emerges of itself—the problem of the relation between human form and

ix

human nature. An intuitive glance stated the question, an exact method gave the empirical facts, and psychological technique unravelled the significance of strange phenomena of being ; an agile pen gave to what was observed the form of its explanation.

I do not doubt that the history of psychiatry will regard the work of Kraepelin on the two classes, manic-depressive madness and dementia præcox, as one of the most important achievements of our medical science. In this doctrine I see, however often actual practice may leave us in diagnostic doubt—an indestructible advance of psychiatric knowledge and capacity. Kraepelin's masterly delineation of the clinical forms of diseases has left only a few additions to be made in the last two decades. A deeper understanding of the symptoms and the individual contents in schizophrenic processes has been opened for us by Bleuler and those who have followed in his footsteps. A great deal that was not clear, and apparently contradictory, seemed to him to require an understanding of the character and history of the pre-psychotic personality and its ancestry. On such connections the clinic at Tübingen, which in its system follows Kraepelin in all essentials, has laid special stress for about a decade and a half. Thus Edward Reiss's book : *Uber die Konstitutionelle Verstimmung und das manisch-depressive Irresein* (1910), shows our attempts to lay bare the relation of disposition to psychosis by means of the orthodox methods of clinical investigation. Other workers have been experimenting in the same direction (on paranoia, paranoiac disposition, hysteria, etc.). Theories of heredity, whose methodical elaboration in the sphere of psychiatry we owe to Rüdin in particular and the recent work of H. Hoffmann, force the clinician to direct his gaze far more than before to the distant past. The theory of internal secretions bring morphology and chemistry closer together. And so the time is ripe for an attack on a field of inquiry which so far has never been brought in the same way, or with such accuracy, into the psychiatric forum : the construction of the human frame is considered in connection with the psychic adnormalities and diseases which Kraepelin's master hand has dragged out of the bewildering chaos of clinical phenomena, and separated off into two great form-groups. But there is more in it than this : when Kretschmer, looking out over the walls of the clinic, saw before him the manifold phenomena of everyday life, and when he brought what had been genealogically established to bear on his investigations, together with historical information, he found that the boundaries between sickness and health became more and more blurred; the circular type of personality passes, without any observable leap, over to the " cyclothymic personality " ; the schizophrenic psychopath finds his abortive form in the " schizoid," and in the healthy " schizothyme " his characterological rudiment, or rather his broad biological frame.   And these two great types of human nature and disease have physical peculiarities which, although they are not always obvious at first sight, nevertheless are startling when they occur with their typical characteristics : such peculiarities are mensurable, and of great significance for the understanding of the whole biological process.   The biologico-clinical study branches out into the general problem of the correlation between physical form and psychic nature, of which we may follow the two largest groups (cyclothymes and schizothymes) in their more extreme culturally important forms into the realm of history.   And so the book is not directed merely towards the psychiatrist, but to all who are interested in psychology, and to whom the grouping of humanity in types seems an important branch of empirical investigation.

R. GAUPP.

Tübingen, January 1921.

PREFACE TO THE SECOND EDITION

WE may here collect the facts and surmises which have turned up in connection with our subject in the short interval ; dealing only with such workers as have carried out careful confirmatory examination or have added large series of facts out of their own experience.

Hitherto there has been confirmatory work, as far as the problem of physique is concerned, done by Sioli, Klott, and Meyer, in the clinic at Bonn.[1] The result of their investigations was that they recognized the validity of the types of physique described in this book, and also their biological relation to the two classes of psychoses ; the investigators also came to the same conclusion with regard to the schizoids and cycloids. This confirmation is important, because it was obtained from a people so unlike the Schwabians as the Rheinlanders.

A little work on schizophrenia and physique, which had nothing whatever to do with our inquiries, was published shortly after this book by Beringer and Düser [2] (Heidelberg clinic). Since this work was carried on from a different point of view, and with quite different terminological differentiations, their results can only conditionally be compared with ours. The more remarkable is the appreciable number of identical and similar results in the two publications : Beringer and Düser also establish the presence of Eunuchoidism and Feminism (and particularly feminine disposition of fat), in a small number of their exclusively male patients ; they mention the prevalence of abnormal conditions of the sexual glands and genitalia, mainly in the direction of hypoplasia, mixed with a few cases of hyperplasia ; further, the prevailingly weak secondary-hair of the schizophrenes ; and finally the frequent occurrence of abnormal sexual impulses, especially in the direction of weakness of impulse. Apart from these facts, which

---

[1] *Report on Rheinische Psychiaterversammlung*, 19, xi, 21.
[2] Beringer and Düser, " Ueber Schizophrenia und Körperbau " (*Zeitschr. f. d. ges. Neur. u. Psych.*, 69, 12, 1921).

are particularly interesting from the point of view of the endocrine glands, and which are in close agreement with our own results, other bodily characteristics are only briefly sketched. All the same, the group which is described by Beringer and Düser as the *weak-infantile* type is undoubtedly a border-line example of the same type which we have described as the asthenic, and the infantile-hypoplastic. Similar observations must lie behind a group of " pronouncedly masculine faces " as behind the group we describe as " athletics," and the " undifferentiated plump " remind us, in the short description which Beringer gives, of such forms as are described in this book when we deal with dysplastic fat-forms, and also sub-classes of athletics. In disagreement with our experience, their work mentions the more common occurrence of considerable layers of fat among schizophrenes.

Bleuler [1] has dealt with the psychological part of the book in two publications ; in summing up, he says that " only a few details in it do not agree with his experience ; he had already known all the other individual facts for a long time, and had even thought of them together and demonstrated such relations."

We may also mention that many points have emerged which touch on the results of Rüdin and Kahn, who are studying the constitution at the Münich Forschungsanstalt. H. Hoffmann's book [2] is the connecting link between the old and valuable observations of Rüdin's institute and those of our clinic.

Kahn [3] is the last to demonstrate the types of schizoid personality in accordance with his own investigations into the heredity of schizophrenic families, and has recognized the " psychæsthetic proportions " as being what is psychologically common ; he also develops very valuable views as to the variety of the hereditary emergence of the schizoid and the schizophrenic " process-psychoses."

And now a few words as to the critical objections to the book. It has been suggested that we should exchange the expression " cycloid " for another, because it includes many cases without periodical variations of emotion. It seems to me that one can

[1] E. Bleuler, " Körperliche u. geistige Konstitutionen " (*Naturuissenschaften*, 9, 753, 1921) ; and Bleuler, Review of *Körperbau und Character* (*Münch. Med. Wochenschr.*, 33, 1057, 1921).
[2] H. Hoffmann, *Die Nachkommenschaft bei endogenen Psychosen.*, Berlin, 1921 (in Rüdin's *Studien über Vererbung*).
[3] E. Kahn, " Bermerkung zur Frage des Schizoids " Jahresversammlung des Ver. bayr. Psych. (*Zentralbl. f. d. ges. Neurol. v. Psychol.*, 26, 567, 1921).

use it quite reasonably in this derivative sense, just as we still say "melancholy" without thinking about "black gall" every time.

It has been thought improbable that there should be only two types of human nature. But we never said there were (cf. p. 177). This book is only a preliminary canter : by means of patient co-operation on the part of others it may perhaps be possible to divide up the types, which we have differentiated for the meantime, into sub-groups, and to discover new ones to add to them.

The numerous mixed forms, alloys, crosses, and a-typical examples have been brought forward as proof against the setting-up of the types. But in human inheritance, which is continually mixing together various dispositions, we must expect that from the very outset. If, in research into botanical heredity twice as many pink sweet-peas occurred as pure red or pure white, no one would use the pink flowers as proof against the red or white ones. The only question is this : are there statistical relational-frequencies between certain forms of physique and certain psychical dispositions ? Here, in numerical relational-frequencies lie the fixed, provable facts, not in individual cases, which may be typical or a-typical.

Now for another technical remark. We think it obvious that psychiatric measurement of the body should keep as closely as possible to the anthropological methods which are in use. The technique which we have sketched out here varies from it only where such variations are demanded by the requirements of practical psychiatry.

In particular, the instruments must be reduced to a minimum, having regard to the restless environment in which the work is done, and individual points of measurement are suited to the peculiarity of our material, which is composed of patients. This is quite sufficient for practical diagnosis. But for more subtle calculations and comparisons one would have to base one's experiments on exact anthropological technique, with complete sets of instruments in accordance with the text-book of Martin.

We have improved many details in the text of this edition, and additions have been made, without any fundamental alterations.

E. KRETSCHMER.

Tübingen, February 1922.

NOTE TO THE SECOND ENGLISH EDITION

INTEREST in Kretschmer's now classical work on *Physique and Character* makes it necessary to go to Press with a new edition while the subject is still in a transitional state. There are now four or five thousand recorded cases published in all countries with regard to the main hypothesis of the work, but although some serious criticisms and modifications have been made by various observers, its broad classifications are generally accepted.

A review of the literature will bring home to any student that the study of human Morphology in relation to mental illness has had a normal line of development. That is to say, while Kretschmer's fundamental views are still held, the complexity of the subject has grown, because the manifold factors involved in type distinctions have been more clearly realized even if they have not been more clearly understood.

In his most recent work, Kretschmer has made certain modifications in his terminology. For example, in place of the term Asthenic, which implies certain physiological peculiarities in addition to those denoted by the physique, the more morphological term Leptosome has been substituted. Furthermore, a term introduced by Bleuler, " syntonic," is now used, and clearly defined. It is intended to convey a description of the harmoniously balanced individual without violent oscillations of mood and free from all schizoid features or reactions. The hypothetical normal person would therefore be regarded as the true syntonic, the cyclothymic and the schizothymic as the divergencies from this Norm.

Merely to concern ourselves with morphological differentiæ, however, would leave the subject clinically barren, although still fruitful to the student of pure anthropometry. But, whereas Kretschmer was dealing in the first instance with the subject of temperament in more or less general terms, he has to some extent found it necessary to restate his problem in terms of fundamental psycho-physical structure. In the present edition, therefore, though the original text has through-out been retained, with minor corrections, in the form in which it is familiar to a generation of students, an Appendix has been added to cover the latest contributions to the experi-mental psychology of Type and the more detailed discussion of temperament.

This Appendix is the work of Dr E. Miller, whose pioneer survey of the whole problem, *Types of Mind and Body*, was published in 1925, and who has since been conducting a series of investigations in this field which will later be printed *in extenso*.

In 1928 a translation of Kretschmer's *Men of Genius* was added to the Library, and to this volume, as well as to the supplementary researches of W. A. Willemse in his *Constitution Types in Delinquency*, those interested in the further develop-ment of the Kretschmerian technique may also be referred.

C. K. O.

February 1936.

PART I

PHYSIQUE

CÆSAR :   Let me have men about me that are fat ;
                Sleek-headed men, and such as sleep o' nights :
                Yond Cassius has a lean and hungry look ;
                He thinks too much : such men are dangerous.
ANTONY : Fear him not, Cæsar ; he is not dangerous ;
                He is a noble Roman, and well given.
CÆSAR :   Would he were fatter ! . . .

Julius Cæsar—SHAKESPEARE.

A

PART I

PHYSIQUE

In the mind of the man-in-the-street, the devil is usually lean and has a thin beard growing on a narrow chin, while the fat devil has a strain of good-natured stupidity. The intriguer has a hunch-back and a slight cough. The old witch shows us a withered hawk-like face. Where there is brightness and jollity we see the fat knight Falstaff—red-nosed and with shining pate. The peasant woman with a sound knowledge of human nature is undersized, tubby, and stands with her arms akimbo. Saints look abnormally lanky, long-limbed, of penetrating vision, pale, and godly.

To put it shortly. The virtuous and the devil must have a pointed nose, while the comic must have a fat one. What are we to say to all this? At first only this much : It may be that phenomena which the phantasy of the people has crystallized into the tradition of centuries, are objective documents of folk-psychology— jottings from the observation of mankind, worthy, perhaps, of a glance even from the eyes of the experimenter.

But this is beside the point. Our investigations do not proceed from such general reflections, but from the special problem of psychiatry, and only eventually, by a certain inner necessity, ever making wider circles, do they stretch out over the boundaries of that study into general Psychology and the realm of Biology. It seems advisable, in the presentation of the results of our inquiry, to choose the order in which they have appeared. On the psychological side, then, we have in the first place the advantage of already possessing, in the two great psycho-pathological types of manic-depressive or ' circular '[1]

---

[1] We use the expression ' circular ' throughout this book to stand for the manic-depressive type in the widest sense of the word, on account of its great linguistic advantages.

3

insanity and schizophrenia (dementia præcox), which have been distinguished by Kraepelin, something which is fairly tangible and with which we can set to work.

As soon as we have worked out the corresponding physiological types by the aid of these psycho-pathological types, we shall see at once that these bodily types not only correspond to the two psycho-pathological types, but that they have far more extensive relations to widespread normal-psychological types of temperament ; which, on their side again, have close psychological and hereditary connections with the psycho-pathological types from which we started. Anyone, therefore, who ventures on this book without special knowledge of medicine, but with only psychological interests, will nevertheless not be able to avoid becoming involved in that part of the book which deals with psychiatry, because the whole work emerged from investigations in psychiatry and can be understood only from that point of view.

CHAPTER I

METHOD

INVESTIGATION into the build of the body must be made an exact branch of medical science. For it is one of the master-keys to the problem of the constitution—that is to say, to the fundamental question of medical and psychiatric and clinical work. Good isolated observations on the part of medical practitioners of the past do certainly exist : they remain unused. Belle-lettristic *aperçus* of a physiognomical nature do not get us much further. There is nothing for it : we must plod along the bitter, wearisome road of systematic verbal description and inventory of the whole of the outer body from head to foot ; wherever possible, measuring it with calipers and tape-measures, photographing, and drawing. And not only must we do this in a few interesting cases, but we must take hundreds of observations, using every patient we can get hold of, and for each must we make out the same complete scheme. Above all, we must learn again to use our eyes, to see at a glance, and to observe without a microscope or a laboratory.

For the purposes of such an investigation the following scheme was worked out :

CONSTITUTION SCHEME

e :

ssion :

Day of examination :
Diagnosis :
Special type of disease:

I. FACE AND SKULL

: large   medium   small
   relation to head)
   long   medium   short
   narrow   ,,   wide
   delicately boned   ,,   coarsely boned
   sagging   ,,   firm
   thin   ,,   fat
   sharply cut   ,,   soft, plastic (surface)
   thin-skinned   ,,   thick-skinned
   shiny   ,,   dull
   fresh red   ,,   pale

yellowish ; sallow ; brown ; congested ; dark red ; bluish ; pasty ; dirty ; smooth ; tight ; wrinkled ; creased ; faded ; hollow ; washed out ; bloated ; well-marked blood-vessels

Eyes : large   medium   small
   outstanding   ,,   deep-set
   shining   ,,   dull
   blue ; green ; grey ; brown ; black
   Upper orbital frame : overhanging ; high ; sharp ; blunt

5

I. FACE AND SKULL—*Continued*

Nose : large   medium   small
long   ,,   short
thin   ,,   thick (cartilaginous part)
narrow   ,,   broad (bony part)
pointed   ,,   blunt
pulled forward   ,,   snubbed
pale   ,,   red
flat-saddled   ,,   deep-saddled
curved   straight   turned up
jutting out   medium   deep-set
strong outline   ,,   weak outline
Root of the nose : well-defined ; weakly defined

Mouth: large   medium   small
firm outline   ,,   weak outline

Lips : thin   ,,   full
turning inwards   ,,   pushed outwards
flabby   ,,   firm
open   ,,   shut
pale   ,,   red
Upper lip : long ; short ; trunk-formed ; pursed ; normal

Cheek-bone : strongly developed medium weakly developed
outstanding   ,,   not outstanding

Lower Jaw : large   ,,   small
high   ,,   low
wide   ,,   narrow
sticking out   ,,   receding
sharp curve   ,,   flat curve
coarse   ,,   delicate

Chin : well-modelled   ,,   weakly modelled
cone-shaped

Larynx : projecting   medium not projecting

Teeth: large   ,,   small
regular   ,,   irregular
sound   ,,   diseased

Gums: steep   ,,   flat

Ears : large   medium   small
sticking out   ,,   lying flat
flat   ,,   rolled
thin   ,,   thick
in-grown   ,,   free

Fore-head : steep   ,,   sloping
high   ,,   low
domed   ,,   flat
broad   ,,   narrow
cornered   ,,   rounded
well-defined   ,,   weakly def
Supercillar arch : strongly developed ; ium ; weakly developed
Frontal protuberance : strongly devel medium ; weakly developed
Glabella : broad ; medium ; narrow

Profile: straight ; weakly arched ; strongly ar angular
sharp ; weak ; indefinite
strongly projecting ; well-developed ; veloped ; stunted

Frontal : broad shield-shaped ; flat five-corr steep egg-shaped

Outline : shortened egg-shaped ; childish oval; cornered ; uncharacteristic

Facial form : masculine ; feminine ; too young ; too suitable to age

Cranium : large   medium small
(in relation to head)
long   ,,   short
broad   ,,   narrow
high   ,,   low
abnormally high top
bladder-shaped cranium ; *caput quadr* tower-skull

Back of head : projecting   rounded   steep
Occipit : well-developed ; medium ; w developed

II. PHYSIQUE

large   medium   small
round   fat   thick-set
broad-shouldered   lanky   slim
long-limbed   short-limbed
infantile ; masculine ; feminine ; senile

Poise : limp   medium   stiff
bent   ,,   upright

Bone structure : delicate   ,,   coarse

Joints : narrow   ,,   wide

Muscu-lature : thin   medium   thick
flabby   ,,   firm
Muscle relief : well-defined ; medium ; w defined

Fat uphol-stery : thin   medium   fat
distribution ; infantile ; masculine ; femi circumscribed islands of fat

Head : large   medium   small
(relation to trunk)
free   ,,   deep-set

II. PHYSIQUE—*Continued*

ong | medium | short
thin | ,, | thick
long | ,, | short
thin | ,, | thick
long | ,, | short
thin | ,, | thick
O-legs ; X-legs
large | ,, | small
long | ,, | short
narrow | ,, | wide
delicate fingers | ,, | coarse fingers
flabby | ,, | firm
soft | ,, | bony
finger-tips : pointed ; medium ; flat
large | medium | small
long | ,, | short
wide | ,, | narrow
flat-footed ; arched ; toe-proportion
ers : narrow | medium | wide
sloping | ,, | level
outstanding | ,, | near together
bent (deltoid inner frame)

Chest : flat medium vaulted deep
long ,, short
narrow ,, broad
phthisic, emphysematous type
pigeon-chested ; cobbler-chested ; concave

Stomach : thick medium thin
firm ,, flabby
compact fat stomach ; small pot-bellied ;
loose-bellied ; wasted

Spine : firm medium loose
lordose scoliose kyphose
neck- chest- loin-spinal-cord

Pelvis : Skeleton : well-developed ; medium ; weakly
developed
Fat : well-developed ; medium ; weakly
developed
well-built ; masculine ; feminine ; infantile ;
flat
Flexure of the groin :
steep medium flat
well-defined ,, weakly defined

III. SURFACE OF THE BODY

(A) Skin

thin | medium | thick
delicate | ,, | coarse
flabby | ,, | stretched
elastic | ,, | unelastic
shiny | ,, | rough
transparent | ,, | opaque
t : strong | ,, | weak

ous

on : strong medium weak
Eczema ; acne ; ferunculous ; mucous-mem-
brane pigment

(B) Blood-vessels

lood-vessels : clearly visible ; dimly visible ;
invisible : in face, on hands and feet, on body
Dermography : strong ; medium ; weak
Vaso-motor-system of head ,, ,, ,,
Head : bluish ; dark-red ; medium ; pale
Hands : ,, ,, ,, ,,
Feet : ,, ,, ,, ,,
General colour of skin : dark-red ; medium ;
pale
Hands and feet : damp ; medium ; dry
Body : ,, ,, ,,
Hands and feet : warm ; medium ; cold
Body : ,, ,, ,,
Sweat of arm-pits
s : strong ; medium ; thin and delicate
hardened ; coarse ; soft
winding ; standing out

Pulse : .....beat, strong ; medium ; weak ; easily
excited ; sluggish
full ; tense ; respiratory irregularity ; extra-
systole
Gräfe. Aschner

Veins : outstanding ; visible ; invisible
varicose

(C) Hair

fair brown black grey white

Head-hair : strong medium weak
(relation to sex)
Brows : strong medium weak
Beard : ,, ,, ,,
Trunk : ,, ,, ,,
Arms : ,, ,, ,,
Legs : ,, ,, ,,
Genitalia : ,, ,, ,,
Arm-pits : ,, ,, ,,
Head-hair : long medium short
average limit
receding from forehead ; temples ; nape
growing into ,, ,, ,,
Angle of
Temples : indented medium covered
horizontal frontal boundary
delicate hairs medium coarse hairs
smooth bushy brushy
sleek wavy curly
Baldness : on forehead ; temples ; back of
head ; separated ; not separated ; shiny-
dull ; ' moth-eaten ' ; incomplete

III. SURFACE OF THE BODY—*Continued*

Brows: Intermingled : at forehead ; on temples
      (distance apart — cm.)
    bushy   medium   sleek
    broad   ,,   narrow

Beard : soft   bushy   brush-like
    sleek   wavy   curly
    narrow   medium   broad
    growing well into face ; into neck
    even ; irregular
    predominating : moustache ; chin-beard ;
        cheek-beard
    female-beard

Pubes : masculine—   feminine-limits
    long   medium   short
    fine strand   ,,   coarse strands

Trunk : lying down   ,,   upright
    long   ,,   short

Lanugo : nape of neck, spine, chest, arms, legs

Hair on a-typical places

IV. GLANDS AND INTESTINES

Testicles :   large   medium   small

Genitalia :   ,,   ,,   ,,

Thyroid gland :   ,,   ,,
    Goitre : thick ; soft ; smooth ; knotty ;
        pulsating

Lymph-glands : normal ; numerous ; rare ; la..
    small ; hard ; soft

Mammary-glands : large; small; masculine; femin..
    firm ; flabby ; fat ; well-formed
    Nipples : well-developed ; badly developed

Internal diseases :

V. MEASUREMENT

Height : Weight (naked)
    (assimilation of food ?)
Circumference : chest ; stomach (to top of groin)
    hips (to top of trochanter)
    fore-arm 1 ; hand (over roots of fingers with-
    out thumb) 1 ; calf 1
Length : legs (upper symphysis—base) ; arms (lateral
    shoulder-joint to top of middle finger)
Breadth : shoulder (akriomion, both sides) ; pelvis
    (crest of ilium and trochanter on both sides)
Skull : *Horizontal circumference.* Glabella (forehead
    above base of nose)—ear-muscles—
    occipital protuberance

Skull : *continued*—
    Sagittal diameter. Glabella—occiput
    Frontal diameter. Max. over ears
    Vertical diameter. Angle of jaw—top of sk..
    Length of face. (*a*) Hair limit—root of no..
    (*b*) root of nose (meeting of brows..
    mouth ; (*c*) mouth—lowest point
    chin
    Length of nose. Meeting of brows (pressed w..
    in)—tip of nose (utmost point)
    Breadth of face. (*a*) Cheek bone to cheek bo..
    (*b*) angle of jaw on both sides

VI. TEMPORAL

Commencement of mental disturbance
    ,,   ,, puberty
    ,,   ,, involution
    ,,   ,, fattening

Commencement of emaciation
    ,,   ,, baldness
    ,,   ,, certain physical diseases
Sexual abnormalities

VII. SUMMING UP OF PHYSICAL STATES

VIII. TYPE OF PERSONALITY

IX. HEREDITY

An indiscriminate inventory of single bodily characteristics, which strike us at once when we look at separate
patients lying on their sick-beds, can never serve our
purpose ; for the simple verbal description must be as
precise as possible, ever making use of the same comparable expressions and fixed categories, and, in particular,
we must have clear spatial measurements and also notice
the differentiations of skin texture. It is only in this
way that we can avoid indistinct and ambiguous descriptions, and the omission of many points of detail. The
schema was carried out as follows : We noticed, and
immediately filled in point for point, the foregoing list,
the patient standing naked before us in bright daylight,
and we ruled a red line under whichever member of the
groups of descriptions fitted the case. According to the
pronouncedness of the characteristic, whether it was
strong or weak, we drew a single or double line, so that
we saved the time which a written description would have
required, and obtained a diagram that provided a perfectly intelligible survey, which conveyed to us at a glance,
later on, with no trouble at all, not only the general impression but each detail of the physique ; and thus we could
make a comparison between every single point in different
diagrams in a second. Such a verbal description naturally can, with any degree of certainty, include only the
most obvious differences. When we obtained no clear
optical or tactile impression, then we always underlined
the expression " medium ", which meant nothing for our
later statistics and served only to prevent our attempting
to force a characteristic where no characteristic was to be
found. That a severe training is required in order to
obtain a rough feeling for the average and the variations
from it, I need not say. In each scheme only such
characteristics are included as can be observed quickly,
at a glance, or with but few touches ; while everything
is excluded which requires a special technique of experimental examination. Not that the beating and oscul-
ation of heart and lung, for example, are less important
for an inquiry into the constitution, but because such an
examination cannot be carried out within the limits of a
serial investigation into general type. Naturally, such
special examinations must later on be included to fill in

the more general data, in order to establish the important constitutional relations between the internal types and the psychiatric ones.

The defects of such a verbal description, however carefully chosen, are obvious. Against this objection it must be urged that such a method is unavoidable as the basis for any investigation into bodily structure, and that it offers much which cannot be replaced either by measurement or by means of photography. In the first place, there are numerous important characteristics, such as the colour of the skin, vascular conditions, thickness of the hair, which can be described verbally in familiar language but which cannot be measured or portrayed, or only with disproportionately complex methods. In this way much comes out in direct optical impression far more significantly and definitely. We shall soon be convinced by consideration, say, of a slight form of " Tower-Skull ", which for every observer is clearly recognizable at the first glance, while it finds only insignificant expression in the results obtained from a pair of calipers and a simple tape-measure (the kephologram is clearly excluded in the examinations of large numbers). Besides this, there are also many dimensions in the living man which can be obtained only inaccurately and approximately : that is to say, it will soon be borne in upon one that in the investigation of the body, accurate measurements and optical impression must support one another.

We place in our schema the optical description of the measurement first, for both should be obtained as far as possible independently of each other, and the eye must not find an asses' bridge already prepared for it in the shape of accurate measurements. Everything depends on a complete, artistic, and sure schooling of our eyes, for a scholarly list of single measurements without any idea or intuition of the general structure will not bring us much further. The tape-measure sees nothing : it never leads us to a grasp of the biological types which are our object. But if we have learnt to see, then we shall notice that the calipers bring us exact statements and numerical formulations, and also in some places important corrections of what we have discovered with our eyes. Certain conditions which are not prepared for in this schema will emerge here and there, and may then be written in; occasionally at certain points a much fuller and more distinct description of the æsthetic impression is required. It is very profitable, while the impression of the examination is yet fresh, to give a short résumé of what are the essentials, for which a half-sheet is left free at the end of the foregoing schema.

The large schema is worked out more for the purpose of investigation, and we now use for hurried clinical purposes a shortened schema, which can be filled in according to the same headings as the big one.

CONSTITUTION SCHEME

[*Date of examination*

Name :
Age :

Profession :
Diagnosis :

I. MEASUREMENT

Skull ·
Horizontal circumference
Sagittal diameter
Frontal   ,,
Vertical   ,,
Height of face
Breadth of face
Length of nose

Circumference : chest
            stomach
            hips
Weight :
            forearm 1
            hand 1
            calf 1

Height :

Length :   legs ; arms
Breadth :   shoulders ; pelvis

II. FACE AND SKULL

Shape of head :   high-head ; pyknic flat-head ; small round-head ; tower-skull ; bladder-shape skull ; indefinite

Frontal outline : broad shield-shaped; flat five-cornered ; steep egg-shaped ; shortened egg-shaped ; childish oval ; seven-cornered ; indefinite

Profile :   angular profile ; long nose profile ; hypoplastic ; pyknic profile ; indefinite

Height-proportions · (middle-face ; chin)
Nose :
Description :

III. PHYSIQUE

Bones :
Musculature (Relief) ?
Fat :
Neck :
Shoulders :
Chest :

Stomach :
Pelvis :
Extremities (esp. length) :
Hands and feet :
Description :

IV. HAIR

Head-hair :

Brows :

Beard :

Pubes :

Arm-pits :

Skin-condition :

Vascular condition (esp. colour) :

Trunk :

Arms :

Legs :

Description :

V. GLANDS

Thyroid :

Mammary :

Testicles :

Genitalia :

Sexual anomalies :

VI. TEMPORAL

Commencement of Mental Disturbance :

     „   „ Puberty :

     „   „ Involution :

Commencement of Fattening :

     „   „ Emaciation :

     „   „ Certain physical
                      diseases :

CONCLUSIONS

With regard to the method employed in mensuration there are a great number of not unimportant details to mention, which anyone who deals fundamentally with this question will find out best for himself. Technical instruction can be found in text-books on anthropology.[1] If we refer to what Riezer, in his witty concise way, has said about the value of figures and simple body-measurement in his monograph *Die Mess-stange*, we can thereby save ourselves many a word. The measurements given in our schema give the majority of those measurable body-proportions which are of importance for us, and they also, particularly in the circumference-measurements of the stomach and extremities, provide certain complex points of vantage from which we can study the development of the fat, bone, and muscle. The following remarks

[1] R. Marter, *Lehrbuch der Anthropologie*; Jena, Fischer, 1914; and, on many points to do with Psychiatry see the work of Riezer and Reichart, to whose painstaking and meritorious studies on the exact and clear technique of microscopic body-mensuration special reference may be made in this connection.

have to be made from a statistical point of view with regard not only to our tables but also, in principle, to all the rest of our numerical values : (1) that, almost without exception, they have been obtained from individuals springing from the Schwabian people ; that is to say, they are comparable only among themselves, and without further work they cannot be compared with numerical values obtained from patients belonging to other races ; (2) that the smaller of our sub-groups (particularly the athletic), divided between men and women, includes only a few individuals—a few dozen or less—so that the average figure so obtained is to be regarded only as a provisionary halting-place—as an approximation, but not as a statistical constant. It would be impossible to procure, during any reasonable period of time, such statistical values for every single measurement of the body, and, besides, in any case it is superfluous, because (3) even within a single people we can give only approximate figures, since, when dealing with body-forms, we have not to do with clearly-marked unities but with ill-defined types, where, with regard to certain border-line cases, it depends on the investigator himself whether he includes them on the list of the one single type or not. With these obvious precautions, however, the average-figures afford us extraordinarily valuable objective support for the working out of the fundamental characteristics of the types.

And now a few words about pictorial reproduction. Even if the investigator is not endowed with any talent for drawing, it is advisable every time to jot down on the diagram-sheet certain important details which are easily drawn, such as, for example, the shape of the face as seen from in front—paying attention only to the essential outlines. Little sketches like this provide us with valuable foundations when we come to the task of manipulating the material. I usually fix graphically the disposition of hair about the body in a small diagram. In cases of particular interest we make considerable use of photographs. These are most valuable for the shape of the face and skull. Large-size pictures are for the most part an unnecessary expense, and, paradoxically enough, large pictures are often worse than small ones. A picture of the size 8 × 12 cm. has almost always served our purpose. The important thing is correct lighting and, particularly, a satisfactory manipulation of the perspective. This remark applies specially for photographs of the front view of the face. When they are having their photographs taken, patients tend automatically to hold their heads up stiff in the air : this results in a quite distorted perspective, and very often completely false pictures. The head should be somewhat sunk rather than raised. For the rest, we take our pictures of the face with an apparatus for sharpening the outline when the picture is taken from quite close to, so that the head fills the entire picture and only the naked neck and the lie of the shoulders come in. We use a monochromatic background—black, if the silhouette is most important ; grey, if the shading is of chief interest. Beginners usually use too much light ; this spoils the shading of the contours of the muscles and bones. For scientific purposes there are only two positions from which to take the photographs : exactly frontal or exactly profile—and this is so whether you are dealing with pictures of the face or of the whole body. Accuracy suffers in any midway position between these two, and particularly the exact comparison between the pictures themselves. For pictures demonstrating the general build of the body, illustrations of the whole figure are not to be recommended ; such pictures—where one is not dealing actually with quite outstanding anomalies—are not characteristic. Abnormal length of extremities, femininity of the pelvis, etc., even when according to the figures of mensuration they are obvious, usually come out badly in a photograph. For this reason we make use mostly of pictures of the half of the body about down to the navel, which thus includes the most distinguishing characteristics of the type of physique and shows them in a more distinctive way.

When we have worked through a larger series of patients with all these methods—viz., a combination of exact diagrammatic description, measurement, and registration by drawing and photography—then we are left with solid data, which satisfy all the demands of physical science, for our purpose, namely, an exact clinical diagnostic of physique, as a broad physiological basis for a psychiatric theory of the constitution.

The exposition which follows rests on material which has been worked through by use of the above-mentioned methods, and which is composed of about 260 cases divided in the following way :

	Circular			*Schizophrene*	
Men	.	. 43	Men	. .	. 125
Women	.	. 42	Women	.	. 50
		85			175

Since the closing of these statistics over 100 further cases have been examined, which have not been included in the reckoning but whose examination has confirmed the results obtained from the earlier cases. The total material is therefore made up of about 400 cases, of which about one-third are circular and two-thirds schizophrene.

The clinical boundaries were stretched as wide as possible, so that although among the schizophrenes the great majority of cases were taken from the range of typical catatonics and hebephrenes, common-or-garden dementia præcox, yet every now and then isolated cases of paraphrenia on the one hand, and schizoid " neuras- thenics ", psychopaths, and degenerates, on the other, were also included. In the same way with the circulars (manic-depressives)—by the side of the great mass of average cases, a few cases of involution mania, of senile and arterio-sclerotic depression, and finally of non-lunatic hypomania and habitually-depressive tempera- ments, were dealt with. This practice has, as we shall see, proved itself to be correct in the end. Finally test-cases were taken here and there, among those whose diagnosis was not clear, and in these cases the sureness of aim of the diagnostic inferences from body-build was impressively demonstrated.

Great stress was laid on the inclusion in all the types of a carefully arranged mixture of fresh and old cases, people of every age, and every occupation, in order to avoid those causes of error which otherwise spring from the influence of such isolated causal factors, and also, so that we might be in a position to observe the changes of the single types throughout a long period of life. As an addition to the cases of the Tübingen Clinic, which were mostly recent, the rich material of the Institute in Winnental was chosen ; for the kind permission to use which I am most gratefully indebted to the Doctors at the Institute, and particularly to Dr Camerer, the Obermedizinalrat.

Diagnosis by means of body-build is as vast and complicated a region as organic neurology. For its establishment is required the accuracy and co-operation of numerous observers. It is in this spirit—as a stimulus to further research, and not as anything dogmatic—that we lay before our readers the results which we have so far obtained.

CHAPTER II

TYPES OF PHYSIQUE

THERE does not yet exist an exact ' theory of the constitution ' which deals with the build of the body.   There are
no systematic investigations which enter thoroughly into
the examination of details.   The strides made in the
study of the ductless glands were so swift and surprising,
that, so far, they have been able to give only a few very
general indications with regard to the study of the
physique.   Questions which would be of the utmost
value in these investigations of ours, such, for example,
as the relations between acromegaly and the growth of
the muscles, are hardly touched upon even in the most
complete exposition of the subject.   Nevertheless we
have, in the physique of the cretin, the acromegalic, and
the eunuchoid (only to name the most important), at
least in their most obvious characteristics, a little which has
been already tangibly worked out, and is of great use to us.

We find far less work on the general theory of physique,
in the sense of individual constitution types, than we find
within the small special range of endocrine dysplastia.   For
the greatest work in this direction, due to investigation
of the internal organs, we are indebted to the increasing
activity of Julius Bauer,[1] which must be most warmly
recognized.   What has already been said, particularly
from the paidiatristic point of view, about the exudational,
lymphatic, and arthritic types of constitution, however
valuable for clinical purposes, is so obscure and so vague
as far as the physique goes, that we have not been able to
make any use of it whatever for our purpose.

Recently in Germany the French nomenclature of
types as ' cérébral ', ' respiratoire ', ' musculaire ', and
' digestif ' has taken root.   Much excellent intuition
lay behind these French types.   We think that in the

[1] Julius Bauer, *Die Konstitutionelle Disposition zu inneren Krauk-
heiten*, Berlin, 1917.

true kernel of observation which is the basis of the
' Type musculaire ' and the ' Type digestif ', is much
that will be described later on when we deal with the
athletic and pyknic types of constitution. The fundamental mistake of the French grouping is, however, this,
that their occasionally correct observations of detail are
forced into a scheme which has been constructed purely
speculatively, and at the bottom of which—if we may
express ourselves somewhat naïvely for the sake of clarity
—lie the following ideas : there are (1) men of reason,
these must have a big head ; (2) eaters, these must have
a fine belly ; (3) acrobats, these must have splendid
muscles ; and (4) runners, these must have a fine pair of
lungs. These deductions are not followed out to their
logical conclusion, for in the case of the ' type respiratoire ',
not only the lungs, but the whole breathing tract, the
nose, even the sinus maxillares and frontales must be
over-developed, while the ' type digestif ' naturally needs
the appropriate jaw-bones to go with his belly. I am
afraid that here we are impinging on an idea which,
since the time of Lavater, has been the ruling principle
of physiognomists and popular racial-biologists, namely,
that a strongly-developed under-jaw is, as it were, a
shameful little inheritance from the gorilla, a hall-mark
of those people who make up for the incomplete development of their higher moral cerebral centres by a pro-
portionately generous endowment of vegetative apparatus,
and who are thus condemned by nature to untamed
animality and criminality (this in the older physiognomical literature), or, in the modern view, to a somewhat
milder form of materialism. As we should expect, the
' type cérébral ' presents us with the diametrically opposed
picture of the man who stands in the forefront of mankind, who is almost all spirit, and on to whose abnormally
large head the remaining fragments of matter hang like a
small atavistic appendix.

The worst fact about the whole method of grouping
is really this, that a naïve connection between bodily and
psychic peculiarities is presented—sometimes more or
less implied in the nomenclature itself—which by its very
simplicity strikes the doctor who is a trained psychiatrist
as foreign to all his notions.

If with this constructive method of grouping we compare the new types of physique empirically established by biology which the study of the ductless glands has brought to our notice so far (cretinism, acromegaly, eunuchoid, etc.), we meet here with no single vegetative system (respirative, digestive, cerebral), which has become hypertrophied on its own account, but exactly the opposite ; we find a bewildering complexity of the most disparate manifestations of the same inner cause, which could not in the least have been logically deduced —an interaction of trophic stimulation and trophic inhibition which becomes apparent at the same time in the most different organic systems, here in the skeleton, there in the skin, now in the muscles and now in the disposition of fat, and, again, often only in the general characteristic of an organic system—and that the bodily indications stand in no logically inferable relation with the psychic symptoms which are simultaneously called forth, but that such relations can only be discovered empirically.

We take up our position then, here : we can consider the constitution types which include the whole of mankind, bodily and psychically, and which have a real biological significance as discovered, only when we have found relations between purely empirically-established complex types of physique and similarly complex endogenous psychic types (such as the circular and schizophrene categories) which can be expressed in the form of some law. For under such circumstances we have a sure proof, since the real conditions of the psychic syndrome may be controlled as regards its somatic basis, while the somatic group of symptoms may be controlled as regards the psychic development which accompanies them. The following grouping is to be regarded as being in accordance with such an attempt. We shall notice that in the description of the physique and the tabulation of the average values only schizophrenic and circular material is made use of, while the illustrations show also isolated patients of other groups. This is an important point.

The types, as they will appear in what follows, are no " ideal types " which have emerged, consciously created in accordance with any given guiding principle or collection of pre-established values. They are, on the contrary, obtained from empirical sources in the following way: when a fairly large number of morphological similarities can be followed through a correspondingly large number of individuals, then we pause and register the measurement. From this we reckon the average value, and thus the outstanding common characteristics come out clearly, while those peculiar marks which only occur in isolated cases disappear in the average value. In exactly the same way we treat the remainder of the characteristics which can only be described from mere optical observation. So we proceed, as if we were copying at the same time the picture of 100 individuals of a type on the same picture-surface, one on top of the other, in such a way that those characteristics which cover one another become sharply outlined, while those which do not fit over one another disappear. Only those characteristics which become strongly marked in the average values are described as 'typical'. We must not believe that it only requires careful observation to discover such a type clearly delineated and that we can do without wearisome practice of our eyes on our material; we find, on the contrary, in concrete cases, the typical elements always veiled by heterogeneous 'individual' characteristics, and, in many respects, blurred. It is the same here as in clinical medicine, or in botany or zoology. The 'classic' cases, almost free from any mixture, and endowed with all the essential characteristics of a perfect example of some form of disease, or zoological race-type, are more or less lucky finds, which we cannot produce every day. From this it follows that the description of types to be found in the ensuing pages, refers not to the most frequent cases, but to ideal cases, to such cases as bring most clearly to view common characteristics which in the majority of instances appear only blurred, but which, all the same, can be empirically demonstrated. The same applies to the description of psychological types in the second part.

With the methods we have described, three ever-recurring principal types of physique have emerged from our clinical material, which we will call 'asthenic', 'athletic', and 'pyknic'. They are to be found among men and women, only, on account of the fact that the

PLATE I

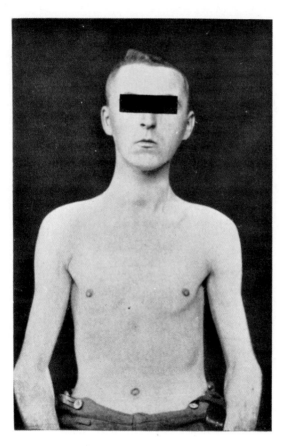

ASTHENIC TYPE. Frontal
(Schizoid psychopath)

[face p. 20

FLATE 2

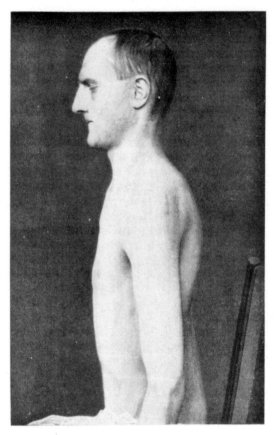

ASTHENIC TYPE. Profile
(Schizophrenia)

[*face p.* 21

female body is less strikingly morphologically differentiated, the most pregnant forms are less often found among women. The way, however, in which these three types are correlated with the schizophrene and circular categories, is very varied and remarkable. Among healthy people we come across these types on every side ; they have no foundation in disease, but they indicate certain normal biological tendencies of which only a small proportion comes to pathological culmination—whether in the region of psychiatry or in certain established internal diseases. By the side of these great principal types we find various small groups, which we have placed together and regarded as special dysplastic types, in that they form striking digressions from the average, and in that they are morphologically very closely related to the clear cases of dysglandular syndrome in endocrine-pathology.

We give first only the outline of the three principal types in their most general characteristics, and, for the sake of clarity we examine the details of the morphology of the physique—particularly the face and skull, and the surface of the body—in the next chapter. In general we must emphasize the fact that the morphology of the physique must be studied first always in the case of men and not women. The female physique is far less ' significant ' on the average, particularly with regard to the form of the face, and the development of the muscles and fat. We find, therefore, among women, many more indefinite and a-typical forms.

(a) Asthenic Type

TABLE I

PRINCIPAL AVERAGE MEASUREMENTS OF ASTHENIC TYPE

	Men	Women
Height	168·4	153·8
Weight (kilos)	50·5	32·8
Shoulder.	35·5	44·4
Chest [1]	84·1	77·7
Stomach	74·1	67·7
Hips	84·7	82·2
Forearm (circum.)	23·5	20·4
Hand (circum.)	19·7	18·0
Calf (circum.)	30·0	27·7
Leg (length)	89·4	79·2

[1] Mean between inspiration and expiration.

The notion of the asthenic habitus[1] was coined by Stille and was then corrected and narrowed down, in a manner which calls for the highest praise, by J. Bauer. The typus asthenius which we have obtained from our psychiatristic material is identical in essentials with the same internal type of Bauer. In respect to detailed points, mentioned in the short description of Bauer, the majority are completely confirmed by our investigation. The only point which we cannot confirm is the theory that the asthenics are mostly dolichocephalous ; according to our reckoning (see below), the asthenic skulls, compared with those of the other types, are, on an average, of small circumference, of middle width, but short and low.

The essential characteristic of the type of the male asthenic is, in a few words, taking the general total impression, *a deficiency in thickness combined with an average unlessened length.* This deficiency in the thickness development is present in all parts of the body—face, neck, trunk, extremities—and in all the tissues—skin, fat, muscle, bone, and vascular system throughout. On this account we find the average weight, as well as the total circumference and breadth measurements, below the general value for males.

We have, therefore, in the clearest cases, the following general impression (Figs. 1 and 2) : a lean narrowly-built man, who looks taller than he is, with a skin poor in secretion and blood, with narrow shoulders, from which hang lean arms with thin muscles, and delicately boned hands ; a long, narrow, flat chest, on which we can count the ribs, with a sharp rib-angle ;[2] a thin stomach, devoid of fat, and lower limbs which are just like the upper ones in character. In the average values for the measurements in males, the way the weight of the body lags behind the

[1] We take the expression ' asthenic ' as established for us in clinical usage, although it is connected with a biological judgment of values which has nothing to do either with general biological descriptions of types or clinical ones. ' Asthenic ' stands, then, for us as a purely descriptive expression, and has no connection with the notion of diseased or healthy, or having great or little value.

[2] Stille lays great stress on the 10 free ribs. I should like to ally myself with Bauer in a warning against the over-estimation of such details. The general diagnostic rule in the theory of physique is not to underline the isolated symptoms, but always to direct the attention to the total picture.

length (50·5 : 168·4), and the chest measurement behind the hip measurement (84·1 : 84·7) stands out clearly.

A variant of this type has wide shoulders, but with a plank-like, flat chest, and very sharp outstanding shoulder-bones. Instead of the thin stomach, in some cases we find a loose, small, enteroptotic pendulent stomach, or a disposition of fat in eunuchoid or feminine form, which must not be confused with the pyknic fat stomach. Often we find a variety of the asthenic type distinguished by stronger or weaker manifestation of symptoms of the dysgenital group—of infantilism (akromicria), of feminism (waist, enlarged buttock-circumference, enlarged hip measurements, feminine arrangement of puberty hair), and particularly a streak of eunochoidism with abnormal height and abnormal length of extremities. We shall return to this later in the account.

A favourite form of variation is a mixture between asthenic and athletic types, where we find either asthenic and athletic characteristics standing immediately next to one another (e.g., long, narrow chests, with coarse extremities, an incongruity between face and physique, etc.), or else a middle-type of slim muscular figure, which, again, may tend more towards the gracile thin side, or more towards the strong muscular side.

If we observe the asthenic type over a long period of development, it seems to be fairly constant in its fundamental peculiarities through all ages. Already, as children, these people are often characterized as weakly and frail ; at puberty they often rapidly shoot up their narrow forms, and when grown-up and in old age they show not the least tendency to inordinate muscle or fat. As peasants they can perform hard bodily labour, and yet they train their muscles, as far as the circumference measurement goes, only a little. They can be nourished on the fat of the land even (as many old inmates of the institute at peace-time), eat ravenously, and still remain as thin as they started. Age does alter the disposition of hair in the case of certain asthenics (see below). The form of the face often only gets its characteristic form, which will be described later, from the age of about 18, and with the oncoming emaciation of later years it may grow thinner and thinner.

In one class of asthenics their premature ageing strikes us as an important biological stigma. In extreme cases, I found men of ages between 35 and 40 already quite senile, with wrinkled fallen-in skin, which was completely dry, flabby, and sallow, and well-marked protruding veins on the temples. (See Plates 7 and 8, which represent a 32-year-old patient.) One frequently finds in such cases, in spite of a normal mode of life, a quite astounding degree of general atrophy of fat and muscle, which points to extreme chronic disturbances of the metabolism. Even patients who are constant large eaters fall a victim to this, and the muscles, without becoming paretic, can, all the same, even when there is constant work in the fields, attain such a degree of atrophy that a diastasis of the thigh adductors comes about, in a way that one only sees, otherwise, in cases of cachectics, with extreme loss of flesh ; the inner contours of the thigh run no longer, as in normal cases, in a line together, towards the perineum, but they remain separated up to the perineum, so that there is a gap between both thighs.

As regards the pubertial development of the asthenic constitution in the case of men, among our patients the growth in height was mostly normal, occasionally striking and premature. A 16-year-old young man of our material, suffering from hebephrenia, already measured 165 cms. (which is decidedly above the average for that age with our Schwabian folk) ; an 18-year-old measured 176. All the same, we cannot pronounce this to be the rule. A few asthenics always remain small, even in the cases of men. The smallest of our adult male asthenics measured 158, the largest 178 cms. ; still, outstanding smallness of growth is not common among them. The case we have just mentioned is the only one among 50 cases with a height under 160 cms. One finds surprisingly childish, undeveloped facial expressions, in the cases of some asthenics, even between 20 and 25 and later, and especially among the women ; many asthenics, on account of the sharp, thin forms of their faces, already at these ages look older than they are. With regard to sex impulse and distribution of hair, see below.

The asthenic women, as far as the type shows itself clearly among them, are, in their general appearance,

PLATE 3

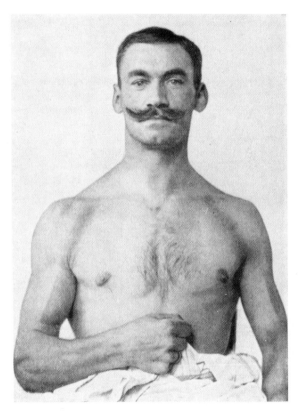

ATHLETIC TYPE. Frontal
(Schizophrenia)

PLATE 4

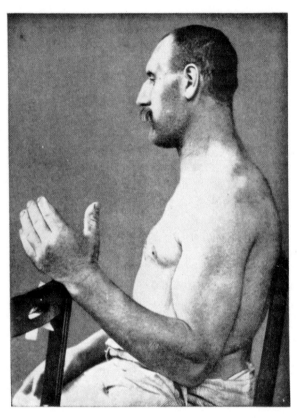

ATHLETIC TYPE. Profile
(Acromegaly)

[*face p.* 25

like asthenic men, up to an important point : they are
not only thin, but also of very small growth. The normal,
and even abnormal height of the men is to be found among
asthenic women, but it is far more often absent among
them. Of 20 female cases, I have only one of 169 and one
161 cms., the rest all measure 160 and under, and the
smallest 145. This group of women is thus not merely
asthenic, but asthenic-hypoplastic ; in this work, by
asthenic we mean merely under-development in thickness,
while by hypoplastic we mean general undevelopment of
the body, and the parts of the body, especially with
reference to the height. Thus we have, among asthenic
women, the very low average height of 153·8, while the
average height of the asthenic male is 168, more or less
corresponding with the average height of the male sex
among the whole Schwabian folk. The result is that the
difference between the height and weight among asthenic
men is very large, among women far smaller (cf. table).
In the case of men, it is about 18 (the weight subtracted
from the last two figures of the height), in the case of
women, only about 9.

(b) *Athletic Type*
TABLE II

CHIEF BODY MEASUREMENTS OF THE ATHLETIC TYPE

	Men	Women
Height	170·0	163·1
Weight (in kilo)	62·9	61·7
Width of shoulders	39·1	37·4
Breast	91·7	86·0
Stomach	79·6	75·1
Hips	91·5	95 8
Forearm (circum.)	26·2	24·2
Hand (circum.)	21·7	20·0
Calf (circum.)	33·1	31·7
Length of leg	90·9	85·0

The male athletic type is recognized by the strong development of the skeleton, the musculature and also the skin.
The rough impression of the best example of this
species is as follows :
A middle-sized to tall man, with particularly wide projecting shoulders, a superb chest, a firm stomach, and
a trunk which tapers in its lower region, so that the
pelvis, and the magnificent legs, sometimes seem almost

graceful compared with the size of the upper limbs and particularly the hypertrophied [1] shoulders.

The solid long head is carried upright on a free neck, so that the sloping linear contour of the firm trapezius, looked at from in front, gives that part of the shoulder which is nearest the neck its peculiar shape.

The outlines and shadings of the body are determined by the swelling of the muscles of the good or hypertrophied musculature which stands out plastically as muscle-relief. The bone-relief is specially prominent in the shape of the face. The coarse boning throughout is to be seen particularly in the collar-bones, the hand and foot joints, and the hands. Next to the shoulders the trophic accent often lies on the extremities, which in some cases are reminiscent of acromegaly. The largest hand circumference among our material reached the very remarkable figure of 25 cms., that is to say, a measurement which oversteps the male average value of about 20 cms. by 5 cms. Hand circumferences of 23 cms. are quite common. Besides the hand circumference, the width of the shoulders is with this type specially remarkable, which, in two cases, reached the astonishingly high figure of 42·5 cms., which defeats the average figure of our people of roughly 37·5 to 38 cms. by about 5 cms. The length of the extremities is rather long than short. Together with bone and muscle the skin has its share of the general hypertrophy. It has a very good, firm, elastic turgor, and, particularly in the face, it looks solid, thick, and often pasty. In contradistinction to all this tissue, the fat is relatively only moderately developed, and, speaking absolutely, is more or less normal. It is on this account, above all, that the distinctive muscle-relief is conditioned, since the over-developed musculature stands out through only a thin sheath of fat.

The height lies above the average ; length measurements of over 180 cms. are not rare, the tallest athletic of our material measured 186 cms. At the other end of the scale the boundary cannot be fixed, because the morphological transition stages between the athletic type and the

---

[1] The expression ' hypertrophied ' is throughout to be understood not in the sense of a pathological disturbance, but simply in the sense of a development which oversteps the average.

type of hypoplastic broad shoulders (see below) cannot be defined. At the tall end we must notice transitions to certain gigantic types which are to be described later.

For the rest, within the athletic type, variants are found, particularly in the form of the face (see below). In the build of the body, side by side with the type with relatively slim lower portions of the body, and a plastic construction of the body-forms, is another variant, which is remarkable for general plumpness. The difference between the shoulder and pelvis developments is here not worth noticing, all is ugly, massive, clumsy, the skin on the face, pasty, while the muscle-relief is obscured by a more diffuse development of fat. Whether we have to deal here with a variant, an alloy, another stage of development, or, which is more probable, with a type on its own, with fundamentally different biological foundations, cannot be determined from purely morphological considerations. There are only a few instances of this kind in my material ; one of them had, besides an advanced katatonic idiocy, epileptic attacks as well. Another patient had, besides an infantile development of fat, a stunted genital organ with double-sided kyptorchism. Among these pasty, plump athletics, I also met in the Institute certain few cases, in which a massive upper body sat on a not absolutely slim, but a miserably thin lower portion, an infantile pelvis, and asthenically thin legs.

Again, we find numerous morphological connections between the athletic types and the dysgenitals. Mixtures of the athletic elements with a growth in length which indicates eunuchoidism, are not unusual, e.g., abnormal length of the extremities with large-handedness, partial thick-bonedness, muscular shoulders, etc. ; similarly we observe striking femininity. I recently saw a schizoid patient with an otherwise quite athletic body-build, but with it narrow, sloping, rounded shoulders, a waist, and a strongly contoured female pelvis with a large circumferal measurement. Whether the type of broad-shouldered small-grown people with akromikry, later to be described, is due to an interference of infantilistic and athletic structure-principles, which is quite likely, or whether it is a type on its own, is a question we must for the time being postpone.

The development of the athletic type throughout various ages offers little worthy of notice. In our material it is already apparent in the puberty period—from about 18 years old onwards ; with the maturing of the body beyond 25 years old it becomes more plastic and more significant. In the 50th year I have found it still unaltered in many cases. At yet more advanced ages than the beginning of the 60th year I have no case at my disposal, which is probably only due to chance since the athletic group is much smaller than the asthenic—men and women together only numbering about 30 cases. That this very clearly-defined type should become in more advanced ages so quickly and completely degenerate that one cannot recognize it at least by the build of the head and shoulders, is not to be thought of. In fact, among middle-aged idiotic katatonics in the Institute, who lay there or wandered about dully year in year out, often the musculature was remarkably weakened and no longer so large in circumference, while the solid bone and the total measurement of the body seemed to point to a very strong development in earlier years. This case may very well be accounted for as atrophy due to inactivity ; still, the question would remain to be carefully dealt with, whether endogenous trophic factors can lead to the degeneration of muscle, as also with asthenics, even in the case of patients where there is no inactivity factor.

The athletic type among women, as far as it is recognizable, corresponds to the male form, with certain characteristic deviations. The development of fat, especially, is often not restricted with women, but rich ; in any case it is in good proportion to the rest of the issue, particularly to the bones and muscle, and is, anyway, in the cases of our material, not electively abnormal as with pyknics. By the side of these athletic women with feminine rounded figure, we find, indeed, also those who have outstanding musculature in face and body. Many such cases, which are quite masculine in muscle-relief, and the proportions of shoulder and pelvis, are described in Chapter V. We must particularly notice that the trophic accentuation of the shoulder is often observable in the case of female athletics (to a breadth of 29 cms.) which does not lie within the boundaries of

PLATE 5

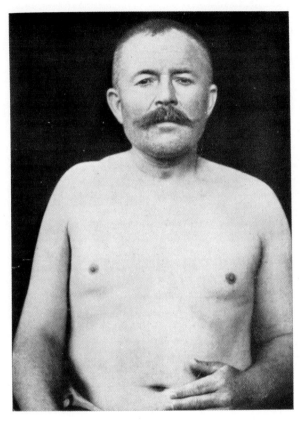

PYKNIC TYPE. Frontal
(Circular)

[face p. 28

PLATE 6

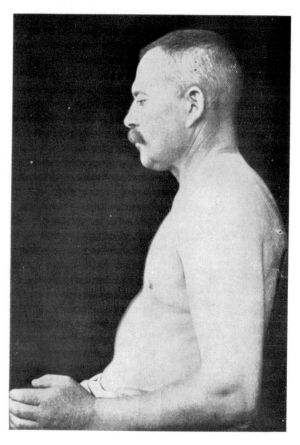

PYKNIC TYPE. Profile
(Circular)

the secondary sex characteristics, but rather oversteps them. This proves that it represents nothing incidental, but denotes a specially directed tendency to grow in that particular direction. Besides the breast-shoulder complex, the pelvis is often very strongly developed among athletic women.

The bodily constitution of the athletic woman gives us on an average more the impression of abnormality, of extreme over-development, of unpleasant stolidity and massiveness, than does that of the athletic male, and for this reason : these men at times come quite near to our æsthetic ideal, while our ideal of female beauty is far overstepped by the athletic female. Here is the place where we must warn our readers that we do not bring the subjective valuation of the laity into our diagnostic of bodily constitution. As regards our three main types, we have not much to do with the judgment ' normal ', or ' abnormal '. All these may be found among healthy people, as well as among those suffering from organic and psychic disorders. All these are normal, in so far as they belong to the anthropological type which is most frequently met with, and abnormal in so far as they contain within them the dispositions for recognized pathological states—each in a different direction. Neither can one say that any one of these types would be in general better fitted, as far as bodily relations go, for the battle of life. The athletic is better built for wrestling, the asthenic for flying ; in many professions it is absolutely immaterial whether they are carried on by the one or the other. Many asthenics are healthy throughout their lives, and live to a hoary old age, while their more magnificent brethren have already died from heart-failure. For this reason it is so fundamentally wrong (and here I agree entirely with Bauer) to speak of a ' morbus asthenicus ' ; also designations such as ' an arthritic habitus ' or ' a phthisic habitus ', belong only to a very narrow clinical sphere of discourse, and they cannot be used for a theory of bodily constitution which is completely objective, and scientifically complete, because they are solely concerned with a tendency in one particular pathological direction. If the asthenic is more highly disposed to tuberculosis he is, perhaps for that very reason, more immune from rheumatism, diabetes, and arterio-sclerosis, than the pyknic, and vice versa. With regard to the disposition to organic disorders among athletics, we have been unable to discern anything accurate ; in the realm of psychic disorders on the other hand, the direction of their tendencies can be easily formulated. One cannot, therefore, mark down any one of the great classes of constitutions as fundamentally healthier or unhealthier than the others.

(c) *Pyknic Type*

TABLE III

CHIEF BODY MEASUREMENTS OF THE PYKNIC TYPE

	Men	Women
Height	167·8	156·5
Weight (kilos)	68·0	56·3
Width of shoulders . . .	36·9	34·3
Chest	94·5	86·0
Stomach	88·8	78·7
Hips	92·0	94·2
Forearm (circum.) . . .	25·5	22·4
Hand (circum.) . . .	20·7	18·6
Calf (circum.)	33·2	31·2
Length of leg	87·4	80·5

The pyknic type, in the height of its perfection in middle-age, is characterized by the pronounced peripheral development of the body cavities (head, breast, and stomach), and a tendency to a distribution of fat about the trunk, with a more graceful construction of the motor apparatus (shoulders and extremities).

The rough impression in well-developed cases is very distinctive : middle height, rounded figure, a soft broad face on a short massive neck, sitting between the shoulders ; the magnificent fat paunch protrudes from the deep *vaulted* chest which broadens out towards the lower part of the body.

If we look at the limbs, we find them soft, rounded, and displaying little muscle-relief, or bone-relief, often quite delicate, the hands soft, rather short and wide. In particular the joints of the hands and the clavicle are often slim and almost elegantly formed. The shoulders are not broad and projecting as with the athletics, but (especially among older people) are rounded, rather high, and pushed forwards together, and they are often set down against the breast with a characteristically sharp depression on the inner deltoid curve. It seems then as if the whole mass of the shoulders were slipping downwards and inwards over the swelling chest ; and the head also plays a part in this static displacement : it sinks forward between the shoulders, so that the short thick neck seems almost to disappear, and the upper portion of the spinal column takes on a slight kyphotic bend. In profile the neck no longer seems, as is the case with the other types, a slim round column, which carries the chin like a sharply cut-off, widely projecting capital, but in well-developed cases of middle-age and over, the point of the chin is directly joined with the upper forehead, without any definite bends, by a sloping line (Plate 13).

The breast-shoulder-neck proportion is, apart from the shape of the head and face, and the manner of the disposition of the fat, the most characteristic mark of the pyknic character. The ratio of the moderate-sized breadth of shoulder to the large-sized breast circumference—36·9 : 94·5—stands out strongly by the side of the characteristic proportions of the athletic, where the chest circumference is completely dominated by the huge breadth of the shoulders—(39·1 : 91·7). While the athletic torso seems especially broad, the pyknic appears deep ; in the former the trophic accent lies on the shoulders and extremities, in the latter on the width of the trunk, or the bowl-shaped chest which widens towards the lower region of the body, and on the fat abdomen. The extremities are on an average rather short than long.

The pyknics tend emphatically to a covering of fat. And besides this the manner in which the fat is disposed is characteristic and must be accurately distinguished, not in comparison with the asthenics and athletics, who have as a general rule no noticeable tendency to fat, but in comparison with certain purely dysplastic special types (see below). The obesity of the pyknic is restricted for the most part within *moderate* limits, and is primarily an obesity of the trunk ; the fat deposit in the case of the male results usually in a compact fat belly. All the other body-forms are softened and rounded by a diffuse covering of fat, but not disguised and disfigured. Thus the face is to be distinguished by its round, soft lines, and the hips, and often (but not always) the calves share in the increased covering of fat. The forearm and hands, and the lateral parts of the shoulders, on the other hand, are often only moderately provided. The legs also in the case of older pyknic males can be surprisingly thin.

The skin is neither loose, as in the case of the asthenic, nor tight as with the athletic, but smooth, well-fitting, of moderate thickness, and following strongly-marked contours, as, for example, over the cheek-bones, and well-rounded over the outer side of the upper arm. The muscles are of medium strength but of a soft consistency.

The average height of the pyknic males is a moderate one (167·8). The characteristically strong covering of fat is shown in the fact that, contrary to the other types, and even to the athletic types, the weight of the pyknic exceeds the last two figures of the height (68·0). Weights of one to two hundredweight have been found in certain phases of the lives of isolated cases ; the maximum weight found among our material was 107 kgs. with 171 kms. height. On the other hand we do find occasionally, especially among older people, remarkable cases of under-weight (in one case the ratio was 163 : 49) as a result of strong involution. Pyknics not seldom show striking and at times abrupt changes in weight, particularly in connection with the life periods and the psychotic changes of phase. In the above-mentioned cases there began from about the 30th year onwards a rapid increase in weight, which in middle-age, with numerous significant vacillations, reached the height of 107 kgs., to fall rapidly at the age of 60, coincident with psychic depression, to 76 kgs., and after that, even when the depression was removed, no more to rise. Small undersized figures are very common among the pyknics of our folk, but there is in our material only one single instance below 160 cms., though outstanding height is rare ; only two cases, both strongly mixed with elements of the athletic constitution, overstep the limit of 180, with 181 and 182.

The pyknic type is very regular, and contains no very strongly marked variants. We must notice that it is clearly distinguished by the build of the skeleton, especially the skeletal proportions of the skull, face, and hand, apart from the overlay of fat, and often by the breast,

shoulder, and neck proportions, and that an outstanding
overlay of fat is not necessary to its diagnosis. The
rough peripheral form of the body is outwardly very
varied, according as the fat stomach and the thick neck
give it the characteristic appearance or not. When one con-
siders that with the majority of hard workers (see Chapter
VII), and also the majority of young people under 35–40
years of age, the compact pyknic overlay of fat is absent,
one will realize how many errors in diagnosis will occur if
one limits oneself to this symptom, which, however striking and important, is not an unvarying criterion. Perfectly
definite instances (see Chapter VII) may, at first sight,
remind one of nothing remotely connected with the
pyknic average form, and yet, after careful observation
and measurement, typical pyknic components will be
discovered. Mixture with athletic elements is not rare,
in which case the shoulders are wider, and the limbs
solider, and more bony. Asthenic-pyknic interference in
structure is found in, *e.g.*, the following arrangement :
small fat stomach, long thorax, long thin extremities,
and, in addition, in the shape of the face and skull, a
slight form of ' tower-skull ' over a pyknically soft and
wide cheek and jaw formation. We could reel off here,
and with other types, innumerable mixtures of such a
kind : there is absolutely no single criterion which cannot
be varied by, and combined with, marks of another type.

The morphological differences between single life periods
is far greater among pyknics than among other types.
The pyknic type usually reaches its most typical form
early in the riper years between 30 and 40, and after
the 60th year can become again somewhat disguised by
strong involutionary processes. These differences have
in the first place to do with the layer of fat, and the
changes in the thorax which are induced secondarily on
this account. There are cases where the pyknic fat belly
and the broadening of the lower thorax aperture which
grows parallel with it makes its appearance shortly after
the 20th year. This is, however, an exception. We
generally find among young pyknics between 20 and 30
the following characteristics (Plates 14 and 15). The
broad soft face with good moderate height proportions,
and the characteristic under-jaw is already fairly clear,

C

the neck is short, rather thick, but not strikingly depressed, and is well set away from the under side of the chin. The coming-together of the neck and shoulder proportions above the blown-out thorax has not yet made its appearance, and no kyphosis, and no depression of the head forwards between the raised shoulders is visible. Thus the young pyknic at first sight can easily be confused with the athletic. The following little table, however, in which the relevant average values in the three main groups for the years between 18 and 30 are reckoned, shows how closely the essential mass-relations approximate to those of later years.

TABLE IV

MALE AVERAGES FOR YEARS BETWEEN 18 AND 30

				Pyknic	Athletic	Asthenic
Head	.	.	.	57·7	56·3	55·6
Shoulder.	.	.	.	37·9	39·4	35·9
Chest	.	.	.	95·7	90·9	83·9
Stomach.	.	.	.	84·4	78·7	70·6

We see here plainly already the characteristic pyknic proportions, since even the young pyknics stand well in advance with their head, chest, and stomach measurements and thereby betray their tendency to breadth and rotundity. And particularly we notice again the ratio—so important for diagnosis—between shoulder-breadth and chest : for on an average the pyknic stands below the athletic in shoulder-breadth, though above him in chest measurement. The depression of the shoulder on the inner deltoid curve is usually already observable among quite young pyknics.

The tendency to fat is more diffuse among young pyknics, and is particularly observable in the face, and in the smooth modelling of the trunk and extremities, which show but little muscle-relief.

In old age the pot-belly is usually still in evidence, but it has often to a certain extent fallen in, so that the chest is not pushed up so much. The skin is loose and flabby. The principal bodily criteria of the type remain, however, as they were.

The bodily characteristics of the pyknics are slightly modified when we come to deal with women, in accordance with their sexual characteristics. We find here as before that the main covering of fat is round the trunk, but more strongly concentrated over the breast and hips. The ratio of chest to shoulder is the same as in the male. With regard to chest and hip measurements the pyknic women do not exceed the athletic absolutely but only relatively, when the height is taken into consideration. All this hangs together with the greater covering of fat among the athletic women, and the fact that the pyknic women are relatively smaller than the pyknic men. Remarkably small stature, under 150 cms., is not seldom found among them. The smallest of our material measured 145 cms. Very young pyknic women, who so far show no marked covering of fat, can at first glance, on account of the grace of their bodies, be confused with asthenics. The accurate observation of the measurement ratios, the shape of the face, the vaso-motor system (see below), and the body-forms, which are already noticeably full and round, will guard against this mistake. Young pyknic men may look, at first sight, very athletic, when they have good musculature, and fresh skin. Where the shape of the face and the breast-shoulder ratio are typical they cannot be confused. Otherwise in isolated cases the diagnosis may be very uncertain.

When we look at the photographs of old circulars when they were young, it is particularly remarkable that certain men and women exhibited quite a-typical bodies, longish faces, and a narrow build in their twenties, while later on they have developed along distinctly pyknic lines. When dealing with young circulars, therefore, one must be very careful in one's negative judgments in this respect, because from the state of the body before it is 40 years old one cannot say for certain that there are not, at any rate, pyknic components present. These episodically appearing pyknic components play an important part when we come to the question of change of dominance (see Chapter VII).

There are only two quite young circulars under the age of 17 among our material. They both show, along with well-formed, rounded bodies and limbs, clear retardation in their development. Whether there is some law lying behind this, we cannot say, for lack of sufficient evidence.

(d) *Distribution of the body-types among the schizophrene and circular classes*

Before we go on to a more detailed account of the diagnosis of the type by means of the head and periphery, and to the description of the smaller special types, let us first take a bird's-eye view of the numerical distribution of the body-types over the area covered by the circular and schizophrene classes.

It must be noticed here that a sharp line can obviously not be drawn between the individual types, and that therefore the distribution of border-line cases can never be exact. Among the circulars, we have underlined the number of cases with indubitably strong preponderance of pyknic structural elements (58). Fourteen others are cases of mixture, which show clear pyknic body symptoms, but alongside them, equally well-marked heterogeneous streaks, *e.g.*, pyknic-athletic (5 cases), and pyknic-asthenic (3 cases), all mixed forms.

Among the schizophrenes also the asthenico-athletic forms are very prevalent. Among a large number of "pure cases" we shall, of course, be able to establish minor traits in physique, indicative of alien types; they must be very carefully observed in each single case, and are often very interesting in connection with questions of heredity, characterology, and the development of psychotic symptoms. They may, however, be ignored in the bird's-eye view of the statistics of the whole.

TABLE V
PHYSICAL AND PSYCHIC DISPOSITIONS

	Circular	Schizophrene
Asthenic	4	81
Athletic	3	31
Asthenico-athletic mixed . . .	2	11
Pyknic	58	2
Pyknic mixture	14	3
Dysplastic	—	34
Deformed and uncataloguable forms .	4	13
Total .	85	175

The general survey which this table gives us is surprising and of great biological importance. Naturally one can lay no weight here on the actual figures. One must allow for the border-line cases, and also for the possible sources of error from exogenous factors (see Chapter VII). One will have, above all, to bear in mind that the material under examination, although in all groups drawn from the most varied environments, professions, and ages, belongs quite definitely to the Schwabian folk ; and for this reason the physical characteristics of other races will have to be carefully compared for purposes of definite proof. Our widespread comparison of portraits of healthy people belonging to the most varied German peoples and other European races (see Chapter XIII) makes it probable that there also, fairly similar, if not in certain cases identical, relations will be found to subsist between the physical and psychic dispositions. With these provisos then, we can set out the following remarks as true of our Schwabian material.[1]

In the case of *circulars*, among a number of mixed and indefinite forms, we find a marked preponderance of the pyknic bodily type on the one hand, and a comparatively weak distribution of the standard asthenic, athletic, and dysplastic forms on the other.

In the case of *schizophrenes* on the contrary, among a number of heterogeneously mixed and indefinite forms we find a marked preponderance of asthenic, athletic, and dysplastic types (with their mixtures) on the one hand, and a surprisingly weak distribution of typical cases of the pyknic bodily type on the other.

Thus we can formulate our results straight away.

(1) There is a clear biological affinity between the psychic disposition of the manic depressives and the pyknic body type.

(2) There is a clear biological affinity between the psychic disposition of the schizophrenes and the bodily disposition characteristic of the asthenics, athletics, and certain dysplastics.

(3) And vice versa, there is only a weak affinity between schizophrenes and pyknics on the one hand, and between circulars and asthenics, athletics, and dysplastics on the other.

[1] These remarks have been examined and confirmed with Rhenish material by Sioli, Kloth, and Meyer.

CHAPTER III

FACE AND SKULL

GALL's brain theory dealt the anatomic examination of the head of living man a blow, from which even to-day we have not yet recovered. The seat of the soul is the brain, and the skull is its capsule. Labouring under this idea, people have expended untiring assiduity in the attempt to discover from the size and shape of the skull the key to the contents hidden within it, with the end in view, as they supposed, of finding out something about the intelligence and psychic disposition of its owner. So long as psychiatry looked at things from this exclusive standpoint, " Psychic disorders are Brain disorders," just so long must the brain capsule, as the receptacle of the brain, enjoy a peculiar preference in the eyes of the psychiatrist, so far as he interested himself in the morphology of the body-build. And this was the case even after the phantasms of Gall had long been left behind. So it was that the finest methods for measuring the skull were very early formed, and that craniometry very soon developed into a distinct scientific speciality, without scientists going on to pay as much attention to the morphological examination of the other parts of the body as they had paid to that of the face and skull.

As soon as we bring ourselves to look anew at the problem of psychiatry from the point of view of the whole constitution, our anatomical interests also undergo a fundamental change. We no longer say " Psychic disorders are Brain disorders," but we see besides the brain the whole complex of ductless glands (the ultimate stronghold of the chemistry of the body), which, though, indeed, always through the brain, has the profoundest influence on the psychic development. And then we remember that it is precisely the inner secretions, which have an especially obvious parallel influence on two things : the general psychic disposition and the physiological development. This has been clearly demonstrated in

38

the case of the thyroid. The physical appearance of the cretin bespeaks a certain psychic type, so that when we see such a body, we go further and say : in this body there is probably a mind with certain clinically-known peculiarities. This psychological correlation is not absolutely accurate, in so far as there is a wide range of variations in the bodily and psychic nature of cretins, and in so far also as a well-marked indication of endocrine causality in the growth of the body is not always accompanied by an equally well-marked set of peculiarities of a psychic nature, and vice versa.

In the majority of cases, and consequently, on the average, however, the psycho-physical correlation may be clearly and unmistakably recognized. We see a similar correlation between the physical and psychic characteristics in the pathology of the generative glands among castrates and eunuchs. In the same way we have come upon similar indications of a correlation between the general form of the body and the psychic disposition in the case of schizophrenes and circulars : a correlation, which, it is true, is not hard and fast, but which on the whole is unequivocal. It may therefore be said that there are absolutely no physical characteristics of a patient which can be regarded with indifference by the psychiatrist. We have no longer any " individual peculiarities " which we may regard as chance phenomena, and which, therefore, have no interest for us. Just as the external detail which forms the Babinski sign can betray subtle changes deep hidden in the central nervous system, so every centimetre of the compass of the hand, and every degree of the angle of the jaw may serve as an index for drawing up the constitution formula of the patient. Not a hair of his head, and not a peculiarity of his nose is indifferent to us.

All this is true, with this proviso : the single morphological characteristic is always to be regarded as being important only in the framework of broad typical forms of bodily constitution. Only in this way do we avoid that type of investigation which clings to petty isolated peculiarities, and also the over-valuation of " symptoms of degeneracy." In this way the lobes of the ear, which have for so long enjoyed a regard that has almost amounted to a cult, return to the rôle which they should play, as being merely of relative importance. For not every detail has the same value. What is more important, and what is less important, we can only decide empirically, by comparison with the form as a whole, according as the detail in question shows itself to be more or less regularly connected with the type.

So long as we have no general form, no amount of diligent collecting of detail will help us. For " the criminal " or the " degenerate " is no biological type, either from a physical or a psychological point of view. For this reason " the criminal " can have no ear-lobes which belong only to him.

Now that we have, in the last chapter, discovered certain general types which have up to a point psycho-physical correspondences, and are therefore of genuine biological importance, we may start on the problem of the isolated anatomic symptoms with a different attitude, and a well-grounded position from which to pose our questions.

At this point, in our observation of the head, the centre of gravity of our interest shifts from the skull to the face. For the cranium is not of importance for us here in its relation to the brain, but as a detail in the formation of the body, and, indeed as a detail which is particularly poor in articulation, very obscure as to the laws of its growth, and extremely liable to secondary formations (trauma, overlaying in childhood). The face, on the contrary, undergoes the richest morphological development of all the parts of the body, and the final form to which this development leads is far less obliterated or modified through secondary influences, such as a sedentary life or a tendency to work ; far less than, *e.g.,* the extremities and the trunk, less indeed than any other part of the body whatever. Only in a few cases does the face also exhibit fundamental modifications by secondary influences, notably as a result of the serious loss of teeth at an advanced age, and of the operation of the weather and of poison on the soft parts (cheeks and nose) ; in the case of the bony tissue (nose) one must keep one's eyes especially open for syphilis, which, however, played no important part in the material from which our patients were drawn, it being principally rural.

Altogether we have discovered that the face is an epitome of a great part of those structural principles

PLATE 7

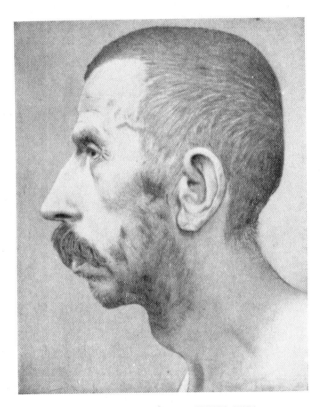

ANGULAR PROFILE. SMALL ASTHENIC SKULL
Premature senile involution
(Schizophrene congenital idiot, age 39)

PLATE 8

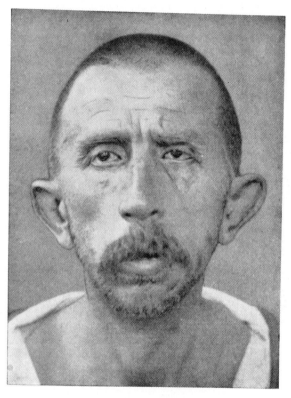

SHORTENED EGG-SHAPED FACE
(Schizophrene. Same as Plate 7. Frontal)

[face p. 41

which find expression in the general form of the body, and also of those trophic impulses which spring from its general neuro-chemical constitution. The face is the visiting-card of the individual's general constitution.[1] In the everyday judgments of men regarding one another, it is emotionally used as an index on account of two classes of facts which we do well to distinguish. On the one hand the expression of the face compresses the psycho-motor formation of a man into a narrow space. This falls outside our subject. On the other hand, however, the constitutional formation of a man, or, if one wants to narrow the notion down, his endocrine formation, is impressed on the build of the face. And in this indirect way the anatomical structure of the face becomes at least as important an index of the psychic character, as its mimetic innervation. For the layman, when he comes forward as a judge of mankind, the two components flow together into a general emotionally-toned judgment, when, after a first look at a face, he says: I like the chap—or, I don't like him. The anatomical components, as we have already pointed out in the introduction, are, for our practical-empirical emotional judgment, at least as decisive as the mimetic expression, though, in our rationalizations, we usually only make clear its relations to the latter.

And it is only with this anatomical structure of the face as the condensed expression of the psycho-physical formula, that we have to do here.

(a) *Type of face of the asthenic schizophrene: angular profile, long nose, shortened egg-form.*

TABLE VI

HEAD MEASUREMENTS OF THE ASTHENIC SCHIZOPHRENE

	Men	Women
Round the skull . . .	55·3	53·6
Sagittal diameter . . .	18·0	17·0
Max. frontal diameter . .	15·6	15·0
Vertical diameter . . .	19·9	19·2
Height of face. . . .	7·8 : 4·5	7·1 : 4·1
Breadth of face . . .	13·9 : 10·5	13·0 : 9·7
Length of nose . . .	5·8	5·2

[1] Excepting for the small number of those alloys and mixtures (see below) in which the face goes an entirely different way from the rest of the body.

As soon as we enter on the description of the more delicate morphology of the body, certain precautions have to be taken. We were speaking above, not of the facial types of the asthenic, but of the asthenic schizophrene. For we know that among schizophrenes in general a certain type of body, viz., the asthenic, appears to preponderate, but we do not know, vice versa, whether the schizophrene, or more correctly the schizothyme (see below), is the only type which stands in biological correlation with the asthenic characteristics. We can give this probability on the basis of considerations which we will go into later, but we cannot prove it. We also do not know beforehand whether certain isolated marks of bodily construction are common to all asthenics, or only to the schizothymes among them. Again, we do not know for certain whether the degree of pronouncedness of certain isolated stigmata stands in any relation to the degree of constitutional peculiarity which lies behind it (as is usually the case with acromegaly) ; whether, that is to say, certain stigmata are on an average more pronounced in the case of schizophrenes who are in a pathological condition, or in a condition which is tending in that direction, than in the case of a healthy schizothyme. Such a graduation would naturally, from a medical point of view, very much interest us, on account of its prognostic value ; from our material, we can, so far at any rate, not give any decisive answer to these questions. Besides this, it must be mentioned that in many cases the structure of the face does not harmonize with the total structure of the body, so that we may sometimes find a head such as otherwise belongs to the pyknic type, set on an asthenic body, and vice versa ; in such circumstances the mixture of types is usually indicated also in other ways in the body-build. Particularly within the schizophrene group do we find isolated stigmata of the various types often strikingly entangled. We find, therefore, here as everywhere else in the study of the constitution, the tendency for symptom complexes to appear which can be brought under more or less fixed laws, but which are not incapable of variation.

These considerations having been put forward once and for all, we have the following remarks to make about the form of the face among asthenic schizophrenes in well-marked cases : the general trophic tendency conforms to the characteristics of the rest of the body. The skin and soft parts are thin, pale, poor in fat ; on the bridge of the nose, particularly, the skin is stretched thin and smooth over the sharply outstanding bone. The bone-formation is throughout delicate ; where, as is the case with the malar bone and the supra-orbital arch the conformation is well marked, this is not due to strong bony growth but to the transparency and thinness of the soft covering flesh. The circumference of the skull is small, measuring 55·3 cms.—by far the lowest measurement of the three types of head. The asthenic skull is, compared with the other types, on an average short, low, and of a middling breadth. In the figures representing the measurements one is surprised by the smallness of the sagittal diameter (18·0), while in width (15·6) it is larger than the skull of the athletic type. We find that the shape of the back of the head is usually steep, with but little roundness. On this account, and because of the shortened sagittal diameter, we often find among asthenics also the visual appearance of the ' high-head ', without this necessarily being justified by the actual proportion of the height to the width. In the face the general principle of growth of the asthenic men is repeated, so that the upward growth is undisturbed, while the sideways growth lags behind. The breadth-diameters of the asthenic face lie between 13·9 and 10·5, and are by far the lowest, while the height, at least of the face itself, measures about 7·8, and equals that of the pyknics.

The asthenic face gives the impression of being long and narrow, sallow, and thin, and, in addition, sharply moulded. On account of its narrowness it often appears longer than it is.

When one examines a considerable series of asthenic schizophrene faces, one comes over and over again across one characteristic proportion, which is exceedingly important for diagnosis. This is the disproportion between the great length of the nose and the hypoplasia of the under-jaw. In the portraits of the schizophrene inmates of the Institute—schizoid degenerates—just as in those of the healthy intelligent schizothyme, this æsthetic motive is always cropping up. It has long ago struck the drawers of caricatures, *e.g.*, Resnizeh in a well-known comic drawing, *Die Familie von Krach*, has made variation on this theme through a whole family, and Menzel has raised it to the eminence of monumental stone in the profile of old Fritz.

This disproportion between the length of the nose and the shortness of the under-jaw often shows up particularly well in the shape of the profile. Out of this comes a form of profile which should be called the angular profile (Plate 7). Here, especially where the forehead is rather sloping, the upper half of the contour of the face runs straight forward along the sharp dominating bridge of the nose to its tip, and from the tip of the nose it goes straight back to the feeble short little chin, so that at the tip of the nose two arms of an obtuse angle run together. In such faces the nose is usually narrow, thin, sharp, and long, the tip of the nose does not seem turned up, but rather pulled downwards, while the bridge of the nose may be either straight or curved. In cases which are constitutionally less pure we find indications of the angle-profile, even in fuller faces with snub noses. It is important to look out for it.

Supposing we look at such an asthenic face from the front (Plate 8) ; in the purest cases, it manifests a shortened egg-shape in the lines of its circumference, while the contour of the lower jaw runs downwards from the ears to the tip of the chin unexpectedly quickly and sharply. This is particularly due to the smallness of the angles of the jaw, which, in the case of fuller faces, accentuates the lateral contour of the face, and also to the lack of fatty upholstering of the cheeks at the side ; it is also due to the thinness and delicacy of the branches of the lower jaw, and the narrowness of the flesh round the mouth which lies between them. The whole contour of the lower jaw from one ear over the tip of the chin to the other ear seems for this reason, from the front, to be very sharply bent back and angular, while with fuller faces it looks more obtusely bent and rounded into the shape of a shallow curve. Where the cases are not very typical the shortened egg-shape does not stand out very clearly ; we have then a wizened shield-shape or else an altogether

indefinite outline. We also find in many instances pronounced long faces with a high middle face.

The nose-jaw proportions of the schizophrene asthenics,
which we have described, are observable in the majority
of our material, while the average length of the nose in
relation to the height of the face is 5·8 : 7·8, which is
large (whereas, *e.g.*, the length of the nose of the circular,
with the same height of the face, is only 5·6). The
difference between the breadth of the malar bone and
the breadth of the lower jaw in asthenics is 3·4, while
with both the other types it is only 3·2. It is on account
of this that the extreme degree of hypoplastic narrowness
of the lower jaw of the asthenic in relation to the rest of
the face comes out so clearly ; and in addition we must
remember that the breadth of the malar bone is itself
already on an average 0·3 cms. narrower in the asthenic
than in the other types. The lower jaw of the asthenic is
on an average not less than half a centimetre narrower than
that of the pyknic or athletic. Measurement and visual
appearance therefore agree completely in the case of the
nose and lower jaw ; which shows how astoundingly
good and sure is the discrimination of our eyes for small
millimetre differences of measurement when we have to
do with the proportions of the face ; far more reliable
here than when we are dealing with the rest of the body.

For the rest there is a considerable range of variation
in the way in which the hypoplasia of the face comes out.[1]
Only a few of the asthenics exhibit the classical angle-
profile, for it is not in all of them that the hypoplasia of
the jaw in the sagittal axis shows itself so strongly, and
thereby gives the distinctive backward-springing of the
chin in the profile. The nose, too, does not always
spring so strongly forward, often it is only long, thin, and
with the tip drawn downwards. In all these cases we
have a simple long-nosed profile (Plates 2 and 16). The

---

[1] One must always investigate separately the hypoplasia of the
lower jaw as a whole, and that of the tip of the chin. The latter comes
to view in a lack of clear formation of the dent in the chin (*i.e.*, the
hollow between the underlip and the chin), and a scanty rounding and
swelling of the tip of the chin itself. The hypoplasia of the lower jaw
as a whole, on the other hand, is to be observed visually especially in
the short distance between the larynx and the tip of the chin, and,
from the front view, in the tendency to a concave sweep inwards of
the contour of the lower jaw near the chin.

height of the chin need not always be so small ; it may be that the hypoplasia of the lower jaw comes out very clearly when viewed from in front without its being perceptible in the profile. With practice one gets an eye for the variants of the face, which are all based on the same fundamental trophic principle—long noses, with hypoplasia of the lower jaw.

The angular profile, and those facial shapes which are connected with it, belong to the commonest special stigmata of the physique of the schizophrene class. Even in the faces of the athletics and dysplastics, which are built up in quite a different way, this motive constantly occurs here and there. And when, which is not often, we find a hint of it in faces of pyknics of advanced age, we must always search for the inheritance of schizothymic characteristics, and we often find them. In my material of 74 pyknics and pyknic-mixed circulars, only 7 cases have long pulled-out noses, which are too long for the rest of the face. It is interesting to observe them from a clinical and hereditary point of view. *Case* 1 : (♂). Impure case, old age depression with sullen paranoiac humour, stupor, uncleanliness, and a tendency to feeble-mindedness. *Case* 2 : (♂). Mother severe degenerative hysteria. Brother suffered from schizoid derangements at puberty and went to the bad. *Case* 3 : (♂). Father epileptic, harsh, autistic, peculiar, and an inventor. *Case* 4 : (♀). Mother's sister peculiar. Mother's brother suffered from clinically impure cyclic psychosis with strong delusions of persecution and domination. First cousin, indefinite psychosis with occasional suspicions of a schizophrene tendency. *Case* 5 : (♀). Parents bigoted. One sister schizophrene. *Case* 6 : (♀). Mother autistic, retiring, serious-minded. *Case* 7 : (♀). Mother strikingly autistic, quiet, preferred to be alone, unsociable, unfriendly, fell a victim at 60 to an incurable psychosis, refused to speak, sat about stupidly, sometimes screamed aloud (? late katatonic).

This brief review speaks for itself ; especially when one has mastered the characterology and heredity of schizophrenes. When we find long noses, we often find along with them impure paranoiac psychoses, cases of schizophrenia, and schizothymic personalities in the

PLATE 5

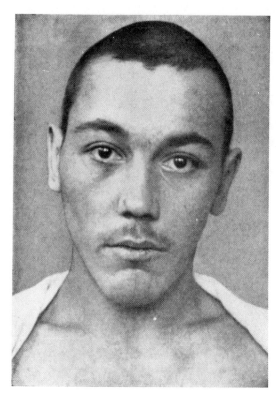

STEEP EGG-SHAPED FACE. LONG MID-FACE. LONG CHIN
(Schizophrenia)

PLATE 10

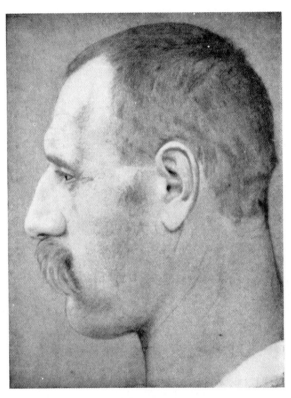

COARSE "HIGH-HEAD." PROMINENT BONE-MODELLING
(Acromegalic)

immediate family. At the same time we should not deny
that in many cases the connection may remain undis-
coverable, because the laws of inheritance are notoriously
no simple reckoning matter.

With regard to the variation in the shape of the head
of asthenic-schizophrenes we find, besides the simple
small skull which we have described, a rich group of other
characteristic shapes. We have sometimes observed a
light degree of ' blister skull ' (Blasenschädel).[1]

In these cases the cerebrum stretches bitemporally
over the ears, and may narrow down strikingly towards
the forehead. The rest of the face, otherwise built quite
on asthenic principles, widens in such instances slightly
towards the upper part, in order to join on to the wide
basis of the skull. One must not let oneself be led astray
by this appearance, which might easily appear to be a
fuller wider face than is the case. Whether this shaped
skull is due to a light hydrocephalus, or is a manifestation of a separate law of bone-growth, we cannot decide
off-hand.

Side by side with the high-head, the tower-skull
motif (Turmschädel), which plays so distinctive a rôle
in certain elongated schizophrene dysplastics (see below),
is not seldom to be found in asthenic morphology. From
the front view, we find the forehead tapering off conically
above, or, from the profile view, we find the back of the
head rising sheer and unrounded ; the top of the head is
raised, tending to pointedness, and falling away too
sharply towards the forehead, so that, from in front
the bushy growth of hair stands out like a rampart,
which gives many schizophrene faces a peculiar expression.

In my whole schizophrene material, I found only two
instances of the scaphoid skull (Kahnschädel), but in
these cases it was very prominent. From its rarity, we
cannot infer that it stands in any direct inner relation to
the schizophrene class. We must rather suppose that

---

[1] Even in cases which offer no evidence of congenital lues, etc.
On such doubtful points, we must be very careful not to seize immediately on an endogenous or exogenous cause. Why do we find such
blistered skull formations among schizophrenes oftener than among
circulars ? At first sight this does not indicate a purely exogenous
cause. We withhold our judgment, and give a merely descriptive
account.

heterogeneous causal factors are here at work, probably, also, of a degenerate variety.

That athletic, and in many cases also hypoplastic (see below) forms of face may be observed on an otherwise asthenic body, has already been mentioned. Mixed forms are especially numerous here.

The facial build of asthenic women shows the same deviation from that of males as their stature. It is, that is to say, smaller not only in point of breadth, but also in height.

The length of the nose reaches only that of the female circulars, the height of the face even lags behind. Thus, the faces of the asthenic women give the appearance of being not narrow and lengthy, like those of the men, but generally under-developed — even dwarfed. The small pointed nose, and the hypoplastic jaw are, however, often exactly the same. Heterogeneous face-shapes, sometimes hypoplastic, sometimes bony, are seen among asthenic women perhaps rather oftener than among the men, and certainly far more shapes which are uncharacteristic and morphologically indefinite. Many of these female asthenic faces appear themselves round and soft, because their slender bone-structure is covered by a certain bloatedness of the skin.

(b) *Type of face of the athletic schizophrene. Steep egg-shape. Substantial high-head.*

TABLE VII

HEAD MEASUREMENTS OF ATHLETIC SCHIZOPHRENE

			Male	*Female*
Skull circumference	.	.	56·0	54·8
Sagittal diameter	.	.	18·7	17·6
Max. frontal diameter	.	.	15·3	15·4
Vertical diameter	.	.	20·6	19·6
Height of face	.	.	8·3 : 5·2	7·6 : 4·6
Breadth of face	.	.	14·2 : 11·0	13·7 : 10·5
Length of nose	.	.	5·8	5·7

We can deal far more shortly with the athletic type of face. It also, just as the physique, is primarily characterized throughout by the pronounced trophism of the bones and skin (the muscles play but a small part here) ; the skin is thick, firm, sometimes fresh and of a good turgor, sometimes unclean, with a tendency to pimples, and often pasty and somewhat puffy. The colour is generally pale. The bony relief has in many cases a plastic appearance, which can be easily observed on account of the pad-like shading of the bony supra-orbital arch, and the compact formation of the malar bone and the prominent under jaw. The occipital pro-tuberance also is a good manifestation of the general growth of the bones, though, indeed, that degree of visible shovel-shaped projection which occurs in acromegaly is not reached among athletic schizophrenes. The develop-ment of the fat in the face is not particularly great ; I have, however, seen it richly displayed in cases of pasty, spongy, shield-shaped faces, particularly in combination with diffuse deposition of fat about the body in cases of certain dysgenital types.

The circumference of the skull is of a medium size. The shape of the skull is on the average high, narrow, and of a fair medium length. The shape of the back of the head varies, sometimes it is strikingly steep, sometimes projecting. A tendency to tower-skull is every now and then observed.

The shape of the athletic profile offers but little which is characteristic. The prevailing type is heavily boned, snub-nosed, with projecting, well-moulded chin, and a gently curving profile line [1] (in contradistinction to the well-marked total curve of the contour in angular profiles). But by the side of these we find many instances of angular profiles, and large-nosed profiles.

The athletic faces are often very long, the mid-facial length can attain an astonishing measurement (up to 9 cms.). The chin also is on the average long, in some cases it is moulded into a cone shape. So it happens that many athletic faces, in spite of their not inconsiderable absolute breadth, still have the appearance of being pre-eminently long.

The circumference of the front face is derived from the proportions which we have mentioned. With great values of the height-diameter we have the elongated, egg-

---

[1] By a profile line we mean a line drawn from the forehead over the tip of the nose to the tip of the chin.

D

shape (Plate 9), where the tip of the chin is as it were pressed down, and the contour of the jaw rises steeply to the ears. This kind of egg-shape has quite different anatomical foundations from the shortened asthenic oval, in so far as it is not conditioned, as is the case with the latter, by hypoplasia of the lower jaw, but, on the contrary, by lengthwise hyperplasia of the mid-face and chin. The whole of the athletic head, the cerebrum and the face taken together, often have a decisive influence on the appearance of the profile, compared with which the sagittal diameter takes a minor place in the visual impression. The general impression is then that of a massive high-head. This shape is exactly the opposite of that of the typical pyknic head, which, viewed in profile, with its smooth contour of the top of the head, its well-rounded hind portion, and its rather forward-projecting jaw-bone appears larger and lower (compare Plates 10 and 13).

If the length development of the face dominates, and the bend of the lower jaw is wider and smoother, we have a shield-shaped facial circumference, which, looked at from a purely morphological point of view, can only in detail, through its greater height, be distinguished from the five-cornered pyknic shape, and in this particular there is no sharp demarcation between the two. The shield-shaped athletic face is only about half as frequent among our material as the elongated egg-shape, which is by far the commonest athletic type. We find, besides, a few shortened egg-shapes and also some morphological transition forms between the elongated and shortened oval.

In the facial formation of the athletic woman, elongated egg-shapes are again not rare. But besides these we often find the hypertrophy of the mid-face tending more towards breadth, so that there emerges a very massive wide face with surprisingly plump cheek bones. With this, just as in the build of the body, is combined a rich overlay of fat. In contradistinction to the pyknic broad faces, the malar bone is here equally prominent, so that the contour appears not five-cornered, but seven-cornered, or even only consists in a formless massive rotundity.

PLATE 11

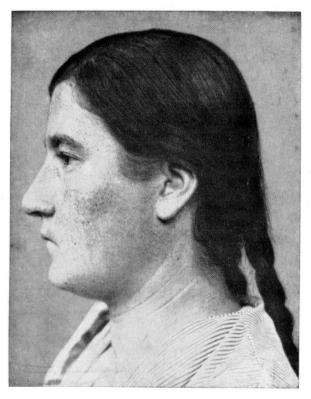

COARSE MASCULINE FACE OF AN ATHLETIC SCHIZOPHRENE (AGE 25)

(c) *Type of face of the pyknic circular. Smooth
five-cornered type.*

TABLE VIII

HEAD MEASUREMENT OF THE PYKNIC CIRCULAR

	Men	Women
Circumference of skull . .	57·3	54·5
Sagittal diameter . . .	18·9	17·1
Max. frontal diameter . .	15·8	15·0
Vertical diameter . . .	20·3	19·1
Height of face . . .	7·8 : 4·8	7·3 : 4·3
Breadth of face . . .	15·3 : 11	13·3 : 10·4
Length of nose . . .	5·5	5·2

A typical pyknic face is the true mirror of the pyknic physique. It has a tendency to breadth, softness, and rotundity. The large skull, therefore, is round, broad, and deep, but not very high. The skin of the face is stretched softly on the unprojecting bony structure, letting the blood-vessels of the skin show through, the cheeks and nose having a tendency to redness. On account of the fullness of the individual parts the skeleton tends to breadth and flatness, and is not very prominent. The overlay of fat is rich ; it is mainly concentrated, especially among old people, on the lower lateral parts of the cheeks, in front of the angle of the jaw, and in the region below the chin (a filling out of the angle between the chin and the larynx, double-chin). On the other hand, the delineation of the characteristic parts of the face, of the forehead, nose, malar bone, and chin, is in no way blurred on this account (in contradistinction to the diffuse indecisive character of the facial elements of many fat dysplastics), so that among the older circulars, we frequently find very beautiful heads with strong and distinct characters (Plates 12 and 13). In fact, among the older pyknics, the rich upholstery of fat under the skin seems to bring out in their rotundity, and almost like pads, certain curves of fundamental importance for the facial expression, particularly the crease between the nose and the lips, whereby results a quite remarkable plastic modelling which has great artistic attraction. The younger pyknic faces do not show this strong modelling yet ; they are full, round, soft, and, when they are suffused with red, blooming, and with certain cyclothymic temperaments this softness unites with the pyknic expression of kindly good-nature (Plates 14 and 15).

The profile line of the pyknic is, as a rule, only gently curved, not particularly high ; clear and complete in the particulars of the nasal and lip contours, and yet not sharp and projecting. The mutual relations in length of the forehead and mid-face, nose and chin, are, in general, very harmonious, and their proportions can often be used as an index for the average. We may say, with regard to the general æsthetic impression (excluding the dysplastics) : schizophrene faces are on the whole more interesting, circulars more balanced. While the faces of socially valuable schizothymes of good breeding make their impression through their very significant structure, their queer profile angle, their sharp prominent nose, or the distinguished restfulness of a long drawn-out pale face, the bright faces of the older cyclothymes have the advantage in the plastic modelling of the surface and in the harmony of the head proportion. This is only mentioned here in passing, it connects up with the portrait diagnosis which we shall describe later.

The front-view circumference of the pyknic face varies in the typical cases about the characteristic flat five-cornered shape (Plate 14). The faces are of middling height, and distinctly broad. The lower jaw, viewed from in front, has a smooth curve, and appears wider than it really is (the absolute breadth measurement being no greater than with athletics). This impression of a broad jaw is emphasized by the layers of fat on the lateral portion of the jaw, which, when the shape of the jaw itself is not very distinctively pyknic, makes the five-cornered shape full. It is on this account often clearer with older people than younger. When the turgor of the skin has somewhat degenerated, the fat lateral portions of the cheeks begin to drop, through their own weight, into pouch-like formations. This action pulls the lateral contour of the face almost completely vertical, so that a straight line runs from the corner of the temple to the angle of the jaw which is not broken by the weakly marked malar bone. At the angle of the jaw, the contour bends round fairly decisively into the horizontal sideways-running lower contour of the face, with

BROAD SHIELD-SHAPED FACE. PLASTIC SURFACE MODELLING
(Circular, age 65)

PLATE 13

PYKNIC PROFILE AND SKULL
(Same as Plate 12)

[*face p.* 53

its slight dip downwards for the tip of the chin displaying the flat arching of the lower jawbone, so that the two jaw contours run together from right and left, meeting in a very obtuse angle at the tip of the chin. The result is that the circumference of the face, if it is outlined, takes on the shape of an obtuse-angled pentagon, formed by a horizontal line from one temple to the other across the upper forehead, two vertical straight lines at the side (temple to angle of jaw) and below the two branches of the lower jaw meeting in a shallow angle.

This complete wide pentagonal form is to be found among youthful circulars as well, when the jaw is very wide and flat. Otherwise one finds in youthful cases, the side boundaries of the pentagon (temple to jaw angle) usually not vertical, but running obliquely downwards and inwards, without the general visual impression being very much modified thereby.

As to the shape of the nose, a middle-sized type dominates, at least among our folk. The bridge is straight or bending inwards, it springs clearly from the roots, rather broad, but not flattened ; the tip, fleshy and even thick, blunt, but neither snub nor pulled forward ; the nostrils often wide and sideways-springing. Redness of the nose is particularly common among older pyknics, and acne rosacea is not uncommon, and even, in some cases rhinophyma.

The eyes of the circulars are observed to be often small and deep set ; isolated cases of exophthalmia are sometimes found.

The forehead is usually beautifully developed, broad, or domed. The skull, as we have said, is large, round, and especially among men, it decidedly exceeds the other types in circumference, measuring 57·3. Plate 13 shows an excellent example of the pyknic-shaped head, with the full contour of the skull, and the well-formed roundness of the hind part of the head. In sagittal and cross diameters the pyknic skull exceeds the others, while its height is not particularly great. A comparison between Plates 10 and 13 makes the difference between the athletic and pyknic skulls very clear. With the athletics the height diameter dominates in the general optical impression of the whole skull (particularly on account of the length of the face ; cf. in both pictures the vertical distance from the lower lobe of the ear to the base of the lower jaw), while the dominating element with the pyknics is the depth diameter.

With regard to the variations in the shape of the pyknic face, we may remark that the full five-cornered shape of the front face circumference does not always come out clearly. We see far more usually simple, soft, broad, round faces, which are, as far as anatomical structure and proportion go, fundamentally analogous to the pentagonal type, without attaining its morphological obviousness.

We have already mentioned that we may observe between the ages of 17 and 30 longish oval-shaped faces among pyknics who later betray typical characteristics. It seems, indeed, as if at this age heterogeneous factors in the constitution come out clearest (e.g., temporarily longer necks, narrower build, or again, athletic musculature), while as time goes on, such foreign elements may be quite overgrown by the typical pyknic fat deposits, and the characteristic displacement in the proportions of the neck and shoulders. Still, this is only true of a small number, while the majority of pyknics already in youth have quite typical characteristics, even to the shape of the face.

If the length of the mid-face is rather above the average, then the full pentagonal shape of the face goes over into the broad shield-shape (Plate 12), which is often common among pyknics. On the other hand, pronounced length of the mid-face, as also pronounced narrowness or any other form of hypoplasia of the lower jaw, is extremely uncommon. And, therefore, one must always think of heterogeneous hereditary elements if the breadth of the face is not due equally to the malar bone and the lower jaw, but primarily to the malar bone. The massive, prominent cheek-bones project, and, viewed from in front, stick out of the otherwise clear lateral contour lines of the face. We have already spoken of very long, pulled-forward noses among circulars. Finally it seems to me that we must also turn our thoughts to foreign elements in the constitution in those cases where instead of the full round head we find a tendency to pointedness.

PLATE 14

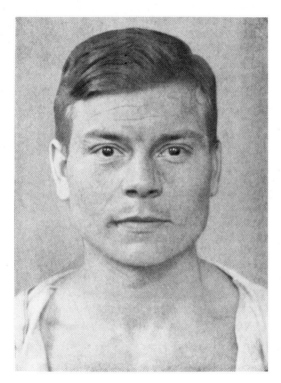

FLAT FIVE-CORNERED FACE
(Young pyknic type, age 20. Endogenous depression)

[*face p.* 5]

PLATE 15

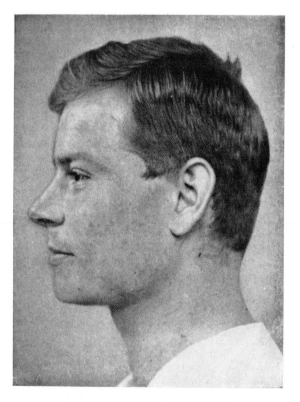

YOUNG PYKNIC TYPE. SOFT SURFACE
Weak delineation of profile. Harmonious proportions
(Same as Plate 14. Profile)

face p. 55

The shape of the face and skull of female pyknics offers no peculiarities, except that, in conformity with the smaller size of the body they often lag behind the athletics as regards the absolute measurement. The round faces of young female circulars can be quite small and delicate. In differential diagnosis one must above all beware of confusion with the broad faces of athletics, as sometimes these can have quite a rich overlay of fat. Apart from the general physique, the far coarser bone-structure of the athletic face and the prominence of the malar bones keep one from this confusion.

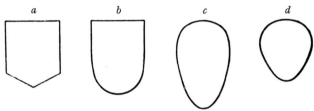

a. flat five-cornered.   *b*. broad shield-shape.   *c*. steep egg-shape.
d. shortened egg-shape.

PLATE 16.

CHAPTER IV

THE SURFACE OF THE BODY

OF those constitutional symptoms which can be established on the surface of the body, the hair is by far the most important, particularly with men. Stress is also to be laid on the colour of the skin, the vaso-motor system, and the state of the blood-vessels. The consistency of the skin, its thickness, firmness, and elasticity, can unfortunately only be very inexactly estimated, and therefore is of value only when gross variations are observed. The same is true of the moisture of the skin, which is far too dependent on external conditions, movement, and the temperature of the room.

The close connection between the hair and the endocrine conditions is well known, particularly from the phenomena of puberty as well as from the pathology of the generative gland, hypophysis, and the thyroid gland. We may therefore expect to find in the hair an excellent indicator of constitutional conditions.

What are the normal hair conditions of the adult male? That is a senseless question. We shall soon observe that the hairage (Behaaren) may be divided into various types, which can only be stigmatized as abnormal when they are excessively developed. In order to understand these types we must first make the following preliminary statements about hairage in general. We differentiate primary hair, and secondary hair. The primary hair of the child consists of the hair on its head, brows (and eyelashes), and the almost invisible lanugo hairy covering of the rest of the body. At puberty is added the secondary hair, which takes the place of the foregoing in some respects, in the following chronological order: genital and arm-pit hair, beard (and generally the chin-beard and the moustache first), and hair on the trunk. Synchronizing with these processes, there occurs gradually, and therefore not to be arranged in exact chronological sequence, the change of the lanugo hair of the extremities into fine secondary hair, and this occurs on the legs more pronouncedly and also earlier than on the arms.

Of these groups of secondary hair, the earliest are at the same time the least subject to variation. A defective development of the pubes and hair under the arm-pits is rarely found among adults, and when it does occur it is always accompanied with serious disturbances of development in other quarters of the physiological and psychic domains. It is therefore always to be considered as a dysplastic abnormality. The same may be said of a lasting and striking lack of development of hair on chin and upper lip, while the hair on the cheeks is very variable even in the cases of perfectly well-developed men. This is still truer of the hair on the trunk, which varies among healthy men from faint markings to what forms a covering for almost the entire surface. It is important to know its exact localization. We find a typical region of hairiness on the lower half of the breast-bone. Here, even with men who are not hairy, we seldom fail to find indications of hair. About this centre, when the chances of growth are favourable, is found a triangular hairy zone. The two angles at the base of the triangle contain the nipples of the breast, while its upper part reaches about to the manubrium sterni. Even when there is this wider scattering, the hair is usually thickest at the pit of the stomach. From there, in the case of hairy individuals, there is a continuous bridge connecting with the upper extremity of the pubes. With most men, the hair on the back is thin, sporadic, or even non-existent. The centre of growth here seems to lie primarily in the region between the shoulder-blades, from which, in the case of hairy people, a faint line may stretch over the deltoid muscle, joining the breast centre, so that there is a ring of hair lying round the breast and shoulders. Below this the interscapular hair fades away without any sharply defined boundary, and at a point which varies with different people.

Visible hairiness of the legs belongs to the more constant characteristics; it is at any rate less variable than the hairiness of the trunk. When, in adult age, it is absent or quite weak, one must attribute it to dysplastic abnormality.   Fundamentally more variable, and, on an average scantier, is the hair on the arm, and yet its complete absence is surprising.

One must, therefore, reckon the strength of the trophic impulse lying behind the growth of the hair of any individual, not only from the strength and thickness of the hair itself, but also from its grouping and distribution, so that thinness of hair on the chin, and complete lack of pubes, must be counted *eo ipso* as an advanced degree of hair weakness, while scarcity of hair on the legs betokens mere hair weakness.   Conversely one finds clear indications of hair outside the described trunk hair zones, for example on the lateral regions of the stomach and loins, in general only among those who are otherwise pronouncedly hairy.[1]

The secondary hair of women corresponds with all this ; it is to be regarded simply as a generally weaker form of the male type in that those regions which are constant in their hairiness in the male (pubes and arm-pits), are also hairy in the female.   With regard to the next weaker points in the male hairage, the upper lip, chin, and legs, a light down is often observable on them in women, and there is a notorious tendency to growth of beard after the involution period, while the trunk and arms, as also the most inconstant regions in males, often remain free from hair in females.   The degree of abnormality in hairiness in the female is reckoned approximately according to this scheme.

The moment of commencement of the male secondary hair varies considerably, at least among our people. Only the pubes and hair under the arm-pits must be considered as completed between the ages of 16 and 17, while a lag in the growth of the beard up to 22, and of the hair of the trunk up to 25 cannot be regarded as anything remarkable.   Synchronously with the appearance of the secondary hair there occurs a certain tendency to a retrogression of the primary hair.

Finally, notice must further be taken of the length, consistency, and mode of growth (upright or lying down) of the hair, especially in the case of the hair on the trunk,

---

[1] Our investigations have produced so far nothing determinate about the biological meaning of the colour of the hair.

PLATE 17

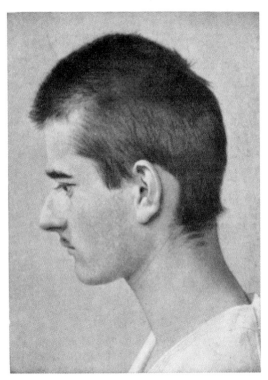

' FUR-CAP HAIR '
(Asthenic schizophrene. Age 21)

[*face p.* 58

and also we must observe the uncustomary regions in which it grows, beyond the described centres. The further behaviour of the earlier lanugo hair is (as we shall see) of importance. After these preliminary remarks, we can proceed to the description of the individual types of hairage which, on their side, betray clear correlations with the types of physique which we have already outlined.

We will deal first with the circular pyknics, because they are least prone to serious deviation from the above described average. The hair of the head in the male, being in many ways dependent on the cut and the barber, is in general not very easy to judge. Among circulars one is constantly coming across a form of soft hair, which does not stand up bushily or like a brush, and yet does not lie flat, but falls in soft, often wavy, curves, and, where it is plentiful, may be easily parted. In my records I have mention of remarkably soft hair in 26 cases, and remarkably bushy hair in only 6. These are, of course, naturally very subjective judgments. The hair on the head of the pyknic usually does not grow downward to the face, but rather recedes ; on the temples the ' Geheimrat's corner ' may be often observed, but horizontal forehead boundaries are just as common. The tendency to baldness seems far greater among pyknics than in the schizophrene groups. I have noted about 30 per cent. of schizophrenes and about 40 per cent. of circulars who were bald. A good example of a pyknic bald head is like a polished billiard ball. Here and there, on the shiny surface, stand upright or lie wavily single long delicate hairs distributed with fair regularity. They form a kind of bay from the temples of the forehead towards the middle of the head, or they group themselves more at the back of the region of the crown.

The bald heads, as they often occur among schizophrenes,[1] offer a peculiar contrast. We find among them, for example, a type of baldness that looks as if the region of the hair had been gnawed by mice. The bald part is incomplete, indefinitely marked off, and partially bald patches alternate with such patches of short woolly hair

---

[1] Of course, great care has everywhere been taken, that no case of artificial modification of the hair (through rubbing or pulling out) has been described.

as remain. The bald surface shows no reflecting polish, but is, rather, distinctly dull, and has a tendency to peculiar sharp wrinkles, each of which may cross the skull in a direct line, so that they look like knife-cuts from a distance.   Then one often finds among schizophrenes quite unusual localizations of baldness.   One form for example affects the forehead only, right in front, cutting in a straight line across the remaining growth of hair, so that it looks as though the tip of the hairy region, which usually curves forwards from the temples, forming a bay, to the middle of the forehead, had been marked across and removed.   Again, occasionally we find quite grotesque tonsures in the middle of the cranium (not behind, near the vertebral region), where towards the forehead is left a ring of hair, or even only a compact woolly tuft of hair, which marks the remains of the forelock.

Let us now return to the hairage of the circulars. The brows are of middling thickness. The growth of the beard—this is diagnostically important to determine— is usually remarkably evenly distributed, without pre- ference for any region ; it has fairly wide boundaries, so that it may grow right into the face and down the neck. The hair of the beard is of middling consistency, rather soft and wavy.   We notice from old photographs of the time of the fashion for full beards that pyknics had beautifully shaped, even, full beards.

The pubes and hair under the arm-pits have often a peculiar form among pyknics.   It is surprisingly well developed, very coarse, and so long that more often than not it outgrows the arm-pit, and a small, short genital organ often almost disappears in it.   The hair on the trunk varies from middling to plentiful in the regions which we have described as typical in the general outline above. The individual hair is of middling strength, standing rather upright, and curling over crisply at the tip.   I have seen individual cases of circulars where the hair on the trunk is exceptionally plentiful, but I had doubts of the purity of their constitution ; remarkably scant distri- bution of hair on the trunk is decidedly rare.   The hair on the extremities is of a mean degree of plentifulness among circulars.   I have found that the secondary hair puts in its appearance rather late than early in the young pyknic.

Now for the characteristics of the hair in the schizophrenes. Among young schizophrenes up to the age of
20 we often find an excessive formation of primary hair,
particularly among the asthenic group. The hair on the
head is not only very thick, but seems to try to spread
itself over its usual boundaries. It grows down the neck,
and also inwards over the forehead and temples, so that
the bay formed by the corner of the temples spreads its
arms out, and in the lateral region of the temple, the
hair of the head links up with the brows in a more or less
narrow bridge. The brows also take part in this excessive growth, they are very wide and thick and often join
over the root of the nose. In this way a continuous ring
of hair—formed by this closed circle of head-hair and
brows—surrounds the forehead like a wreath. This type
of head-hair which we have just described, with its thick
bushy growth and its tendency to advance well into the
face and neck, we may designate by the name of ' fur-cap
hair '. A small asthenic skull with its angular profile
poking sharply out of what is left free from hair, often has
the same general æsthetic effect as the head of a martin.[1]
Quite often the lanugo shares the profuse growth of the
primary hair-covering, especially in the form of well-
marked visible stripes of lanugo, which grow in continuous
lines from the head-hair at the nape of the neck down the
spine : similar phenomena may be observed also on the
outer side of the arm, and on the chest.

This primary hair which we have just described, is retained more or less unchanged beyond the age of puberty
only by a certain number of the schizophrenes in whom
it was originally present. We constantly find even
among elderly schizophrenes thin hairy bridges at the
temples, still often quite clearly marked, and, in the case
of well-developed brows, a marked junction at the root
of the nose (hence the old theory of the growing together
of the brows as a sign of degeneration). Indication of con-
fluence of the eyebrows is found by accurate observation
to be altogether general, and is quite a common thing
among circulars too. On the other hand I have only met
with isolated cases, among circulars, of thick growing
together of the brows, and especially of the clear junction

[1] One often reads the expression " bird-like head."

of brow and head-hair at the temples. The three cases
of junction at the temples have the following characteristic hereditary symptoms: *Case* 1: (♂). Daughter
schizophrene (under our treatment). *Case* 2: (♂). Brother
schizophrene. *Case* 3: (♂). Mother schizophrene.

The head-hair of the older schizophrenes remains on
an average stronger and longer-lasting than is the case
with circulars. Bald heads are, as we have observed,
rather less prevalent among schizophrenes, and in any
case they seldom are as large in area or as complete;
but they have the form we have described above. More
often than with circulars do we find the individual hairs
coarse and even brush-like, growing bushily, and not lying
down so easily and softly. On the other hand, however,
among asthenic and hypoplastic schizophrenes is to be
found a type where the hair is quite fine and not very
thick, lying smooth and tight to the head like fur.

While the primary hair in schizophrenes is on an
average extensively and intensively very developed and
also relatively lasting, we find just the opposite to be true
of the secondary hair. The growth of the beard is, and,
in the majority of members of the schizophrene class of
physique, remains weak (cf. Plates 7 and 8); it is often
confined to a narrow area, and is unevenly distributed
with preference for the chin and upper lip. Of 92 schizophrenes who were carefully examined with reference to
this point, I found 60 with weak beard growth, 21 where
the growth was of medium strength, and only 11 whose
beards were distinctly strong. We observe a weak growth
of the beard in many asthenics, and also among dysplastics, especially the eunuchoid group, where the beard
may remain latent, to the extent of only showing mere
indications. Even among athletic schizophrenes I found
a tendency rather to weak than strong beards. The
strongly bearded schizophrenes fall generally into two
sub-groups of physique. There are the plump pasty-faced
athletics with the shield-shaped facial circumference, and
the small characteristic group of elongated ' tower-skulls ',
which we shall describe later. Here the growth of the
beard is often extensive, and of a pronouncedly brush-like,
upstanding nature.

The pubes and the hair of the arm-pits are of medium

strength in the majority of schizophrenes ; one seldom meets with very hairy individuals, but on the other hand there is a striking percentage of distinctly weak, un-developed hairage of the genital and arm-pit regions, which, as we have already remarked earlier on, has an important biological significance. This scanty hairage is to be found above all among asthenics and those dys-plastics impinging upon the eunochoid group. After closer examination I have noted among schizophrenes two cases of strong hairing of the genital region, 25 of medium strength, and 18 weak.

As we might expect, the hair of the trunk remains still further behind the average (8 strong, 10 medium, 29 weak). Profuse hairage with normal distribution we found mainly among the athletic group. Among asthenics, on the other hand, we found, among those who tend to scant hairage, a small interesting class where late hair development occurs.

Here, at a riper age, is developed a fairly profuse growth of hair on the trunk and extremities, with this peculiarity, that the individual hairs (and this is opposite to the pyknic cases) remain rather short and straight and lie flat on the skin. Hair round the genitalia and under the arm-pits often possesses this characteristic of straightness of growth. This crop of hair is often found, besides on the legs, on the upper parts of the breast and shoulders, which it may encircle in the way we have described before. This strong, straight growth of hair is often observed by physicians between the shoulder-blades in cases of asthenic phthisis, and to a certain extent has been taken as a direct stigma. It seems to me, also, that this late crop of hair in the asthenic has a tendency to be localized rather higher up the chest, and to grow right up to the laryngeal cavity, leaving the lower sternal parts free. But my material is not sufficient to enable me to make any certain pronouncement on this question.

The distribution of the hairs on the extremities, among schizophrenes, is usually found to be of weak to medium profusion, and is seldom remarkably plentiful.

There is far less to be said of diagnostic significance about the growth of the hair among women, in the first place on account of its special limitations, and also because external conditions often stand in the way of a more detailed investigation. The behaviour of the primary hair seems to be analogous to that occurring in the male type ; with circular women the head-hair is middling to weak, and with schizophrenes there is often the tendency to a growing inwards towards the face, with strips across the angle of the temples. The individual hair of the schizophrene woman is often coarse, long, and luxuriant, like the hair of a horse's mane; but on the other hand, especially in the case of many asthenics and dysplastics, it may be also like the hair of a child, short, silky, and thin.

With regard to the brows, hair under the arm-pits, and pubes, the same may in general be said as was said of the male. As regards the beard, and the hair on the trunk and extremities, apart from the schizophrene tendency to hypertrichosis of the lanugo, which we have already described in dealing with young men, I have not been able to discover any fundamental difference between the women of the schizophrene and circular classes. One finds here and there a tendency to a downy bearded-ness, and the appearance of a few isolated hairs on the mammæ, but these do not seem to fall under the working of any ascertainable law.

The nature of the skin

The most important differences here lie in the region of the vascular systems of the skin. We find, for instance, that the colour of the face in the case of circulars is generally red, while that of the schizophrenes of all groups is mostly pale. I have the following notes of male circulars : colour of the face, pale 8, medium 12, red 21 ; and of the schizophrenes : pale 87, medium 21, and red 10. These proportions are also valid for women. I believe these vaso-motor differences to be fairly import-ant for diagnosis. I have often been surprised to find how, among healthy schizothymic men, in spite of an otherwise quiet asthenic physique, a ruddy colouring and a high degree of vaso-motor sensitivity of the skin on the face betrays inherited cyclothymic characteristics, which then come to light characterologically in good-tempered or humorous components.

The complexion of the circular is spread usually over the cheeks and nose. It is very common among older people to find the smaller veins showing through quite red in these parts, which points to the fact that the plentiful vaso-motor provision in these regions later often leads to chronic dilation of the veins. In this way is explained a certain disposition to acne rosacea, which we have already mentioned. Apart from this heightened normal colouring, there is also a high degree of sensitivity of the facial vaso-motor system to thermal and affective stimulation. As far as the rest of the vascular system is concerned, on account of my necessarily summary investigations in this particular, I have not been able to establish a great tendency among circulars to arterio-sclerosis ; isolated instances of apoplexy and raised blood-pressure are naturally found among my material. This question should be investigated in detail,[1] since some constitutional connection with kinds of physique, which at any rate are very like the pyknic, is quite rightly suspected by physicians.

In my observations the occurrence of pale complexions among circulars was noted particularly in young male patients. On the other hand I saw remarkable blooming fresh complexions in the case of young circular women. I was unable to decide whether there lay any law behind these phenomena.

In contradistinction to this, the complexion of schizo-phrenes of all ages is generally pale, often with a dash of yellow or cheese-like pastiness on the one hand, or with a tendency to a sallow brown pigmentation on the other. Among the small minority of reddish schizo-phrene faces I find, among other colours, which may be attributed to acne, isolated instances of a peculiar cherry-red colouration of the cheeks, which varies slightly in a bluish direction ; the surface over it is a thick, almost myxœdemic stiff skin, so that it is possible that this colour is simply dependent on the optical laws covering the passage of light through a thick medium. I have already mentioned the tendency to acne of many athletics.

[1] In the older psychiatric literature there are many remarks on somatic subjects, which, however, are valueless from a modern clinical point of view.

E

Many athletics are also subject to a dark reddening of the face behind an otherwise brownish pale complexion. In connection with the vascular system of the rest of the body, one must mention particularly the often very surprising thinness, delicacy, and smallness of pulse-wave, of the radial arteries, in the case of asthenics. Atrophy of the heart has also long been a well-known clinical phenomenon of asthenics. Distal cyanosis as a chronic peculiarity, *i.e.*, blue-red hands and feet, is notoriously very often met with among schizophrenes and especially in the asthenic group. This dystal cyanosis contrasts with the paleness of the face and the rest of the body.

The other qualities of the skin can be dealt with shortly. We have mentioned that the skin of the asthenics is thin and poor in fat ; it is flabby and not very elastic ; with people who are no longer quite young it falls into long thin flaccid creases. Among prematurely aged asthenics we frequently find a delicately wrinkled zero-derma, such as Bauer and others have described, particularly in dysplastics. The covering of the body may then be remarkably dry and inclined to peel. The skin of the athletic is, as we saw, generally thick and firm, with a moderate amount of fatty upholstering (at any rate among the men). Myxœdemically thick, stiff, unelastic skins were found, particularly among certain dysplastics (q.v.) ; this quality of the skin is most easily felt over the malar bone, and on the outer side of the upper arm. The skin of the pyknics, with its richer, softer upholstering of fat, possesses otherwise average characteristics. At the ends of the extremities, where, even in the case of pyknics, the covering of fat is not particularly plentiful, it may more or less disappear at a later age, so that a soft flaccid skin is left loosely stretched over a graceful, never very wide, short rounded hand.

PLATE 18

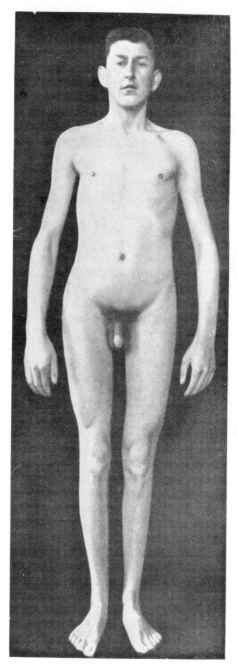

ELONGATED EUNUCHOID
(Schizophrene. Age 18)
Abnormal length of extremities. Ample curving of the hips
Measurements—Height 173 ; Legs 95 (!) ; Chest 86.91 ; Hips 91 (!)   [*face p.* 66

at all.   Striking disturbances of individual bodily proportions, too, are rare.   Where we do find such, as for
example a tendency to ' tower-skulls ', marked irregularity
of the features, etc., we also find, running parallel with
them, many signs of a heterogeneous constitution on the
psychic side as well, in the general attitudes, personality,
and heredity.   Well-developed symptoms of rickets are
also only found in isolated cases.

It is quite otherwise with the schizophrene class.   Here
the dysplastics number 34 cases of our total material,
that is to say, a very striking proportion, among which
we have not included the numerous dysplastic indications
occurring among athletics, and particularly among
asthenics.   Now while these dysplastic types among the
schizophrenes are more or less isolated in relation to
the circular class, they have so many and such marked
connections in other directions, specially with epileptics
and dysglandulars, that from a purely morphological
point of view they often cannot be differentiated from
one another.   This observation is very important, because
it points to the possibility that the biological causes, *e.g.*,
of a secretional nature, are in all three groups the same
in a certain number of cases, and that only the clinical
development in the one case into a schizophrenic attack,
in the other into an epileptic seizure, and in the third, into
harmless debility, is different, in as much as accessory
factors lead now in the one direction, and now in the other.
Still these are only suggestions, which one must allow to
pass through one's mind, but which, particularly with
regard to their bearing on epilepsy, are very far from
being ripe enough for anyone to pass judgment on them.

In our exposition of the psychic constitutions, we have
left epilepsy altogether out of our considerations ; we have
done so, in the first place, because characteristics which
are not determined constitutionally, but primarily through
trauma or damage to the generating cells, play a disproportionately large part, and are also very difficult to
distinguish from characteristics which are in the main
constitutionally genuine, so that to-day it would be
difficult, and only possible with the very greatest caution,
to make use of epilepsy as a clinical unity in any investigation into constitutions ; but above all, because we

PLATE 19

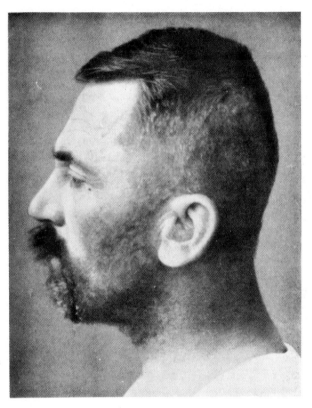

'TOWER-SKULL' WITH EXCESSIVELY COARSE BEARD
(Schizophrenia)

[face p. 68

cannot find from our inquiry into characterology so far, that epilepsy plays anywhere near as important a rôle as the pathological representative of similarly widespread personality-groups, of fundamental importance for normal psychology, as is the case with the circular and schizophrene classes.   Probably the 'epileptic personality' only characterizes a small group of men with some excessively developed defect.   That great mischief has been done by the diagnosis of epilepsy in regard to talented historic personalities, on insufficient evidence, is known to everyone.   Among the few certain cases of epileptic geniuses (Dostoievski), how far significant connections can be shown between their psychiatric nature and their creative genius in the positive sense, and not with regard to the checking of their genius by the disease, is a question which naturally demands further careful investigation.   In any case we must be prepared later on, if necessary, to rank an epileptic type between the schizophrenes and circulars.

Now for the dysplastic physiques among the schizophrenes.   If we do not want to waste time in the description of startling individual forms we shall do well to collect them together under broad headings.   These headings are provided for us by the morphology of the disturbances of the internal glands.   It is particularly to the physique forms of the dysgenital groups that so many of the schizophrene dysplastics bear unmistakable morphological resemblances.   The question immediately arises whether this similarity of form points to the same endocrine etiology, which is not improbable, but which by itself naturally cannot be strictly proved yet.

The following are our groups :

(a) *Elongated Eunuchoids*

In the application of the notion we follow Tandler-Grosz [1] and Bauer,[2] and of the characteristics of the elongated eunuchoid we take the following as the most significant and most tangible : the extreme length of

[1] Tandler - Grosz.   *Die biologischen Grundlagen der sekundaren Geschlectscharakter.*   Berlin, 1913.
[2] Loc. cit.

the extremities in relation to the height of the body ; the obliteration of the sexual characteristics in the proportions of the trunk, so that we find in a male an ' asexual' pelvis, which, to an outside observer, has a tendency to femininity ; and finally the scantiness of secondary hair combined with well-developed head-hair.   We number among our material about 20 schizophrenes of all ages, in whom at least two of these characteristics are simultaneously and clearly developed, and 6 cases which show all three.[1] We find this schizophrene-eunuchoid character sometimes alone, and sometimes combined with an asthenic or athletic physique.   The representatives in our group (apart from the 4 athletic mixed cases) are mostly thin, tall figures, with a strikingly graceful build of the bones ; the majority being over medium height (max. 196, min. 164 cms.).   The chest often seems narrow, and long, and frequently runs downwards and inwards giving the impression of quite a feminine waist.   From here downwards the contour of the hips often spreads out into a generous curve, which again produces a feminine impression.   In fact we find that the measurement of the hips equals or even exceeds the chest measurement after inspiration, while in the normal male the hip measurement gives the minimum measurement of the chest at rest, or else does not reach it.   The appearance is particularly striking when the width of the trochanter is greater, while the breadth of the shoulders is less, which becomes equally apparent in the measurement.   There are, then, disproportions such as in the following case of a young 21-year-old heboid, W.W. : Height 172, length of leg 94, chest 80–85, hips 89.   This case had scant secondary hair, and testicles smaller than a nut in size.

In 10 cases of our group we found anomalies of the genitalia, namely : Hypoplasia of the testicles 4 times ; severe hyperplasia 4 times ; hypoplasia of the genital

---

[1] With regard to the length of the extremities alone, where it does not reach an excessive degree, we cannot draw any conclusions. After careful measurement of a great deal of material, one will soon notice that pronounced excess of the length of the leg over half the length of the body is quite common in all physique groups. We have here only paid attention to those lengths of the extremities where twice the length of the leg (measured from the upper junction with the body) exceeds the height by more than 10 cms., and then only in those cases where other eunuchoid stigmata are joined thereto.

PLATE 20

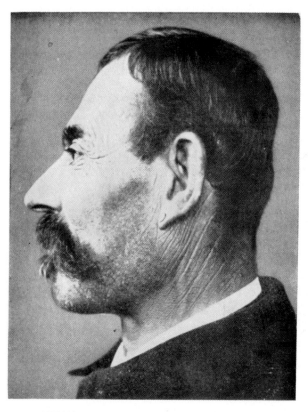

'TOWER-SKULL' WITH EXCESSIVELY COARSE BEARD
(Father of a schizophrene)

[face p. 70

organ twice. The hypoplastic testicles were in one case hard, in another surprisingly poor in substance and hardly palpable, the smallest being only the size of a cherry. The hard hyperplasia of the testicles with a clear increase in consistency reached in one case, where the influence of sexual disease could certainly be excluded, a not inconsiderable degree, and besides this there was in this instance a goitre the size of a goose's egg.

Among the circulars I have only found in one instance two eunuchoid stigmata together, namely, abnormal length of the extremities, and enlarged hips, and that was in the case of a 51-year-old clerk whose measurements were as follows : Height 176, legs 94, chest 91–93, hips 95½, shoulder 35, breadth of trochanter 35. We have here, therefore, which is very rare in the male, the breadth of the hip equalling the breadth of the shoulder. This man, otherwise of pyknic build, with a large round skull, emphysis, and a great fat belly, had, as well, a formidable knotted goitre, almost as big as two fists. He suffered from a particularly severe psychosis which went on for decades without a break, in unceasing alternation of manic and depressive phases. In his mania he was subject to an unusual sexual cynicism, which spent itself in phantasies, writings, and drawings. His heredity showed signs of heterogeneous influences. One must regard this isolated instance, differing from the usual form in so many respects, as, probably a complicated constitutional synthesis, and not as a typical circular, as one must likewise regard all such rare manic-depressive cases with striking dysglandular symptoms.

Elongation with Tower-skulls

I should like to deal with this small sub-group, containing 8 male schizophrenes, next to the elongated eunuchoids, on account of their manifold morphological connections. It is possibly based on a closely related endocrine formation. The outward appearance of this group is significant and characteristic, above all, on account of the peculiar shape of the face and skull, and the nature of the growth of the hair. Under the narrow upward-running structure of the tower-skull, sits a very long bony

face with a prominent snub-nose, having a sharp depression
at the root.   The lower jaw is often high and firm.   The
moustache sticks well out like a brush, and the eyebrows
often share in the excessive growth of hair.   In addition,
the hair on the head is strong and bushy.   This tower-skull
face, often grotesque in itself, with its powerful brush-like
beard, rests on a long, tall ill-proportioned body.   Most
of the examples of our group are over medium size (max.
184, min. 168) and have an appearance which varies
between the asthenic and the athletic.   The posture is
often sloppy and rather bent ; large hands hang on the
ends of long thin limbs ; either the figure is thick-set and
muscular, with broad extended shoulders, or it is femininely
disproportioned, with narrow shoulders, and a long narrow
chest.

In 5 of these 8 cases eunuchoid stigmata were to be
found, namely :   outstandingly excessive length of the
extremities 3 times, feminine trunk proportions with large
hip measurement twice, hypoplasia of the testicles and
the genital organ twice, in one case the testicles lying
very high, almost a case of cryptorchism.   In one of the
subjects there was the following combination : excessive
length of extremity, hypoplasia of the testicles and genital
organ, and homosexuality from youth up.   The hair on
the trunk and extremities varied, but without any significant peculiarities.   The age of these patients was between
28 and 50.

Masculinism [1]

The female eunuchoid is, from a clinical point of view,
not sharply delineated enough for us to be able to use
this notion for our purpose.   We group together here
7 cases of schizophrene women, of whom the most striking
common characteristic is a distinct variation in the
secondary characteristics from the female type ;   and
certain of them remind one of the male eunuchoid, particularly as regards the excessive length of the extremities.
It would seem idle to collect together all the cases of
hypoplasia of the genitalia among schizophrene women,
because such anomalies are so common among them that

---

[1] Cf. Plate 11.

PLATE 21

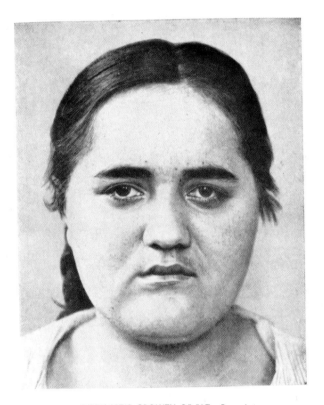

DYOPLASTIC GROWTH OF FAT. Frontal
(Schizophrenic pubertial weakmindedness. Age 19)

Hypoplastic mean mid-face; plump coarse development of cheekbone and chin;
formless obesity

PLATE 22

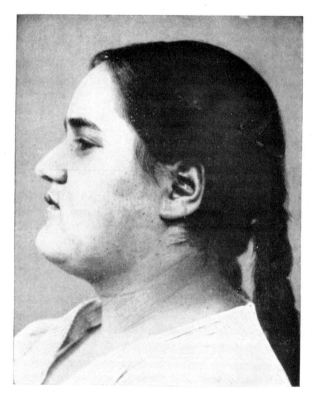

DYOPLASTIC GROWTH OF FAT. Profile
(Same as Plate 21)

face p. 73

one would have to include practically the majority of all the female schizophrenes.   Hauck[1] has recently demonstrated this after the detailed examination of over 100 women in a psycho-pathological condition.

First of all, we have 5 cases showing masculine traits highly developed in the build of the skeleton and musculature.   The proportions of the trunk, particularly, are characterized by a remarkable disproportion between the breadth of the shoulder and the hips.   Here, just as with strongly-built men, the low hip measurements lag behind a high shoulder measurement to a very marked degree. The most extreme case of this phenomenon, a 32-year-old katatonic, E.H., had a medium height (159), a shoulder breadth of 39, and a hip breadth of 27 cms. (from the crest of the ilium).   The measurement round the hips, too, is sometimes very small ; in 2 cases only 79 cms. In addition, 4 cases have well-developed and well-modelled musculature, standing out in high relief ; the muscle substance, itself, is firm and sinewy to the touch ; the normal feminine upholstering of fat is absent.   Two of the cases have a leaning to the asthenic type ; they are thin, wiry, and soft-boned ; the other 3 cases tend towards the athletic group, having large bones, broad joints, and strong muscles.   Two cases show excessive length of the extremities, one of them having the following marked disproportions : height 154, length of leg 85.   The faces are mostly long and heavily boned.   The height varies between 154 and 166 cms.   The breasts are in all 5 cases small and undeveloped, approaching the masculine type in many respects.   In 2 cases there is not even a swelling of the breast, neither fat nor glandular tissue being palpable ; there is only a large, button-shaped nipple of feminine shape on each side of the chest, immediately above the thorax.   Gynæcological investigation was, unfortunately, not practicable in any of the cases.   One patient used to suffer from very severe and painful menstruation lasting 8 days, which had commenced when she was 16 years old.   Three of the patients had well-marked goitres, of which one had a nucleus the size of a hen's egg, and the others the size of a goose's egg.   The

[1] Hauck, " Gynäkologische Untersuchung bei Schizophrenen," *Monatschrift. f. Psych. u. Neur.*, 1920.

hair of the head was generally strong, and sometimes stiff and growing forward into the face ; only in one instance, a 47-year-old patient, had the hair, which was always short and thin, come out in bunches of latter years, so that with the little that remained she could no longer make a plait ; the hair over the rest of the body, including the pubes and the hair under the arm-pits, was also very scanty. A second (both of these are the ones with the most decidedly masculine build, and with no mammary glands), had coarse long hairs round the nipples, distinctly masculine hairiness of the legs, and a fairly well-marked moustache and beard. In the other cases the secondary hair was rather scanty.

In this masculine group is included an isolated case of rather different form, but still of a dysgenital nature. It is that of an 18-year-old domestic servant, with a psychosis which at least approached very near the schizophrene type ; it began with weeping, and persecution delusions, and developed into a complete psychic and motor torpor, with mutism, and a passive indolent disposition. We found here a severe hypoplasia of the whole genitalia, with a uterus hardly the size of a cherry, and an ovary which could only just be felt, and was hardly the size of a strawberry. The menses had suddenly and completely ceased not long before the beginning of the psychosis. The girl had a tall, and remarkably plump and firm body (169) ; the bones and muscles were large and well developed, of masculine measurement, but the disposition of the fat, and the development of the breasts were quite feminine ; the measurement round the hips was excessively so (104), and in spite of the broad shoulders and chest, the proportions of the trunk were on the whole feminine in character. The extremities were abnormally long (legs 92), the hands and feet large and plump. The head displayed a slight tendency to ' tower-skull '. The skin approached the myxœdemic type, being remarkably thick, firm and unelastic ; the colour of the cheeks was cherry-red. There was also a small firm goitre. The hair on the head grew strikingly inwards towards the face ; the trunk, particularly along the spine, was covered with thick masses of lanugo.

Finally, I call attention to the case of a paranoiac

SPECIAL DYSPLASTIC TYPES 75

schizophrene with partial masculinism. It is remarkable, in that the psychosis broke out after an operation
for ovarian tumour when she was 29 years old ; since then
the patient had had a different character, was stubborn,
retired, very suspicious and sensitive, occasionally
depressed, and complained of sensations in the genitalia ;
from this there gradually developed a delusion of descent,
with phantasies, which took its course in jerks, with
aggressive affect, but without imbecility. Physiologic-
ally, combined with an otherwise asthenic build, she
had a strikingly masculine, heavily boned, angular face,
a well-developed protruding virile larynx giving forth a
deep voice, small flat breasts, and a parenchymatous
goitre ; the growth of the hair under the arm-pits was
abnormal.

Other lesser masculine characteristics we have,
naturally, often found scattered among the female
schizophrenes of all groups. The dividing line is particularly blurred between the athletic group and the group
which show distinct masculine traits.

(b) *Group of eunuchoid and polyglandular fat-
abnormalities*

Individuals showing a tendency to pronounced fatness
are altogether in the minority among schizophrenes.
We found, as we have already mentioned, only quite
sporadic instances among them of well-marked pyknic
physique, and these, indeed, may be taken as the result
of crossing with other types (see below). We are not
dealing with them here. Besides these, however, there
remain among our material still about 7 cases of abnormal
schizophrene fatness, all of which cases have, to a greater
or less degree, characteristics which are a-typical and
markedly dysglandular.

While the pyknic fatness only rarely and transitorily
reaches an abnormal and outstanding degree, and even
then is confined to certain localities—particularly cheeks,
neck, and trunk (here, in men, taking the form of the
compact fat belly)—on the other hand we find among
schizophrenes types of fatty deposition deviating from
this, which may, morphologically, be best grouped under

eunuchoid fat-abnormalities, and which by transitional stages ultimately pass over into a kind of fatness which cannot yet be clearly differentiated, but which is probably of a polyglandular nature.   One finds, here and there, deposits of fat according to the eunuchoid plan, as scattered physique-symptoms, among the schizophrene men of all groups, with and without the correlated symptoms in the formation of the skeleton.   Thus we have, in the case of a young hebephrene, combined with an otherwise asthenic physique, an isolated layer of fat round the buttocks, which makes them stand well out, and quite obliterates the normal modelling of muscle and bone ; this comes out in the very excessive measurement round the hips : chest 79–84, stomach 69, hips 90.   The man has testicles hardly the size of a nut, and is homosexual. Among athletics, too, one may observe occasionally such isolated accumulations of fat round the buttocks.   In the case of a very weakly-impulsed, elderly hebephrene, who was formerly of a weak, graceful build, there developed in his 30th year a small pendulous fat belly, just under the navel.   The man is almost beardless, and the rest of the secondary hair is also lacking.   The skin of his face—he is now 36 years old—is delicately wrinkled in a manner typical of senility.   Also among male schizophrenes one occasionally finds, combined with infantile development, such small hemispherical deposits of fat on the lower stomach.   They do not stretch, as in the case of pyknic fat paunches, over the widened lower aperture of the thorax in a compact mass, but they merely hang in a confined area just under the navel.

The lateral arrangement of fat over the crest of the ilium which is also described as being characteristic of the eunuchoid type, was observed in another patient, a schizoid eccentric, who fell sick in his 49th year of schizophrenic hallucinations with telepathic delusions.   He is an albino, and suffers from congenital nystagmus.   His bony structure and his skin are both of feminine delicacy ; the breadth of his hips comes up to the breadth of his shoulders (35 cms.), the measurement round the hips is considerable (99).   He is rather fat over the whole of his body, but, besides that, there is this striking layer of fat over the crest of the ilium and on the calves, which

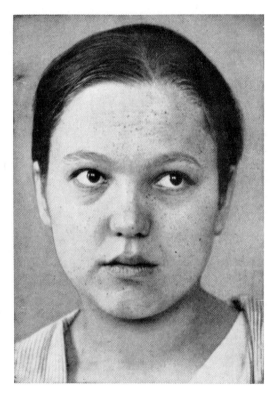

INFANTILE HYPOPLASTIC FACE. Frontal
Profile falling away in a straight line
Undeveloped nose. Spongy bloated skin
(Severe schizophrenic idiocy. Age 19)

[face p. 76

PLATE 24

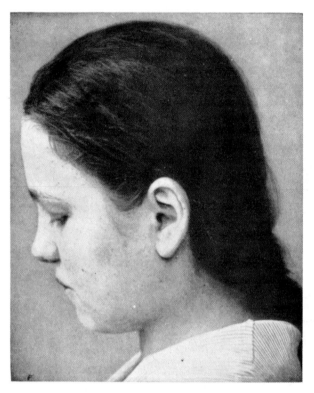

INFANTILE HYPOPLASTIC FACE. Profile
(Same as Plate 23)

measure 39 cms. round, and are such that their rounded contours give a quite feminine appearance. His testicles are hardly the size of nuts, are very soft, and are almost lost in a doughy mass of connective tissue. He is congenitally weakly-impulsed, unmarried, and even in his youth never had a serious attachment.

Two schizophrene imbeciles of my material have in their general physique many points of similarity with Karl K. (Tandler and Grosz, Plate 10, Bauer, Plate 13), who has been portrayed by Tandler and Grosz as the paradigm of eunuchoid fat-abnormalities : thick rounded head, with plump hypoplastic features, a short neck, and the whole body encased in a firm, broad, symmetrical, level, diffuse sheath of fat. One does not observe abnormal length in their extremities, but, on the other hand, thick brush-like hair on their heads, growing inwards towards the face, and at the same time undeveloped secondary hair (one has only slight indications of a beard). Both have moderate hypoplasia of the genital organs. There is a third case very like them in bodily structure and the disposition of the fat, but he has a ' tower-skull ' ; the secondary hair is almost completely absent but for a somewhat bristly beard. In cases of fully-grown men, where infantile fat-distribution persists, the way in which the fat is apportioned seems to bear some close relation to the dysgenital groups. Here we see a light sheath of fat encasing the whole body, trunk and limbs alike, both on the surface and under the surface, even beyond the ages of 25 to 30 ; the outlines of the bones and muscles are hardly apparent through the surface, and the muscles are soft to the touch ; and all the parts of the body have something soft and round about them. One may often observe this type among schizophrenes combined with eunuchoid stigmata, or with infantile under-development.

Here is the place to bring in a particularly severe case among the female material, having the marks of advanced dysglandularity, and striking morphological connections with eunuchoid fat-abnormalities. The factory hand, E.G., who is now 19 years old (Plates 23 and 24) fell ill when she was 17 with chlorosis, tiredness, and headaches ; she then gradually became more and more apathetic and

listless.   There were times when she lay motionless,
sweating heavily, and with some sign of foam at the mouth
(certainly not epileptic).   With her 19th year a typical
severe katatony broke out, the attacks of which tended
to disappear swiftly (apathy and excitement, stupor,
becoming stiff as a poker, negativism, mutism, each in
turn ;   occasionally unfounded anger, laughter, and
weeping).

She has the following physique : very severe hypoplasia of the face, with a rudimentary deeply-saddled
nose, a short flabby upper lip, and large plump malar
bones ; the whole face is fat, wide, pasty, and bloated ; the
mid-face is of medium length (only 6½), and the length of
the nose only 4 cms.   The trunk is plump and ill-modelled,
without a waist, without a proper curve of the hips, with
narrow shoulders, and a deep thorax.   There is a remarkable amount of fat over the trunk, diffusely spread over
the surface, and particularly over the stomach, not concentrated in the usual places (breasts and hips).   There
is an advanced state of acromegaly (see below).   The thin
limbs run into a point at the extremities, narrowing down
from the trunk outwards ;   there are no calves, the leg
runs conically downwards without any curving, and ends
in a small talipes cavus ; the hands, too, are small and
childish (17 cms. in circumference), and the length of the
limbs very abnormal (height 163, legs 90).   The breasts are
rudimentary, quite small, soft, childish, and not rising to
a distinct point.   The hips are not developed.   The outer
genitalia are hypoplastic and infantile (investigation into
the inner genital organs was not possible).   Although the
patient is in her 19th year, she has not yet menstruated.
The secondary hair is almost entirely absent ;   the mons
veneris has no hair on it, and there are only isolated hairs
on the labia and under the arm-pits ; the rest of the skin
on the trunk and limbs is completely smooth and hairless.
The hair on the head is soft and fairly strong, the brows
are weak, childish, and thin, like lanugo hair.   There is
nothing particularly noticeable to the touch in the
thyroid gland.

Thus we have in this instance, in the case of a female
katatonic, a collection of symptoms, composed of extreme
dysgenital arrested development and an ill-proportioned

skeleton, combined with hypoplasia of the face and akromikry, and a remarkably diffuse distribution of fat, particularly over the trunk.

This case leads us from the less distinctive stigmata, which remind us, morphologically, of the distribution of fat characteristic of the eunuchoid, to the cases where there is an advanced degree of dysplastic obesity, which must, very probably, be attributed to a combination of polyglandular symptoms, without our having at this time sufficient data to enable us to make a detailed biological differentiation.

Among my material there is a female case of this kind, which belongs clinically to the schizophrene group. It is the case of the 19-year-old peasant girl C.M. (Plates 21 and 22) : extreme imbecility at puberty, at first anxiety feelings, wild behaviour, unconnected processes of thought, occasional katatonic attacks, rhythmical movements, jerking of the head, sitting with the fingers pressed together, variations in mood, persecution delusions, gradual loss of interest, indifference, childish but tractable, and without autistic obstinacy. This was followed later by a high degree of insanity with phantasies, terminating swiftly and suddenly. This girl was formerly bright, good - natured, sociable, and gifted, and from youth upwards she was small and stocky, well developed both bodily and psychically ; she started menstruating in her 12th year. From about her 16th year there set in a startling cessation of growth of the body, with an asymmetrical distribution of fat ; and in the 18th year the psychosis came on fairly acutely. Just as in the last case, the patient has a hypoplastic, plump, bloated face, childishly small hands and feet, quite rudimentary secondary hair, and advanced hypoplasia of the genitalia (the swelling of the vagina is absent, the uterus is the size of a hazel nut, and the ovaries are not palpable) ; the menses, which, when she was 17, were omitted for months at a time, are now protracted.

Quantities of fat are distributed in shapeless masses over the whole body, not only on the face, mammæ, and nates, but over the rest of the trunk, on the shoulders and limbs. In combination with the thick hard myxœdemic skin, the upholstering of fat obliterates all the

contours of the body ; only the hands and feet are delicate
and thin. The thyroid gland cannot be felt. In contradistinction to the last case, however, this patient is
dwarfish, and has short plump limbs. The ossification of
the junction of the epiphysis is seen under Röntgen rays
to be abnormally far advanced. The following are the
most important measurements : height 147, weight 71
kilos, chest 92–95, round the stomach 88, hip circumference 110, calves 40, circumference of the hand 17, length
of the leg 74. In the constitution of the blood there is
a leucocytosis of 11800.

This girl, then, is a decidedly dysgenital case, and yet
the whole of the symptoms can with difficulty be attributed to the generative glands ; as is, indeed, the case
with even the simplest of the eunuchoid forms, the co-
operation of the other glands must never be lost sight of,
because, as is well known, one cannot regard the generative
glands as an organ which works by itself alone ; it has
always to be correlated with the rest of the glandular
complex.

Occasionally, but not often, one sees such formless
distribution of fat among schizophrenes and among
schizoid personalities, with or without striking skeletal
symptoms.

(c) Infantilism and hypoplastics

General hypoplasia, that is to say, a symmetrical
reduction in all the length and breadth measurements of
the body, would have as its result a well-formed little
manikin—a kind of miniature edition. One sometimes
comes across little figures which conform to this description—a 144 cm. high, rotund, perfectly built circular of
this kind is among my material—but they are very rare,
and for practical purposes they play no important part.
In general, the hypoplastic is also a dysplastic, in whom
the growth has been unsymmetrical, in that the hypoplasia is only found in isolated parts of the body, so that
there is striking disproportion in the measurements of
these parts in relation to other, better-developed, and
even hyperplastic, parts of the body. Instances of
hypoplasia, to any marked degree, are rarely found among

circulars, but often among schizophrenes, epileptics, and other nearly-related degenerate groups.

Now there are certain regions of the body for which such hypoplasia shows a preference, and in which it is to be found over and over again, particularly in the case of schizophrenes, and which may be very clearly recognized for diagnostic purposes. These are the face, and particularly the middle part of the face, the extremities of the limbs, particularly the hands, and also the pelvis. We are not going to go into the question here of smallness in general, e.g., defect of the ear muscles, etc. We shall treat genital hypoplasia, together with all glandular hypoplasia, by themselves hereafter, on account of their relative importance.

Now what do we mean by ' Infantilism ' ? It involves a fairly subjective judgment. In one sense the word has reference to the age of puberty, and means arrested development, where the morphological connection with the childish form which has been laid aside is immediately evident. On the other hand in advanced age, when dealing with physiques whose gradual genesis we have usually not followed step by step, it is more correct simply to speak of hypoplasia without any specialization, because we do not know whether the childish minuteness of the hand or pelvis, as the case may be, is simply due to a passive arrest of growth at the age of puberty, i.e., infantilism proper, or to impulses militating against growth, which have been actively directed towards special parts of the body through local pathological conditions, or, again, to the atrophy of a part which has already been fully developed. By ' infantile ', then, we shall mean in primis those cases where we not only find smallness of form but also where the minor proportions in the total body complex, e.g., the modelling of such morphologically separate regions as the lower stomach and the pelvis, are imitative of the proportions of such regions in childhood, where, that is to say, not only the size but also the shape is typically childish—and more especially those cases where, at the same time, dysgenital stigmata lead one to assign as the cause of this infantile formation a lack of pubertial development in the part of the body in question. As a matter of fact we shall see

F

that from this hypoplastic-infantile group innumerable transitional forms and combinations form a bridge to the eunuchoid type.

We shall first deal with the way in which hypoplasia among schizophrenes shows itself in various parts of the body.

Type of hypoplastic face

Besides cases where there is mis-growth and dwarfism, we often find the hypoplastic type of face in other schizophrene groups, *e.g.*, among asthenics, and quite analogously among epileptics and criminal dégenérés.

The fundamental characteristic of the hypoplastic type of face lies in the scanty insufficient modelling of the prominent parts, of the nose, lips, and chin. The bony relief of the forehead, also, is correspondingly weak. In this way the line of the profile does not look sharply bent, as in the case of the schizophrene angular profile, and yet not gently curving as with pyknics and well-formed faces in general, but often falls almost straight downwards, so that only the tip of the short wizened snub-nose stands out just a little way from the whole contour-line of the face. One often has the optical impression that the whole of the middle part of the face is sheltering under the base of the skull. The eyes are then deeply set, small, and piercing, under low, oppressive, horizontally overhanging orbital arches; the insignificant little nose is deep set at the root, either with a sharply-defined dent, or with a broad, flat, squashed-out saddle. The upper lip often seems similarly scanty; it is strained in the middle, as if its skin was too short. If the lower part of the face shares in the hypoplasia, the distinctive curve which in well-formed faces separates the lower lip from the chin vanishes, and the whole line of the profile stretches down from top to bottom in an expressionless, soft, flat monotony. Some of the hypoplastic faces, especially in the case of women, have pale, bloated, pasty skins.

From the front view, the practised eye recognizes the shortness of the height of the mid-face as being very characteristic; in itself it makes the face look æsthetically ugly and meagre. The measurement of the mid-face may be as low as 6 cms. in height in such cases, and the nose may be less than $4\frac{1}{2}$ cms. long.

Caricaturists have already made use of the hypoplastic face, by the side of the angular profile formation, for the characterization of the criminal type. For the sake of the æsthetic contrast, both may be placed side by side in the same group.

One must be very careful not to confuse slight degrees of hypoplastic facial formation, on account of their round softness and their snub-noses, with the pyknic type. One can, however, very soon learn to differentiate the particularly good modelling of the individual parts of the pyknic face, and their satisfactory proportions of the whole.

It is also important to recognize a very common variation of the hypoplastic face type, in which is found, side by side with an otherwise scanty and mean facial development, a growth tendency in the direction of the long nose of the asthenic. Such noses look as if one had squashed a longish pointed nose by pressure on the bridge from the front. Looked at from the side, such a nose appears pulled downwards with a pointed tip, while from in front it looks wide and plump. In contradistinction to the asthenic nose, these only poke out a little way over the line of the profile. One finds in these cases very often a grotesque disproportion between the fairly long nose and the hypoplastic mean mid-face.

Acromicria

By acromicria we mean an elective hypoplasia of the limbs, for instance the hands and feet. This peculiar formation is common among schizophrenes, and particularly among old inhabitants of the Institute, as an endogenous syndrome ; in some instances it is strongly marked, and in a lesser degree it is scattered here and there. I have 12 well-marked cases of this kind, 9 male and 3 female. In fully-developed typical examples we see how the distal portions of the limbs, from the elbow or knee outwards, unexpectedly become younger and more pointed, and end off in childishly delicate small hands and feet, so that the feet often have a tendency to a talipes cavus formation. There is no proper swelling of the calves, so that the leg below the knee may take on a thin conical shape. In the male the circumference measurement of the hand may sink to 16 cms., and the length of the hand to 17 cms. ; this diminution is found in all the dimensions to the same degree. The individual characterized by this anomaly often has other hypoplastic stigmata, *e.g.*, in the face and pelvis.

In one class the general growth is small and un-developed. A few other cases are remarkable in that the shoulders are of a broad, muscular, and robust build, so that the minuteness of the hands and feet stands out all the more distinctly. This combination of a strong shoulder development with an otherwise small insignifi-cant growth and hypoplastic stigmata is often met with among schizophrenes. Many transitional stages, com-binations with genital hypoplasia, infantilism of the pelvis, scantiness of the secondary hair, infantile distri-bution of fat, lead one to suppose that this mixture of strength of shoulder with hypoplastic minuteness of growth is perhaps only a variation of dysgenital infantilism.

Hypoplasia of the Trunk

The hypoplastic pelvis among schizophrenes is very narrow, and there is but little lateral swelling of the contour ; the inguinal folds are straight, and rise steeply, while the lower abdominal boundary in the case of strong men runs in a curved line. If, in addition to the hypoplastic formation of the pelvis, we also find the small hemispherical stomach which we have described, just under the navel, projecting forward in an energetic curve which springs sharply from the groin, the lower half of the trunk, at least to superficial observation, has quite a childish appearance. This impression is strengthened by a smooth skin, delicate and poor in grease, a soft, rounded, diffuse upholstering of fat, scanty hair over the body, hypoplasia of the genital organs, and an arrested growth in length of the body. One may occasionally find all these characteristics united in one single case, and often isolated or in combinations of a few. Facial hypoplasia and acromicria can likewise occur together.

There are two particularly severe cases of general infantilism among my female material. The girls are both 18 years old, the menses are absent, the pubes and the hair under the arm-pits is minimal, the whole body is thin, meagre, and markedly under-developed, the secondary characteristics, particularly the breast and hips, are almost entirely undeveloped, and in one of the cases the face also is remarkably childish and hypoplastic, so that at first glance one takes her for a 12-year-old. This last has become a typical hebephrene, while the other, ever since her 15th year (the time of the arrest in her growth) has been an example of increasingly severe autism, with refusal of food, childish hysterical outbursts of anger, stubborn apathy, and inability to make decisions, but without any destruction of the thought processes.

For the sake of completeness, it should be added at this point that instances of severe misgrowth and dwarfism due to rickets may occasionally be met with among schizophrenes. Two cases of this kind have simultaneously considerable degrees of hypoplasia of the genitalia, and in one case there is, besides, very scanty secondary hair, and infantilism in numerous respects. Among the circulars, I find one male patient of otherwise pyknic build, with marked crookedness of the lower part of the leg due to rickets.

CHAPTER VI

GLANDS AND BOWELS ; SEXUAL IMPULSES

THE discussions in the last chapter have focussed our thoughts on the problem of the ductless glands. We must now add a few brief words on the constitutional correlation between internal disease and psychic pathology. The most important relations of this kind are those existing between dementia præcox and tuberculosis. The frequent occurrence of tuberculosis among schizophrenes is known from of old, and quite recently, in new works on the subject, has been strongly insisted upon,[1] so that one is almost tempted to regard tuberculosis as a kind of sister disease to schizophrenia.

Even if one does not let out of one's sight the external factor of the often quite unfavourable relations between the movement, posture, and breathing apparatus, in the case of old inhabitants of the Institute, still one cannot avoid accepting a high constitutional disposition on the part of certain schizophrenes to tuberculosis. This is all the more enlightening when one bears in mind the very important part the asthenic physique plays in both these forms of disease.

As regards circular insanity, corresponding to the prevailing physique of this class, one must look out particularly for connections with certain diseases of metabolism, obesity and diabetes, and also arterio-sclerosis, and rheumatic disturbances. And here we must not only notice direct combinations of circular madness with this or that somatic disease in the patients themselves, but we must also pay careful attention to hereditary and characterological relations.[2] As we have already said, as far

---

[1] Wolfer, " Die somatischen Erscheinungen der Dementia Præcox," *Zeitschr. f. d. ges. Neurol. u. psychiatr.*, 60, 1920. Here will be found further bibliographical information.

[2] French literature has dealt multifariously with the same matters. But more detailed differentiations are required for our purpose.

as our investigations have gone, we cannot yet pass any sure judgment on this kind of question.

Now, as regards the inner secretory glands, our material among the circulars offers us no valuable indications. Connections have occasionally been mentioned between exophthalmic goitre and manic-depressive insanity. That such toxin can sometimes produce manic or depressive sets of symptoms, can certainly not be denied. Among a large collection of circulars from our indigene population, one finds only isolated patients with Basedow symptoms or with even a few constitutional symptoms of this kind (eye symptoms, etc.).

Enlarged thyroids are numerically very common among the circulars of our material ; and there are a few considerable goitres among them. In our neighbourhood, which is rich in the production of goitres, this is, absolutely speaking, not saying much, but relatively speaking, in comparison with the asthenic schizophrenes, it is worthy of notice, for among them the number of enlarged thyroids is far smaller, while among the athletics one finds a rich supply of enlarged thyroids, and even goitres. This is one of the questions which can only be answered after investigation of different races.

We have mentioned earlier the somewhat small genitalia of many circular-pyknic males, particularly where the short, sometimes mushroom-shaped penis disappears in the thick long hairs of the pubes. Serious malformation of the genitalia is found hardly anywhere among our circular material. As we have said, circulars seldom suffer from that local dystrophy in the formation of the body which points to severe endocrine disturbances.

Now, as regards schizophrenes, on the other hand, among the asthenics we found well-developed goitres (of the severe and knotted kinds) only in a few cases. In the case of many asthenics, particularly among the prematurely senile, it was surprising to find that in spite of the long neck, which was rendered convenient for investigation on account of its thinness, the thyroid gland was hardly to be felt at all. Whether the thyroid here plays a part, as primary cause of an endocrine nature, in the drying of the stem, the senility and emaciation, or only shares passively in the general emaciation, one cannot say for certain. Symptoms of exophthalmic goitre are also rare among our schizophrenes. In physique, it is only among the hypoplastic group that one finds analogies to the morphology of the thyroid gland disturbances; in particular many hypoplastic facial forms with ill-developed mid-face and a sharply depressed nasal saddle, may be brought into line with certain cretinous facial forms. We must register this fact, but obviously we can draw no conclusion from it.

The same modesty must be shown in our attitude towards the morphology of the hypophysis. Here also we can only mention the simple fact that there are numerous superficial analogies between the physical stigmata of certain schizophrene athletics and the physique of the muscular hyperplastic group of acromegalics, the physique of the schizophrenes in question having the appearance of a faint prefiguration of the massive symptoms of muscular acromegaly. We have, for this reason, given illustrations of such an acromegalic as a gross paradigm of the athletic physique, for the purposes of comparison (Plates 4 and 10).

In both cases we happen to find, differing only quantatively, the tendency to a massive formation of the face, and of the protuberances of the skull, to a disproportionately high growth of the facial side of the skull, and indeed of the skull altogether, to a general over-development of the bones and muscle, and in particular to trophic accentuation of the extremities and the shoulders. Nageli[1] stresses besides this, in cases of chlorosis which is to be attributed to disturbances of the generative glands, enlarged and heavy-boned physique with strong development of the chest.

In the matters with which we have been dealing, we have discussed isolated and superficial similarities, which we have to notice with care, but which we must in no wise use as bases to form hasty judgments; the investigations with regard to the generative glands, accordingly, require a somewhat more exact consideration. When dealing with schizophrenes particular attention

[1] Nageli, " Die Vries'sche Mutationstheorie in ihre Arnwendung auf die Medizin," *Zeitschr. f. angew. Anat. u. Konstitutionslehre*, 6, 1920.

has long been paid to this organ, and, indeed, this is quite understandable. First and foremost we have the fact that the schizophrenic diseases show a marked preference for the age of puberty. It is for this reason that complaints of 'sensations in the genitalia', sometimes direct and sometimes under the guise of phantasy (mishandling, pollutions, electric shock delusions, 'artificial' stimulation and erection), belong to the commonest of the schizophrene symptoms. And however far one may treat these complaints as of the nature of phantasy, there must be some reason why the pathological thought processes of the schizophrene always range with such persistence round the region of the genital organs.

These purely clinical thought processes now link up further with morphological facts. We have seen that variations in physique in a dysgenital direction,[1] and indeed of a eunuchoid as well as of an infantile nature, are relatively common among schizophrenes.

Also the tendency to a scanty distribution of secondary hair, combined with comparatively strong growth of hair on the head and brows, is a frequent characteristic common to both schizophrenes and eunuchoids.[2] Anomalies in the size, consistency, and position of the generative glands and genitalia are seldom found among schizophrenes, as we have shown in the last chapter. In men this may come out most in a high degree of hypoplasia of the genitalia and penis, and also in hypoplasia, inequality, and sometimes severe hyperplasia, or inadequate descent, even to the extent of cryptorchism of the testicles ; abnormal coarseness, as well as abnormal softness and poverty of substance in the glands are sometimes present in these cases. Fundamentally clearer and more common is genital-hypoplasia among schizophrene women, sometimes to a very significant degree, and, indeed, not only in the case of asthenics and hypoplastics, but

---

[1] For the Psychopathology of Eunuchoids, cf. the careful work of H. Fischer (Giessen), *Zeitschr. f. d. ges. Neur. u. Ps.*, 1919 and 1920. The characterological relations and transitions to the group of the schizoid temperament are unmistakable and of great theoretical importance.

[2] Bauer's 37-year-old castrate has an excessively angular profile. Of course, this may be mere chance, and yet careful attention must be paid to such morphological details in castrates, and in the sexually perverse as well.

occasionally even combined with the athletic physique (see Chapter V).

In the last few years, we have now and then come across cases where the outbreak of schizophrenia has synchronized with an operation on the ovaries. Naturally the explanation on psychic lines still remains open. It is well known that the periods of pregnancy, birth, and child-bed, are critical for any woman who has a tendency to schizophrenia or circular madness. It is not unknown for a schizophrenic psychosis to break out in a man at the same time as an engagement; here also one must be very wary before one decides on an endocrine or a psychogenous etiology, or, indeed, on any etiology at all.

Generally speaking, when one reviews all the clinical and morphological facts which we have mentioned, one will have the impression that the phenomena connected with the generative glands are in many ways an oppressive load, at any rate for one section of schizophrene cases;[1] particularly in the direction of functional atrophy or disturbance. And here we must add as a most important factor certain peculiarities in the sexual impulses of the schizophrenes, which we shall describe later. In all this, one must beware of conceiving the possible causal activity of the generative glands in schizophrenic disease in the form of a simple massive, monosymptomatic disturbance of function. Castration of a soundly constituted man has, as is well known, no psycho-pathological results of a schizophrenic nature. If one accepts an endocrine etiology (*i.e.*, co-etiology) as being probable in the case of schizophrenia, one must regard it in the form of a very complicated constitutional syndrome, of a very tangled chemical relation between the brain and the glandular complex, in which the etiology of the generative glands stands out very obviously. The brain as a causal factor in all these matters must never be lost sight of, so

[1] We cannot refer here to the results of the investigations of Abderhalden and Fauser, because the conclusions are too divergent. The investigations of F. Mott, on the other hand, would be of great theoretical interest, if they were confirmed. In comparison with a large number of normal persons, he found that schizophrenes showed decided microscopic modifications in the generative glands and spermatozoa, in the direction of regressive atrophy and malformation. (Cf. *Zentralbl. f. d. ges. Neur. u. Ps.* 27, 280, 1921.)

that in our escape from the brain-anatomy extreme, we
do not fall into another extreme on the endocrine-
chemical side.

The same care must be taken when we are dealing
with the sexual impulses. The sexual impulse is not
a simple function of the generative glands, but clearly
depends on the co-operation of the other glands and the
central nervous system, while the central nervous system
and the endocrine glands have intimate relations with one
another of action and reaction, now on the nerves, now on
the vascular system, regulating each other with positive
and inhibitive impulses. The sexual impulse is not a
product of the generative glands, but of a complicated
system of causal factors made up of cerebral nervous
tissue and glandular tissue, in which the interstitial
glands play a particularly important rôle. This means
that the sexual impulse is no isolated psycho-physical
entity, but an important ingredient of the total temperament, which cannot be separated from it, and which is
closely interwoven with it. We must not separate the
total affectivity from the sexual impulse, nor account for
it entirely in terms of sexual impulse, in the exaggerated
terminology of certain psycho-analysts. We must make
it clear that any observation of the working of the sexual
impulses leads us far down into the temperamental
peculiarities of a man, and that much that we say here
bears very closely on the investigations in the psychological
chapters.

The sexual lives of circulars and schizophrenes show
certain remarkable differences, not so much in individual
cases as on an average. The sexual impulses of men
suffering from circular madness, are generally simple,
natural, and lively. We are speaking here of their
personalities as a whole, and not with special reference
to the time of the psychosis. In the hypo-manic, they are
generally notably strong, but in those whose affectivity is
of medium sensitivity, and even deep down in the depression region, we often find a strength of impulse which is
over the average. Even among severe cases of depression we are met, here and there, with a case where
sexual excitement of a painful intensity breaks through
the otherwise total clogging-up of the feelings. Devia-

tions from the normal direction of the sexual impulse are seldom found among circulars.

The sexual behaviour of the schizophrenes is far more complicated. Anyone who does not take great trouble and does not have good psychic rapport with his patients, will often learn nothing detailed on this matter from schizophrenes. In the first place we find, among individuals suffering from schizophrenia, a by no means insignificant number of weakly impulsed, untemperamental, simple natures, who assure us quite sincerely that as a rule they are influenced by no strong leaning towards people of their own or the opposite sex, and who have satisfied their unenthusiastic and soon conquered impulses in their early years by means of masturbation.

On the other hand, it is well known to be no rarity to find appearances of overwhelming sexual excitement in acute schizophrenic psychosis. In certain schizoid groups an overstrong sexual impulse is a typical personality symptom. The subject then has that kind of general affectivity which is characteristic of the temperamental schizoid (see Chapters X and XI), and which swings abruptly backwards and forwards between the alternatives of excessive heat and excessive coldness, and is uneven in the regulation of the impulse. Premature as well as retarded awakening of the sexual impulses is not a rare phenomenon among schizoids.

After careful exploration we also find, among people suffering from schizoid diseases, some with an abnormal, or not clearly fixed direction of the impulse. We find among them and among their relations frequent tendencies to homosexuality, and, further, cases, without strong sexual impulses, of contrary-sexual types of affectivity—masculine women, and feminine men. Sadism, and the perversions related to it, are occasionally met with, but these things do not hang together with the sexual impulse as such, but with the general schizoid temperament, and particularly with the coldness of the affective life, and the convulsive hunger for stimulation. All these abnormal variations of impulse can often be traced in the prepsychotic personality, sometimes as far back as the years of childhood ; but it may happen that they only make their appearance in the schizophrenic psychosis, or at

any rate only break out then with all their brutal
clarity.

Perhaps even commoner than these recognized perversions, one finds, among those who have a schizoid
disease, sexuality which has no one direction, striving
after no clearly defined relief.

In the first place we find, in many subjects in whom schizophrenia has appeared in later life, that infantile feelings
cling to them abnormally far into the period of puberty
and long after, which then modify the development of
the sexual impulses in a peculiar manner, colour them,
or hold them back. There is above all the abnormally
strong affective fixation on the mother (more rarely also
on the father) of which we shall be treating hereafter, with
many examples, in the psychological part; it is an elective,
extravagant tenderness, at a time when normal young
people have cut themselves loose from the narrow bounds
of the family, and have devoted themselves to other
ideals. And, further, we very often find in certain,
schizophrenic groups an abnormally lasting abstinence from
sexual knowledge, a persistence in prudish ignorance or a
system of infantile phantasy at an age when others have
long been clearly conscious of the direction of their impulses.

With many schizophrenes this is very closely connected with the harsh, fitful, uneven functioning of the
regulation of the impulses. Timidity is, as we shall see,
one of the most common characteristics of the late
developed schizophrene. It can reach so high a degree
that it can hinder altogether the attainment of a sexual
end which is, in itself, very strongly desired. Side by
side with this abnormal inhibition we also find, especially
in the case of defective post-psychotics, complete absence
of inhibitions, cynical brutality, and shameless forms of
sexuality.

If we take these two together; the variability and
the absence of firmness in the sexual impulse itself, and
the uneven working of its regulative apparatus, we shall
easily be able to understand certain peculiarities in the
working out of the sexual life in the schizophrene.[1] In

---

[1] In the schizoid psychopathic there occur on these biological
grounds frequent psychic conflicts having further neurotic developments. The Psycho-analytic school has discovered a great deal about
this with admirable perspicacity.

the normal man the sexual impulses develop in the early stages of puberty, divided at first in many ways into psychic and somatic aspects. On the one hand there forms an almost purely psychic ideal enthusiasm for persons of the opposite sex, on the other hand the first local excitations of the somatic genital area make their début. Both go on side by side for a time without having any real connection with one another ; any contact of the two systems of imagery may be rejected immediately and suppressed. Only with the furtherance of the pubertial development does this barrier gradually fall away : the somatic sexual excitations and the general psychic tendencies flow together towards the beloved in an unanalysable and very strongly affectively toned complex, which forms the basis for the psycho-physical love-life of the normal man.

Now, with patients suffering from schizophrenia, we often see this fusion of the psychic with the somatic aspects of the sexual impulse retarded for a long time, and perhaps for ever. It can happen that the somatic sexual excitement, as far as it is present at all, pursues its isolated way, and is satisfied, *e.g.*, by masturbation.

The psychic love-requirements, on the other hand, then retain a form similar to that existing in the early stages of puberty ; they work themselves out entirely in the realm of phantasy, in day-dreams, in the building of palaces of thought or mad imaginations, very often, *e.g.*, as a distant adoration towards a person who has hardly been seen. One finds such worlds of phantasy psychologically developed in the schizoid psychopathic, or even as an ingredient in the growth of a schizophrenic psychosis.

In those individuals who suffer from circular madness, the sexual life takes its place smoothly and naturally in the total complex of the affective life. We do not find with them to such an extent that cleft or disunion which may strike us so forcibly in the case of many schizophrenes, and even among healthy schizothymes : Here stand I, my ethical personality, and over there the sexual impulses, as something hostile, as a continually disturbing foreign body. So that in such cases the moral struggle, which is of the most poignant nature, between these two irreconcilable factors may become a lasting

PLATE 25

HYPOPLASTIC FACE.   EPILEPSY.   AGE 20

Mid-face too narrow.   Undeveloped nose
Piercing gaze.   Short upper-lip
Mid-face $6\frac{1}{2}$ cm.   Length of nose $4\frac{1}{2}$ cm.

[face p. 80

PLATE 26

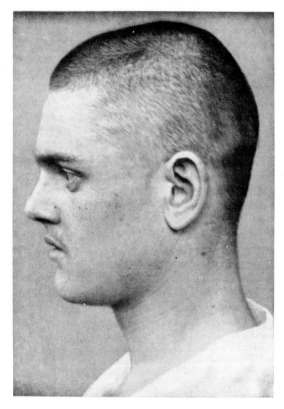

HYPOPLASTIC FACE. Profile
(Same as Plate 25—Profile)

[*face p.* 81

content of life. Much that we shall later on discover in the characterology of certain schizothymes, appearing as prudery, scrupulousness, or categorical imperative and moral rectitude, has, to a certain extent at any rate, its foundation in these relations.

In conclusion, then, we may say, that among schizophrenes, whether we find weakness or abnormal sensitivity of sexual impulses, at all events there is on an average a lack of certainty in the sexual impulses, and we shall also have to place this factor in the balance when we are dealing with the question of the biological co-operation of the generative glands in cases of schizophrenia, if we are going to deliver a decisive judgment on the matter.

CHAPTER VII

THE BUILDING OF THE CONSTITUTION

LET us look back over the whole material as we have so far portrayed it, and once more briefly summarize the conclusions at which we have arrived. We found that in the circular group the pyknic physique, and certain peculiarities in facial formation, hair, etc., were very decidedly predominant. We found, in the schizophrene group, that there predominated, with a series of isolated bodily stigmata, the asthenic, the athletic, and a number of dysplastic physiques, together with mixtures of all these types. Certain physiques seem to show a strong affinity with certain psychiatristic groups.

Side by side with these significant corresponsive types of physique, we also met, however, among schizophrenes as well as among circulars, a certain number of body-formations which were either indefinite or mixed with typical characteristics of the opposite type, and, finally, every now and then we found isolated instances when the physique was, either purely or at any rate predominantly, of the opposite type ; cases, that is to say, where, *e.g.*, a circular is of a decidedly asthenic nature, or a schizophrene of a decided pyknic habitus. It is precisely these cases which lead us into the most interesting biological inquiries, and particularly into the question of heredity.

Let us first take a small example.

Supposing a father of well-defined pyknic build has a son, who takes after his father exactly in appearance, who, that is to say, again shows decided pyknic build, and whose son does the same, and so onwards through several generations. In these cases the son will never be the mere copy of his father, but in isolated parts of the body he will show a series of slight variations which must be conditioned either through inheritance from the mother, or by recessive influences in the germ-plasm of the father, which make themselves manifest in the external appearance of the son. These slight variations of his pyknic physique may appear, *e.g.*, as asthenic or athletic elements, and it is on this never-failing production of variations that what we call individuality or individual peculiarity is based.

These individual peculiarities are never incidental or merely due to chance; they always serve the investigator into the constitution as important indications of deeper lying laws. The same biological agent which, in the case of the otherwise pyknically built brother, only comes into prominence in the rather long and pointed nose, can, *e.g.*, in the case of the sister, come out clearly and overwhelmingly as responsible for an entirely asthenic physique. That is to say : we never, even in the most definite cases, come across a pure example in the strictest sense of the word ; it is always the peculiar individual instance of a type, that is, the type itself mixed with slight accretions from a heterogeneous inheritance. This mixture, in the guise of which the type appears to us in any individual instance, we call the ' constitutional alloy '. This notion of ' alloy ' of course holds equally for the psychic nature of a man ; it covers his whole inherited groundwork, that is to say, his constitution.

There is yet another point about which we must be clear. All along we have assumed, as the basis of our investigations, that the endogenous psychosis is a *pars pro toto* of a man's total psychic type. The psychic constitution of a man expresses itself not in the psychosis alone, but in the inclusive picture of his total personality at any phase of his life, of which the psychosis is only an episodic excerpt. It is only in the rarest cases that it gets as far as a psychosis at all, while analogous correlations between the physique and the psychic nature may well exist even in the case of men who are healthy all their lives, and, as we shall see, as a matter of fact, do exist. We have, therefore, to do not merely with a simple correlation between a physique and a psychosis, but between the former and a perfectly healthy personality. In short, we must collect together all that is manifest out of the transmittable characteristics in the physiological field as well as in the field of psychology, and then

G

we can ask ourselves the question : What is the biological connection between these factors ? There are four main groups of appearances with which we have to do : (1) the physique (and the bodily functions, with which we have only dealt superficially) ; (2) the development of the personality, especially the temperament, *i.e.*, the matters we shall be dealing with in the second part ; (3) any endogenous psychosis (and of course any endogenous pathological condition of the body) ; (4) the hereditary history, *i.e.*, such characteristics mentioned under (1) and (2), as make their appearance among the nearest blood relations.

Neither the physique nor the psychosis are themselves the constitution in the strictest sense of the word ; the constitution is the inherited foundation. Both these two, just as the personality, are only part of the manifest expression of the total inherited mass.

None of these three factors need reflect completely, in their own ways, all the typical characteristics of the type which lies at their foundation. It is far more plausible to suppose that part of the germinal foundation finds expression in the physique, part comes to view in the personality, or else, more strikingly, in a psychosis. On the grounds of our investigations, we may suppose that the circular [1] psyche and the pyknic physique have closely related, and perhaps, in essentials, identical germinal foundations, and similarly with the schizophrenic psyche and the asthenic (athletic, etc.) physiques. Supposing, for example, that an individual has inherited a certain germ-plasm from his parents, half of which involves a tendency to a pyknic-circular nature, and the other half a tendency to an asthenic schizophrene nature. Now, the pyknic-circular foundation, or the asthenic-schizophrene foundation can predominate alone as well in the physique as in the psychic character (and in the psychosis). In this case the external form shows the usual psycho-physiological combination. Or the external appearance may betray an even alloy, in which case you will have a mixed pyknic-asthenic formation as regards the body,

---

[1] We say " Circular " and " Schizophrene " here provisionally for the general types which will be described in the Part II under the names of " Cyclothymes " and " Schizothymes."

hand in hand with a circular-schizophrenic mixture on the psychic side.   It is, finally, also possible that in coming together to form the manifest phenomenon, one of the opposed foundations will predominate in the physique, and the other in the psychic nature, and the external appearance will present an a-typical combination :

Asthenic physique + circular psyche, or

Pyknic physique + schizophrenic psyche.

The constitutional formula of such an individual would, strictly speaking, run thus :

Asthenic (= schizophrene) + (pyknic =) circular, or vice versa, in which the brackets represent the latent, and the rest the manifest parts of the total constitution, in the same way that in heredity, where we are dealing with recessive inheritances, we usually treat certain characteristics as now manifest, now latent.   An organism formed in this sort of way we should call a ' cross '.

As a general rule in human heredity, where the inheritance is of a mixed nature we may expect results to be in accordance with this theory, that side by side with typical affinitive combinations between physique and psyche will always be found a number of indefinite mixtures, and finally a certain number of complete crossings will appear.   This would bear out the empirical facts of the case as we have shown them.

For a matter of that, we can also in the realm of biology easily produce analogous examples of prevalent, but not exclusive combinations of characteristics, in view of the fact that the tendency to variation is one of the most important biological laws, whereas quite rigid, unvarying regularity is the exception.   Quite a simple example, which is like our case, is found in the relation of fair hair and blue eyes.   They are both certainly based on the same constitutional basis from the point of view of pigmentation, and will be typically found together in pure examples of suitably constituted races.   Supposing the fair blue-eyed are mixed with the darker races, then we find in their descendants side by side with a certain percentage of fair blue-eyed, of brown-haired brown-eyed, and of people with a mixture half-way between them, a few rare examples of fair brown-eyed, or of brown-haired blue-eyed.   That is to say, cases where the characteristic ' fair ' has come through more strongly in the eyes, and the characteristic ' dark ' more strongly in the hair, or vice versa, which thus corresponds to what we have called ' crossing ' above.

Of course, no theory can be set up on the basis of all this ; it serves only to indicate certain possibilities, by means of which we may perhaps explain the existence of certain prevalent, but not exclusive combinations of characteristics in the human constitution, and by means of which we may bring these probably highly complicated biological relations within the range of preliminary scientific treatment along a few simple lines.

In all these considerations the notion of ' alternation of dominance ', the importance of which in questions of psychic inheritance has been recognized by Hoffmann, plays its part.[1]   In the description of the individual types of physique, we have already mentioned, and particularly with regard to the pyknic type, that not all the characteristics of a type are present simultaneously at every period of life, that, e.g., so distinctive a mark as the sheath of fat over the trunk of the pyknic may put in an appearance only at a certain phase of life, and then only for a short time, while at other ages, e.g., at the time of puberty, elements of other constitutions may stand out more clearly for the time being.   Quite analogous phenomena in the development of character are known to everyone to occur at different ages in the life of many men, and these also play their part in the psychosis. Where this process may clearly be discerned, in which we have outward manifestations of characteristics indicating a mixed inheritance, not appearing simultaneously, but successively relieving one another during the course of life, we shall speak of variation of dominance.

The considerations we have just advanced about alloys, crossings, and alternation of dominance, have brought us straight to those cases of our material which are strikingly a-typical.   Here are a few examples.

A 48-year-old clerk, A.O., was treated here in 1919 for typical obstructed depression, which ran a periodic

---

[1] For alternation of dominance in cross-breeding see E. Fischer, *Die Rehobother Bastards und das Bastardierungsproblem beim Menschen*, Jena 1913.

course, and was released as cured. His physique was almost purely asthenic : tall, thin, flat-chested, very long extremities, 185 cms. tall, with a weight of only 66 kilos, long thin nose with its tip pulled downwards, and hair clearly growing inwards towards the face ; the broad soft lateral contour of the face, and the fresh colour were the only indications of the pyknic type.

A year later his sister came under our care—with a typical schizophrenia. The constitutional build of this family is extraordinarily interesting, especially when we take in characterological considerations as well (Table IX).

TABLE IX

Father's Brother.	*Father.*	*Mother.*
Extremely well-informed and pedantic, " the mind of a clerk."	Bodily : a typical German shape, very large, strong, big-boned, surprisingly large hands and feet ; died of lung tuberculosis. Psychically : serious, very well-informed, punctilious, careful of externals, correct, very good-humoured.	Bodily : soft, round, blooming face. Later decidedly corpulent. Psychically : bright, sociable, good - humoured, very good-natured.

I ♂	II ♂	III ♂	IV ♀
Bodily : large, corpulent in early life, now thin. Very large hands and feet. Like the father. Psychically : peculiar, unmarried, very shut up in himself, serious, odd, well-informed ; was up to his 30th year more sociable and brighter.	Circular depression. Bodily : asthenic, see above. Psychically : serious, very well-informed, rather pedantic, dutiful, but with all this, very good-natured, friendly, sociable.	Bodily : very corpulent. Psychically : always gay, bright, strong sense of humour, very good-natured. Takes after the mother both physically and psychically.	Late schizophrenia (when about 45 years old). Bodily : typical severe case of asthenic long - growth. When younger the nutrition was average, recently sudden thinness to which no cause has been assigned. Psychically : in early life brighter and more sociable ; in latter years increasingly sickly, serious, reserved, hypochondriacal.

The family offers the following picture (for the foundations of characterological diagnosis see Part II [1]). The father is a typical athletic with a prevailing schizothymic temperament (in his brother the schizothymia reached a grade of abnormality). The mother is of a distinctive

---

[1] Our characterological diagnoses are naturally not founded on the few clues reproduced in these notes, but are based on extensive examinations, which, for want of space, we cannot give here. This is also true of our later cases.

pyknic build, and has a typically cyclothymic temperament.   Both parents are psychically healthy, and in
both physique and character correspond.   The crossing
of the paternal schizothymic-athletic constitution with
the maternal cyclothymic-pyknic produces in the children
the following interesting constitutional mixtures.

Brother I is a decidedly schizoid psychopath with an
athletic physique.   Physique and character are congruent,
and take after the father.   The maternal inheritance
came only temporarily to view in the body in younger
years, manifesting itself as a tendency to corpulence,
combined accordingly with a more open and brighter
temperament.

Brother II has a complicated cyclothym-schizothymic
basis.   His character in health is about equally made up
of schizothymic (pedantic, dry) and cyclothymic (friendly,
sociable) elements mixed.   His psychosis is almost
entirely in the circular direction, while his body is built
on almost purely schizothymic lines.   Thus: psyche
mixed, physique, on the other hand, contrary to the
psychosis.

Brother III is a healthy cyclothyme, with a pyknic
physique.   The physique and the character are congruent, and take after the mother.   The paternal inheritance does not manifest itself externally.

Sister IV seems to have been of a mixed type, both
bodily and psychically, in her younger years.   As the
climacteric was approached, in accordance with the rules
of a partial change of dominance, the maternal basis,
which had hitherto been a favourably compensating
element (just as in the case of Brother I), disappeared,
until bit by bit a purely asthenic physique and a schizothymic temperament were revealed, ending in a transition to a schizophrenic psychosis.   At the time of our
investigations, the physique and character were completely congruent.

From a biological point of view, it is worth noticing
that in the case of II and IV the paternal schizothymic
inheritance manifests itself in combination with an
asthenic, and not, as in the case of the father, an athletic
physique.   Such observations, which are of fundamental
importance for the question of the biological unity of the

schizophrenic group, must be very carefully collected as investigation proceeds. In this individual instance of ours, we naturally cannot decide whether the asthenic physique of the children is merely to be considered as the biological equivalent of the father's athletic nature, or whether it must be traced to inheritance from previous generations.

We give out of our copious notes a few similar examples in brief :

The 32-year-old hotelkeeper, E.F., has a typical circular psychosis, with prevailingly manic and hypomanic phases, interspersed also with depressive phases, which has lasted without a break for years. The physique, however, has quite a preponderating tendency to the schizothymic type : very tall head, long, oval, narrow sharply-cut face, with a pointed nose, thin, wiry frame, with a plastic muscle-relief, profuse hair on the brows, and scanty secondary hair. The strikingly ruddy face is the only indication of the circular nature. The heredity is as follows : The mother, in her 50th year, fell sick of chronic, incurable paranoia with phantasies (everything upside down in the body, sexual organs altered, heiress to millions, etc.). Similarly, the sister has been for many years in the Institute. In her youth she had an attack of simple mania, and was released cured. The second attack began with a manically coloured complex of symptoms which gradually went over into a severe chronic schizophrenic idiocy.

In this family, therefore, we have to do with a mixture of circular and schizophrenic bases, which manifests itself in the mother as an a-typical psychosis with a tendency towards schizophrenia, in the son as an opposition between physique and character, in the daughter as a change of dominance in the form of the psychosis.

The following family series, about which we have very full information, shows similar relations :

The 49-year-old director, S.S., came under our care on account of a typically circular psychosis, with regular manic-depressive alternation of phase. His physique, however, showed a fairly evenly balanced alloy of pyknic and athletic elements : broad, soft, five-cornered face, with a thick nose and fresh colouring, also a certain amount of fat deposit about the trunk. On the other hand he had a large, very broad-shouldered and heavily-boned frame, with a strong plastic muscle-relief. In his character he showed preponderatingly cyclothymic traits, with a few schizothymic elements (reservedness, punctiliousness, strong moral sense).

Of his brothers and sisters, two came under our treatment for simple circular psychoses. A third sister had a typical cyclothymic temperament, with clear endogenous fluctuations, and a small, typically pyknic build. A fourth sister had been from childhood upwards physically delicate, and died later of tuberculosis of the lungs. She suffered from the following interesting psychosis : 1902 and 1905, short periodic psychoses, lasting a few weeks, with healthy periods in between. From 1906 to 1917 (her death) she was all the time in the Institute, with a pathological condition of the mind which betrayed all the symptoms of a severe incurable schizophrenia : long stretches of very severe negativism and mutism, refusal of food, extreme uncleanliness with stool and urine, a high degree of contraction of the muscles, stereotyped obsessional attitudes, grimacing, grotesque incoherent movements, forceful impulsive destruction mania. This severe katatonic picture, lasting twelve years, was blended in her case, however, with a regular alternation of manic and depressive phases.

We have, therefore, a family series in which a schizothymic inheritance-component manifests itself side by side with prevailing circular temperaments. The brother about whom we have been speaking, though suffering from a purely circular psychosis, yet possesses a mixed characterology, and a physique built on a strongly athletic basis (*i.e.*, an incomplete opposition of physique and psychosis). The one sister has a quite congruent cyclothymic-pyknic nature. The other sister, with a physique which leans rather to the schizothymic side, has an excellent example of a mixed psychosis, made up of schizophrenic and circular elements.

And now a cursory glance at a few cases in which the heredity is not known to us in such detail. In our material we have only two instances of a typical pyknic physique correlated with a schizophrenic psychosis. One of these is the clerk, K.S., whose mother's sister had already been, in 1898, and again in 1907, in the clinic of this town for repeated depressive pathological conditions. In 1907 her diagnosis was given as 'manic-depressive mixed condition'. She has since remained healthy, lives an ordered existence, and keeps her own house, but sometimes she makes odd involuntary movements of the head and mouth. The patient, K.S., himself, shows a typical schizophrene symptom complex, with the delusion of physical influences, and classical katatonic motor characteristics, but with this peculiarity, that the psychosis is interrupted periodically with practically sane intervals (since 1915 there have been three attacks of this kind, and each time cured to the extent of his being capable of doing his duties). In this family the supposition of a mixed basis suggests itself very strongly, so that in K.S., the physique comes out with a prevailing tendency to the pyknic side, and the psychosis, on the other hand with a leaning towards the schizophrene side.

Mrs E. N. suffers from periodic mania, but has a strikingly asthenic physique. The records of a previous asylum show that they had observed in her, when she was there, periodic instances of grimacing, incoherence, optical and acoustic hallucinations, and were inclined to a schizophrenic diagnosis. Under my examinations she showed, along with an otherwise typically manic, brightly inconsequent disposition, lack of interest, and automatism. It seems therefore that here again the physique is a good index for a schizophrenic component in the constitution, in the background of the circular manifestations.

Dr E. M. has of latter years suffered from regular periodic psychic disturbances of a manic-depressive variety. His physique is altogether asthenic. During his healthy days, Dr M. was known as a sinister-looking, paranoiacally suspicious, very nervous, reserved man, who did not get on with people. Here the physique is in opposition to the psychosis, while it is in conformity with the schizothymic personality.

I saw recently a fine example of a partial opposition in the case of a patient suffering from periodic depressions, who carried a typical soft round pyknic head with a beautiful bald pate, a broad short well-formed nose, and a pentagonal facial outline, on the top of a well shot-up, thin, asthenic body, which made a remarkable contrast. The healthy sister of the patient showed a completely developed pyknic physique with an undersized stature, fresh colour on the cheeks, and a fine layer of fat, together with a dashing hypomanic temperament.

We will mention two more cases of change of dominance, which we have observed for years in the Institution. Both are now middle-aged women ; both in their youth were surprisingly plump, blooming maidens, and suffered from curable circular psychoses. The one (in spite of normal exercise and nourishment) has grown pale and thin, and the other has fallen into a completely asthenic condition. The first still manifests manic-depressive disturbances, but more and more mixed with paranoiacally hostile traits. She finds everything ' most extraordinary ', thinks people are making faces at her, and complains of influences being exerted on her body. Her mother lay for years incapacitated in bed with ' severe hysteria '. From a clinical point of view disagreements might arise over this case, at any rate if one did not yet know about Hoffmann's investigations into the problem of heredity. The case of the second woman is simpler ; when she was $16\frac{1}{2}$ she passed through a mania, then remained sane for many years, and married ; when she was 30 she passed through a second mania-like attack of a year and a half duration, from which she was released only ' better ', and was taken back into the Institute again after half a year, where she has now remained for three years. As far as psychic characteristics go, she now is hardly distinguishable from the old schizophrenes of her environment ; day in day out she chatters on to herself, incoherent and rambling, without any reference to the world about her ; she is full of fantastic complaints, confabulations, and odd expressions, only interrupted occasionally by senseless abrupt acts of violence. At the same time, although she is only 35 (in spite of good consumption of food and average activity of the body), she has changed physically from a ' healthy blooming undersized maiden in a well-fed condition ' (earlier medical report), into a wizened, hypoplastic, asthenic figure, with a pointed nose, pointed chin, pale face, and thin spare skin, and in this condition I found her, when I commenced my diagrammatic investigations.

Now it is not for a moment asserted, nor indeed is it probable, that the numerous a-typical and indefinite forms, which we have come across in the relations between the physique and the psychosis (or psychic condition), must all rest on ' alloy ' and ' crossing '. Neither the psychiatristic groups nor the types of physique which we have measured side by side can certainly be declared free from all foreign elements, and therefore to be regarded as final. We need only remind ourselves how uncertain our judgment still is, *e.g.*, about many involution melancholias, old-age depressions, paranoiac depressions, agitated anxiety psychoses, with regard to their membership or non-membership in the circular class. And again, our differentiation into somatic types is only a first attempt, and rests on a basis of external observable symptoms. We do not know whether, *e.g.*, the external form of the pyknic type, besides being produced by internal factors, which probably also share in the production of the circular conditions, cannot in less common circumstances be evoked by quite other agents, which have nothing whatever to do with the circular conditions, *i.e.*, that psychological condition which normally corresponds to them. And vice versa, we know just as little whether the inner agency which generally evokes a schizophrenic psychosis in connection with an asthenic body, cannot under certain rarer circumstances manifest itself on the psychic surface as a simple depression. We shall first have to begin to work through our clinical material with the combined method of comparative observation of the somatic, psychic, and hereditary components which have gone to the building of the constitution, and, by going forward carefully, we must hope, by this means, gradually to attain to certain new standpoints for more accurate clinical and general biological differentiation. From a clinical point of view, we have so far obtained the following preliminary impression from our material : that many, but not all cases of depression caused by arterio-sclerosis and age, and some involution melancholias, agree, physically with the circular group ;

that clinically a-typical depressive forms, with strongly marked paranoiac constituents or with a marked tendency to agitations, etc., often show a-typical components, both in their own physiques and in their heredity. The same is perhaps true of those patients suffering from severe manic-depression, who become completely confused and given to violence in their mania, and who for many years have never had sane intervals. On the other hand, with the majority of paraphrenias we have so far not been able to recognize a fundamental difference as far as their physique and heredity go between them and schizophrenes (the same as to heredity was found by Hoffmann).

We must now be perfectly clear about all this : physique and psychosis do not stand in a direct clinical relation to one another. The physique is not a symptom of the psychosis, but : physique and psychosis, bodily function and internal disease, healthy personality and heredity, are each, separately, part-symptoms of the constitutional basis which lies at the bottom of the whole, and are indeed bound together among themselves by affinitive relations, but they are only to be estimated correctly when the coherence of the whole is taken into consideration.

Besides this, these factors reflect not only purely constitutional agents, but also a wealth of exogenous agents as well, the traces of the interworking of the individual with the external world. We add here only a few words with reference to the physique. Chronic exogenous diseases, such as, e.g., syphilis and tuberculosis, dig deeply into the form of the body, and can in many cases change the constitutional build until it is unrecognizable. Where we find a-typical forms we must bear such agencies clearly in mind, besides alloy and crossing. A 25-year-old girl of our material presents a decided asthenic appearance in combination with a simple inhibited depression ; she is altogether haggard, flabby, she has a narrow chest and a curvature of the spine (kyphosis). Her pupil reactions are imperfect, and she has scars suspected of being gummatous. In her 17th year she had already once been depressive, and at that time her weight was reduced from 136 to 86 pounds, and she has since remained in a weakly bodily condition. She was then treated by the internal clinic with quicksilver inunction. For the rest, our material is favourable for our investigations into the constitution, in that it is almost entirely made up of individuals who are country folk, with few signs of syphilis, and who on the whole have grown up under healthy simple conditions of life.

We hold it very probable that external symptoms of an endogenous constitutional condition might become obliterated in the conditions of life in large cities, so unfavourable hygienically.

Rather less important than the luetic agencies are those disturbing external determinants which spring from tuberculosis, because the tuberculosis itself is to a very high degree conditioned by the constitution, and for this reason is less of a hindrance than a finger-post in the investigations into constitution. This holds particularly for the asthenic type, which is only more strongly accentuated by tuberculosis, and perhaps comes into existence in part directly through its collaboration. On the other hand the athletic and pyknic forms may naturally be distinctly blurred by it.

Besides chronic diseases, the effects of nourishment and work are perhaps the most important exogenous factors in the building of the body. On the whole these factors are over-emphasized by the laity, and also by thoughtless physicians. If anyone is pale and thin, it must have been his " sedentary occupation ", if he were fat, then it would be that just the same. If a peasant woman has a blooming complexion and fine muscles, it comes from her " healthy country life " ; if she has collapsed, then she has had " too much drudgery ". Picture two people constantly chatting together in the pub ; one of them gets fatter and fatter, because he " drinks a lot of beer ", the other gets thinner and thinner because he " doesn't drink enough milk ". And just the same thing happens with old age. If anyone in his youth was round, and in old age is thin, then the reason is obvious, just as if he has been slim in his youth, and in old age has developed a paunch. Both phenomena are due to old age—naturally.

We must be clearly understood : all those factors of work, and manner of nutrition which we have mentioned are of importance. They are important secondary factors. But only in a small number of cases have they a decisive influence over the nature of the body. Supposing we feed a pyknic on nothing but turnip-roots and cabbages, then he will get thin, and if we let a slim athletic eat from early till late, and drink Munich beer, then he will certainly develop a swollen exterior. A poor peasant woman who has a baby every year, and has to do ceaseless hard work, very soon looks worn and pulled down, even if she was the most blooming girl, and one even sees young asthenics develop something of a muscle-relief if, with schizoid pedantry, they devote years to sport and gymnastic exercises. All these observations are indisputable.

But we see just as plainly that, within the sphere in which, under natural social-hygienic relations, such work- and nutrition-agencies act on the majority of mankind, they only have an accessory influence in relation to the ruling factors of the constitution, an influence which is sufficient to check or reinforce to a high degree the growth tendencies in question. In this connection a number of schizophrenic and chronic circular patients, whom I had been able to observe in the asylum at Winnental over a period of many years (and particularly since 1911) were very instructive to me. In March 1919, when I investigated their physique, they all enjoyed the same uniform nourishment. I found them after the severe years of the war, a period of enforced underfeeding, very nearly as I had known them before the war. The pyknic circulars were somewhat lighter in a few cases than they were before the war, but they still had round, well-fleshed faces, the parts of the body were rounded, and in some instances the weight was abnormal. The asthenic schizophrenes, such as had not died of tuberculosis, were lanky when they had good food before the war, and after the scanty war-time diet were even lankier and thinner than before. The main differences among schizophrenes are to be found between the severe cases of aged 'stuporous' patients who have been confined to their beds on the one hand, and those who have gone out to work on the other. The latter on an average have more colour, more musculature, and better consistency of the skin, and to a certain extent also a better state of nourishment, while, where there has been a lasting cessation of bodily exercise, the asthenic appearance is exaggerated to the extent of caricature, through atrophy due to inactivity ; the athletic characteristics on the other hand can be very decidedly blurred.   Among circulars the differences between the conditions of nourishment according to the phase of life and illness are very often enormous, for which reason, particularly where one is dealing with thin circulars, one must always inquire after the earlier bodily weights ; on the other hand they do not seem to be very markedly influenced by confinement to bed or by exercise (apart from extreme motor excitation).   In certain professions the pyknic nature (as far as the deposition of fat is concerned) reaches a decidedly higher degree of perfection, *e.g.*, among bakers, innkeepers, butchers, and members of the middle classes who are well-to-do in a small way, and who eat a great deal, and spend a certain portion of their time at the pub, while, on the contrary, among hard workers, particularly among the labouring peasantry and the hard-pressed mothers in humble families where there are a great number of children, the pyknic basis can only be detected by means of the skeletal symptoms, and the rather softer, rounder, redder faces, while the layer of fat on the trunk is slight.   But at any rate in the majority of cases even these strong exogenous agents do not suffice to make the diagnostic picture quite unrecognizable.

Where, however, we have simple average conditions of life, as is the case with most of our private patients at the Institute, who come from the educated official classes, there the constitutional determinants come out fairly clearly in the relations indicated by our general statistics, in which, since they are mixed, the exogenous factors cancel out.

PART II
THE TEMPERAMENTS

CHAPTER VIII

INVESTIGATION INTO FAMILY CHARACTEROLOGY

WE turn now to the description of the types of personality as they correspond to the circular and schizophrene groups. Just a few words on the technical side. As is the case with every important question of an anamnesic nature, so with characterology, it is essential to avoid suggestive questioning as far as possible. Written self-portrayals of intelligent patients are of special value for this reason. In order, however, to get a systematic survey over a large series we have no other resource than direct viva voce questioning of the immediate members of the family, and after that, of the patients themselves. If we ask a peasant woman " Was your brother nervous and peace-loving, energetic, etc. ? " we shall often get a vague and uncertain reply. If, on the other hand, we ask : " What did he do when he was a child, if he had to go alone into the dark hay-loft ? " or, " How did he behave himself when there was a row up at the pub on a Sunday evening ? " then perhaps this same woman will give us concise and unequivocal information which, with its fresh liveliness, bears the stamp of trustworthiness on it. One must be perfectly familiar with the life of the simple man, the peasant, and the workman, and one must put oneself completely in his place, so that by one's investigations one elicits in concrete pictures his experiences in the school, in church, and at the pub, from one end of the week to the other, rather than a scheme of peculiarities of character.

Only in this way shall we get information about the simple colourless psychic life of the average man unfolded in all its detail. For this reason I have laid particular stress on the point, that as much as possible should be asked in this concrete manner, and that direct questions on characterology should only be used to fill out the picture, to save time, and to serve as control questions scattered about among the concrete accounts (and then only in the form of ' either—or ' in order as far as possible to avoid suggestion). Further, it must be noted that, even with the best exploration technique, there are a number of people from whom nothing really precise and unequivocal can be obtained. One leaves such cases on one side, and does not allow oneself to be lured into squeezing answers out of them by means of suggestive questions, answers which are as wasteful of time as they are devoid of value. The best method is to rely on the psychological analysis of a few well-chosen cases where there is a certain anamnesic objectivity and clear intelligent self-portrayal, to get everything out of them, and to lay bare every minute thread of their being. In this way we soon obtain a vivid idea of what is characteristic in the modes of feeling of the circular and of the schizophrene, apart from their psychoses, and of the ways in which they differ from one another. The great number of the other cases which have only been cursorily studied we use to complete the material we have already procured, and to control its validity for generalization.

One should not, however, rest with the pre-psychotic personality of the sick individual himself. Rather, it is the case with characterology, as with physique, that the typical characteristics of a constitutional type may sometimes be more clearly delineated in the nearest relations than in the patient himself. Moreover, where several constitutional types are crossed in one patient, we may perceive the individual components under certain circumstances clearly isolated and split up among other members of his family. In short, if we want to get the completest possible plan of the constitution of a patient, we must always take his heredity carefully into account. For this reason, I have for many years been in the habit of recording, in the instance of important cases, everything that can be found out about the peculiarities of character, illnesses and physique of the blood-relations. The build of a patient's constitution often emerges astonishingly clearly, if at the end we add schematically, using a few key-words, the most important things we have found out in this way, as in the following instance of the paranoid schizophrene, J.F.

TABLE X

TYPE OF SCHIZOPHRENE FAMILY

Father's Sister.	Father.	Mother.	Mother's Sister.	Mother's Brother.
Unsociable and extraordinarily excitable.	Paranoiac eccentric, anxiety, misanthropic, depressed.	Short persecution-mania with alcoholism in pre-senile period; sensitive, humourless, pedantic, depressed. Desire to get away.	Avaricious.	Alcoholism. Vagrant.

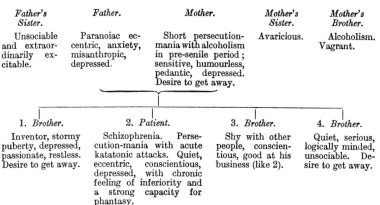

1. Brother.	2. Patient.	3. Brother.	4. Brother.
Inventor, stormy puberty, depressed, passionate, restless. Desire to get away.	Schizophrenia. Persecution-mania with acute katatonic attacks. Quiet, eccentric, conscientious, depressed, with chronic feeling of inferiority and a strong capacity for phantasy.	Shy with other people, conscientious, good at his business (like 2).	Quiet, serious, logically minded, unsociable. Desire to get away.

In this family we find a perfect breeding ground for those peculiarities of character, which we shall later describe as ' schizothyme '.[1] From the healthy, socially sound schizothymic characters (e.g., brothers 3 and 4), through the clear psychopaths, such as the father's sister, and the mother's brother, and those who have hovered their life long on the psychotic boundary, like the father, to the light, senile, abortive psychosis of the mother, and finally on to the severe catastrophic schizophrenia of the son, among these few members of one family we see all thinkable transitions and shadings between health and disease. We recognize at once from this family diagram that a coherent investigation into psychiatristic heredity cannot allow of a limitation to those members of the family who are diseased. A genealogical table in which we have only included the psychoses is like a text full of lacunæ, in which the majority of the words have

[1] Naturally families in which personalities of the same type are so numerous and unmixed as in the example before us are exceptional. The more distant relations of the majority of schizophrenes and circulars are a mixture of both types of personality, but all the same the type to which the patient belongs (in the case of schizophrenes the schizothymic and in the case of circulars the cyclothymic) is clearly prevalent.

disappeared, and frequently those very words which give the meaning. For our method of observing constitution, the psychoses are merely isolated knots in a widely ramifying network of normal physico-characterological constitutional relations.

Supposing, as a counterpart, we look at the type of family which presents itself as being constituted primarily of members who are circulars, we shall at once find ourselves in quite another world, in a sensibly different psychic atmosphere. Here is a typical example out of my material, which has to do with the 65-year-old circular, J.N., who, with a basis of a hypomanic temperament, hovered his whole life long between manic and depressive psychosis.

TABLE XI

TYPE OF CIRCULAR FAMILY, WITH PREVAILINGLY BRIGHT TEMPERAMENTS

Father.	*Mother.*	1. *Mother's Sister.*	2. *Mother's Sister.*
Peaceful, contented, satisfied, industrious, conciliatory, a great favourite, fruit-tree grower, fond of music, a poet.	Bright, lively, always friendly, musical, talkative, very good-natured. House always full of visitors ; beggars never sent away empty-handed.	" A bright life the live-long day," humorous, lovable and friendly.	Ditto.

1. *Brother.*	2. *Patient.*	3, 4 and 5. *Three Sisters.*
Music professor; went to America when young.	Manic-depression, good-natured, bright, satisfied, contented, humorous, industrious, busy.	They " find life a good joke," lively, sociable, full of good works, kind-hearted.

To supplement this cheerful family I now give an example of a family with prevailingly depressive temperaments, belonging to the 49-year-old circular, G.S. (periodic restrained depression).

In this family also we find a continuous series of all transitional types of temperament, from the periodic depressive psychosis of the patient, through the light, occasional age-depression of the maternal grandmother, to the easily moved, emotional man with indications of cyclic disturbances (father), and so on to the serious, harmonious good-nature of the perfectly healthy sister. With regard to such genealogical tables it is particularly enlightening to observe that we can never do justice to the endogenous psychoses so long as we regard them as isolated unities of disease, having taken them out of their natural heredity environment, and forced them into the limits of a clinical system.

TABLE XII

<small>Type of Circular Family, with Prevailingly Depressive Temperaments</small>

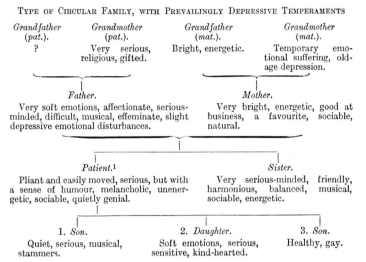

Grandfather (pat.).	*Grandmother* (pat.).	*Grandfather* (mat.).	*Grandmother* (mat.).
?	Very serious, religious, gifted.	Bright, energetic.	Temporary emotional suffering, old-age depression.

Father.
Very soft emotions, affectionate, serious-minded, difficult, musical, effeminate, slight depressive emotional disturbances.

Mother.
Very bright, energetic, good at business, a favourite, sociable, natural.

Patient.[1]
Pliant and easily moved, serious, but with a sense of humour, melancholic, unenergetic, sociable, quietly genial.

Sister.
Very serious-minded, friendly, harmonious, balanced, musical, sociable, energetic.

1. *Son.*	2. *Daughter.*	3. *Son.*
Quiet, serious, musical, stammers.	Soft emotions, serious, sensitive, kind-hearted.	Healthy, gay.

Viewed in a large biological framework, however, the endogenous psychoses are nothing other than marked accentuations of normal types of temperament.

When we get used to taking a comprehensive view of the total personality of the patient and the individualities of his relations together with the psychosis, we soon have the feeling : all this is out of one mould. That which breaks catastrophically through, in the wild seizures and sudden tempers of our katatonic patients, as a persecution-mania, as an absurd set of ideas, as a despairing suspension of activity, as a rigid inflexibility, as hostile autism, negativism, and mutism, that same ' something ' is interwoven as a spiritus familiaris in the most varied patterns ; it runs in healthy and psychopathic variations through the whole fabric of pedants, solid well-informed economizers, hypochondriacs who go through life restless

---

[1] The wife of the patient, whom we have not mentioned here, has exactly the same disposition as he has, and suffers similarly from depression.

and twitching, inventors, and sensitive souls with their shy nervous anxiety, their mistrust, their silence, and their sullen rebuffing hostility towards mankind.

When we come out of the psychic milieu of the schizophrene family into that of the circulars, it is like stepping out of a cool shut-in vault into the open warm sunshine. What is common to both the circular families we have given above, is a certain good-nature, warmth, and easiness of the emotions, an accessible, sociable, human manner, which manifests itself in an infinite number of transitional forms, now rather bright, fresh, and whimsical, active, and energetic, now rather gentle, melancholy, and serious, here at the hypomanic, there at the depressive pole of the circular group.

There are certain families, particularly of the schizophrene type, where we trace this spiritus familiaris through various branches of one family-tree, being handed on with extraordinary tenacity through a series of generations in spite of manifold alien blood-influences, now coming out clearly, now lurking in isolated traits of a personality. Of this kind is the following family, about whose individual members trustworthy contemporary information is at my disposal.

In this genealogical table we find a whole collection of those types of character which have to a certain extent been known for a long time to the psychiatrist as occurring in connection with schizophrenia, and which we shall describe later. We have here to do with a highly gifted old family which has fallen into degeneration in many respects, and in which schizoid individuals who are socially valuable such as II. 2, and V. 4, are mixed with people who have made a mess of their lives and gone off the rails. It is surprising to see how the types correspond to each other generation after generation in the right and left collateral branches. The restless wasters in IV. 2 and 3, have a clear family likeness on the other side in the eccentric loafer IV. 7 (and also a slight echo in V. 3). The bigoted devotee IV. 5, has an almost exact parallel in V. 5. The sensitive, shy, nervous individuals IV. 8 and V. 4 are paralleled by V. 1. As individual representatives we find the schizoid natures of the stern moralist and idealist II. 2, the youthful paragon of virtue VI. 1, and the sour old

TABLE XIII

COLLATERAL INHERITANCE OF SCHIZOID BASES

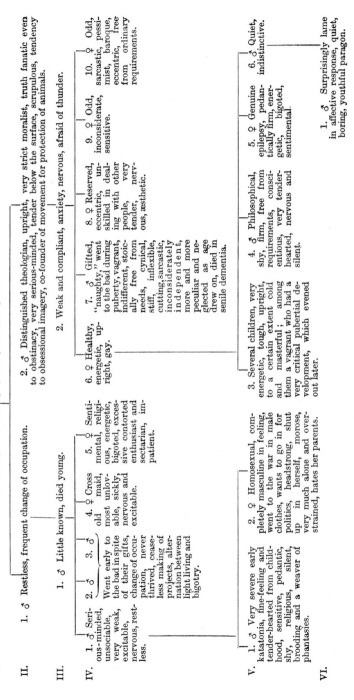

I. 1. ♂ Strong character, upright, unyielding, capable.

II. 1. ♂ Restless, frequent change of occupation.

2. ♂ Distinguished theologian, upright, very strict moralist, truth fanatic even to obstinacy, very serious-minded, tender below the surface, scrupulous, tendency to obsessional imagery, co-founder of movement for protection of animals.

III. 1. ♂ Little known, died young.

2. Weak and compliant, anxiety, nervous, afraid of thunder.

IV. 1. ♂ Serious-minded, unsociable, very weak, excitable, nervous, restless.

2. ♂ 3. ♂ Went early to the bad in spite of their gifts, change of occupation, never thrived, ceaseless making of projects, alternation between light living and bigotry.

4. ♀ Cross old maid, most unlovable, sickly, nervous and excitable.

5. ♀ Sentimental, religious, energetic, bigoted, excessive contorted enthusiast and sectarian, impatient.

6. ♀ Healthy, energetic, upright, gay.

7. ♂ "naughty," went to the bad during puberty, vagrant, indifferent, stoically free from needs, cynical, stiff, inflexible, cutting, sarcastic, inconsiderately independent, more and more peculiar and neglected as age drew on, died in senile dementia.

8. ♀ Reserved, eccentric, unskilled in dealing with other people, very tender, nervous, aesthetic.

9. ♀ Odd, inconsiderate, sensitive.

10. ♀ Odd, sarcastic, pessimist, baroque, eccentric, free from ordinary requirements.

V. 1. ♂ Very severe early katatonia, fine-feeling and tender-hearted from childhood, sensitive, pedantic, shy, religious, silent, brooding and a weaver of phantasies.

2. ♀ Homosexual, completely masculine in feeling, went to the war in male clothes, wants to go in for politics, headstrong, morose, shut up in herself, very much alone and overstrained, hates her parents.

3. Several children, very energetic, tough, upright, to a certain extent cold and masterful; among them a vagrant who had a very critical pubertal development, which evened out later.

4. ♂ Philosophical, shy, firm, free from requirements, conscientious, very tender-hearted, nervous and silent.

5. ♀ Genuine epilepsy, pedantically firm, energetic, bigoted, sentimental.

6. ♂ Quiet, indistinctive.

VI. 1. ♂ Surprisingly lame in affective response, quiet, boring, youthful paragon.

maid IV. 4. The relations by marriage, together with their families, from II. 2 downwards, are known to me by detailed description or personal observation. The wife of II. 2 was altogether easy-going and good-natured, the wife of III. 2, herself harsh and strict, comes from a perfectly healthy family, the husband of IV. 6 has constitutional depressive traits ; he is very righteous, well-informed, strict, difficult, and passionate ; his father died of arterio-sclerosis of the brain, otherwise there is nothing abnormal about his nearer forebears. The family-tree, as far as we can see, has not been weighed down in the schizophrenic direction by incoming influences, at any rate at these points.

We see, therefore, how a rich schizoid basis spreads pertinaciously down both branches of the family like a creeping evil, without any gross manifestation of dementia præcox coming to the surface (only IV. 7 comes very close to it). Eventually, in the fourth generation (V. 1), the lurking predisposition suddenly bursts out with great violence in a particularly severe katatonia which had already made its appearance in the fifteenth year of the patient's age. What has happened here ? Fortunately we know the mother and her family. In the maternal family there is no psychosis to be found. The mother's brothers and sisters are for the most part gentle, sensible, dreamy people. The mother herself, though healthy at the present time, is excessively gentle, sensitive, and fanciful, and she had, at the same age as the young man, a nervous condition in which in broad daylight she saw forms which dissolved after a few seconds ; she passed through this condition in her home without her usual activities being interrupted, and without its being necessary to send her to an asylum.

From the analysis of this family we get the impression that for a manifest schizophrenia to come to a head it is probably necessary in many cases for two generative cells, one paternal and one maternal, to come together, which behave in a complementary fashion to one another. So long as this complementary working does not occur, partial tendencies due to the schizophrenia-producing agent can spread persistently through many generations ; they manifest themselves in distinctive peculiar forms of personality, of the same nature as we find over and over again in the region of the pre-psychotic states of fully-developed schizophrenes, and in their blood-relations. In severe cases they also come out as modifications of the personality at the age of puberty, as in the cases of the restless wasters IV. 2, 3, 7 ; but a real dementia præcox only once occurs, out of all these many pre-dispositions, in the characteristic instance V. 1. All this, however, is to be taken as suppositional.[1] Hoffmann gives an account of a fundamental investigation into these questions.[2] In all questions about heredity which are relevant to this issue we refer to his competent judgment, and for this reason we express ourselves very briefly on the subject of inheritance, but we especially stress the fact that the problem of heredity is obviously to be regarded as one of the most important sides of the problem of constitution. The exposition of our types of constitution is fundamentally confirmed by the genea-logical investigations of Hoffmann.

This much we have already learnt from the few genealogical tables we have sketched, that a fruitful inquiry into the inheritance of endogenous psychoses is only possible if one has intimate knowledge of all the normal and psychopathic types of personality which correspond to these psychoses, both from the bodily and the psychic points of view.

This is particularly true, when, as so often occurs, various opposed inheritance-bases unite themselves in one patient, as happened in the following case of the 43-year-old E.L., who suffered from a manic-depressive psychosis.

This family [3] shows particularly well how the investi-gator into heredity must go astray if he only measures the diseased members of a family against one another. In the case before us, for instance, he must say : here we

[1] As to the appearance of homosexuality, of genuine epilepsy, and of a senile dementia which develops gradually out of a severe schizoid disposition, all in the framework of schizoid inheritance, we here only refer incidentally to the possibility. We have already earlier on thrown some light on the biological relations between schizophrenia and sexual perversion.

[2] H. Hoffmann, *Die Nachkommenschaft bei endogenen Psychosen*, Berlin, Julius Springer, 1921.

[3] Table XIV.

see that the inheritance of a psychosis is quite a polymorphous affair, in that a circular son springs from an epileptic father. Certainly, from a biological point of view, a very unsatisfactory train of thought.

TABLE XIV

CONCURRENCE OF INHERITED BASIS

Father's two Brothers.	*Father.*	*Mother.*
Friendly and sociable.	Epilepsy, whimsical inventive mind, passionate, very strict, unsociable and shy.	Very soft emotions, friendly, kind - hearted, sociable, and still kept in affectionate remembrance by many people.

1. *Brother.*	2. *Patient.*	3. *Sister.*	4. *Sister.*
Tendency to depressive alternation of mood, but always under control; gay, humorous, sociable, very energetic, and decided, rather feared, firm and passionate, very capable, leading manufacturer in a large way.	Manic - depressive, too soft emotions, kind - hearted, friendly, very religious, bright, active, tendency to quick anger.	Soft - hearted, friendly and approachable, somewhat affected, religious sentimentality, gentle but energetic.	Soft emotions, like patient.

Supposing, on the other hand, that we include the healthy members of the family, then we see something completely different. We see, in point of fact, that here the continuity of inheritance goes not from the father but from the mother, as far as the circular son is concerned ; that there is complete correspondence between the temperamental bases of both mother and son, and that this temperament, even as it occurs in the case of the healthy mother, is the very same as we meet with prevailing among relatives of circulars, and in the circular himself. The father, on the other hand, stands on one side as a fundamentally different type of temperament. In the four children we see the parental types of temperament so divided that 1 and 3 exhibit clear mixtures out of the two parental bases, while in 2 (the patient) and 4 the maternal type comes pure to the surface. We now need, at any rate in this instance, no longer fall back on an improbable polymorphism of inheritance, but we can explain quite naturally the mode of inheritance as follows : either the father (his two brothers are friendly and sociable) added an hereditary element of a circular nature, which was not manifested in a clearly recognizable form in himself, to the maternal generative basis which pointed in the same direction ; or the indubitably degenerate tendency of the father worked as an unspecifically depraving influence on the specific maternal generative plasm, in other words, the specific circular tendency comes from the mother, and only its degenerate deterioration, which has gone far enough to allow of a circular psychosis, comes from the father.

And now, after this genealogical survey we turn to a more exact description of the forms of personality.

CHAPTER IX

THE CYCLOID TEMPERAMENT

WE describe as schizoid and cycloid those abnormal personalities which fluctuate between sickness and health, which reflect the fundamental psychological symptoms of the schizophrene and the circular psychoses in the lighter form of personal oddities ; such schizoid and cycloid types we find in the first place in the pre-psychotic personalities of the psychopaths themselves, and then in their nearest blood-relations. These two groups of men give us a secure foundation for our description. If we have investigated them, then we are finally justified in describing as schizoid and cycloid such abnormal individuals as, in their psychic and bodily habitus, are built analogously to these, without having the corresponding psychosis in their own immediate circle.

The direction in which the types of personality in the region of dementia præcox tend on the whole has already been known for a long time. Berze,[1] Medow,[2] Kraepelin and Bleuler have described the nature of these men. Bleuler in particular has prepared the way for an advance from a bare external delineation to a more detailed psycho-pathological analysis of the symptoms of schizophrenia, and all that we shall try to contribute in what follows to the psychology of schizoids and schizothymes is only made possible by the foundations which have been laid down by Bleuler.[3] Besides this we must call special attention to the services rendered by Wilmanns [4] in clearing up the relations between dementia præcox

---

[1] *Die hereditaren Beziehungen der Dementia præcox*, Leipzig and Wien, 1910.

[2] " Zur Erblichkeitsfrage in der Psychiatrie," *Zeitschr. f. d. ges. Neurol. u. Psychiatr.*, 26, 493, 1914.

[3] Contributions to a psychological analysis of schizophrenia are to be found in earlier writings, *e.g.*, in Stransky, etc.

[4] *Zur psychopathogie des Landstreichers*, Leipzig, 1906.

and certain large groups of psychopaths and degenerates among vagrants and criminals.

So far, the outlines of the types of personality in the circular group manifest themselves far less clearly.

Where we have by chance come across the portrayal of such individuals, there has often been little success in a clear formulation of the fundamental essence of the cycloid temperament ; we usually find it far too strongly mixed with factors which do not belong to it, schizoid and otherwise degenerate indications, alien influences of which we naturally find isolated instances often enough in the heredity, or in the pre-psychotic condition, of manic-depressives, without their proving themselves to be typical elements in the majority of cases when a comparison is made over a large characterological series.

Above all, so far, there has been lacking a broad characterological bridge between what one calls a hypomanic and what one calls a constitutionally depressive temperament ; that is to say, the description of those people the tone of whose dispositions lies midway between hypomanic and depressive, in so far as they stand in relation to the circular group, and by this means the disentangling of those traits of temperament which are common to the hypomanics and the depressives, and therefore, to the whole circular class. Though the easily identifiable hypomanic type is not yet disentangled from all alien symptoms, the difficulties really begin with the notion of constitutional depression. Reiss has clearly pointed out these difficulties and indistinct transition stages in his well-known treatise.[1] Above all we shall have to attempt to characterize the temperamental depression which bears a close relation to the circular group more or less in contradistinction to that which points rather more in the schizophrene direction.

In order at first to get a general survey, we shall make use of statistics, involving over a hundred sick-charts of schizophrenes and circulars, in which we have calculated the frequency of occurrence of all the pre-psychotic character-peculiarities of the patients, obtained by the method described above, taking them one by one, and

---

[1] " Konstitutionelle Verstimmung und manisch-depressive Irresein," *Zeitschr. f. d. ges. Neurol. u. Psychiatr.*, 2, 347.

which, for control purposes, we have compared with the certainly quite impartially and unsystematically described characteristics in the sick-charts of the asylum at Winnental.

The Diathetic Proportions

The following characteristics of temperament came out as the most frequent and constantly recurring among manic-depressive patients :

    1. Sociable, good-natured, friendly, genial.
    2. Cheerful, humorous, jolly, hasty.
    3. Quiet, calm, easily depressed, soft-hearted.

For the purposes of our survey we have separated out these peculiarities into three groups. The first includes, as it were, the fundamental marks of the cycloid temperament, the characteristics, that is to say, which, more or less independently of the colour of the mood and the psychic tempo, recur everywhere from the hypomanic to the depressive poles, and which give, equally to the cheerfulness and to the melancholy, the tone which makes them criteria for the cycloid individual. The individuals in the region of manic-depressive madness are prevailingly sociable, good-natured men, people with whom one can get on well, who understand a joke, and who take life as it comes. They give themselves naturally and openly, and one soon makes friends with them ; they have often something soft and warm in their temperaments.

This exactly corresponds to the observations which we have made on the diseased circulars ; it is well known that even manics in a state of excitement have usually something childishly good-natured, trustful, and tractable about them, they are far more up to mischief than harsh acts of violence, they seldom make a serious attempt to do anyone any harm ; they just flare up all of a sudden, but they are soon quiet again ; one can seldom take anything they do in bad part. And the pure typical circular depressives have some soft quality in their moodiness. If the psychic flow is not hampered by a high degree of repression, one usually has a sympathetic feeling for them, one can always say something friendly to them when occasion arises, in spite of all their despair ; they long for encouragement, and, as the obstructions fall away, they have an impulse to express themselves ; and when their trouble gives way to tr atment, they are unassuming, friendly, and grateful. Pat ents in whom the obstruction is overpowerful often actually complain very loudly at their lack of warm, kindly feeling for men and things, a sign that this feeling is their very life element ; and in spite of their subjective consciousness of obstruction, when seen objectively, in comparison with a schizophrene, they still seem affable and kind-hearted.

Side by side with the clearly sociable natures, we often find also among circulars, especially where there is a more depressed colouring, affable " cats that walk by themselves ", people who take things rather to heart, who like to live their lives quietly and in contemplation. They may be differentiated from the corresponding schizoids in that there is no internal antipathy, no hostile turning away from human society, to be found in them, but at the most there is a certain melancholy, and, occasionally, anxiety and a tendency to a feeling of inferiority. If one seeks their company, they are friendly, natural and approachable, they generally have some quiet pub, or a small genial family circle or group of friends, where they can enjoy themselves gently and comfortably.

It is important to notice that one does not find constitutional depressives, *i.e.*, people in whom the sadly-toned disposition comes to the fore with marked continuity, nearly so often in the region of manic-depressive madness. One could collect together a superb series of typically hypomanic temperaments out of our circular material, far more easily than a correspondingly large group of constitutional depressives. And this is so although the Schwabians are a particularly melancholy race of men. When people with a strong tendency to periodic depression are described by their relatives as to their personality apart from the psychosis, we do not usually at first get the statement : " He is depressed and downcast," but generally the negative formulation : " He could never enjoy himself like other folk ; " and very often only : " He is gentle and quiet, he always takes things a bit hard, he has a soft heart." If we ask directly about his temperament, then we get something like this : " In normal times

I

he is friendly ; people like him ; he never grumbles ; he has a sense of humour ; he joins in a laugh, and even makes a bit of a joke himself at times. Only, tears come easily to his eyes, he can't get over even quite little things, and he grieves longer and deeper than other people over sad situations." That is to say : in the case of such individuals, it is not that the temperament itself is sad, but only that it is more easily roused by sad conditions. And what is particularly significant is this : in difficult, responsible positions, when there is any danger, in thorny, exasperating situations, and in sudden precarious crises in business, they are not nervous, irritated, or agitated, like the average man, and particularly like a great many schizophrenes. But they are *unhappy*. They cannot see any distance ahead, everything stands like a mountain in front of them.

This is the conclusion we have reached : men of this kind have a soft temperament, which can swing to great extremes. The path over which it swings is a wide one, namely between cheerfulness and unhappiness. It does also swing towards the cheerful side, but not so often and not so far ; on the other hand it lingers over in the unhappy direction. There is, however, another swinging-path which is very little used, namely that which leads in the direction of nervous excitability ; for to the emotional stimulations which lie in this direction, they do not usually react in this way, but with their typical pre-formed symptom complex : sadness with a feeling of obstruction.

We observe the same thing the other way round in purely hypomanic temperaments. Not only is the hypomanic disposition well known to be a peculiarly labile one, which also has leanings in the depressive direction, but many of these cheerful natures have, when we get to know them better, a permanent melancholic element somewhere in the background of their being. " There has always been something of that kind hidden away in me ", a man told me, who, in earlier life, had always been cheerful and happy, and who only later, in old age, developed a depression. Goethe's mother, a woman of the sunniest hypomanic temperament,[1] gave

---

[1] " Hypomanic " in this book always means something characterological, and has nothing to do with the distinction between " healthy " and " diseased ".

her servants the strictest orders never to tell her anything unpleasant, so greatly did her emotions need this
artificial protection from themselves.

We ought not, therefore, to describe cycloid individuals,
even apart from intermediate grades, as simply hypomanic,
or simply depressive.   For in many hypomanics there is
hidden a small depressive component, and in the majority
of cycloid melancholics there is a vein of humour.   The
hypomanic and melancholic halves of the cycloid temperament relieve one another, they form layers or patterns in
individual cases, arranged in the most varied combinations.

This relation between the hypomanic and melancholic
elements in the individual cycloid personality, we call its
diathetic or mood proportion.

The hypomanic is 'hot-headed', he is a man of a
quick temper, of the 'knightly hot-bloodedness' of a
Fritz Reuter, who flares up all of a sudden, and is soon
good again.   He cannot halt behind a mountain ; when
anything gets in his way, he sees red at once, and tries
to get what he wants by making a row.   He is not made
so that he can swallow his indignation, and carry it
around under a gentle exterior while it causes him internal
agony ; but for that reason he bears no malice ; lying in
wait, intrigue, and brooding, are foreign to him ; when
he has indulged in a hearty outburst, then all depression
has disappeared, and only the refreshing feeling of having
got a load off his mind remains.   Of the typical hypomanic person we cannot say he is never sorrowful, but
we can say he is never nervous.   "I don't know what
nerves are."   "I have the nature of a horse."   These are
the favourite descriptions of the hypomanic temperament.
And, in point of fact, they do not know what it is to be
tired, neither have they the brooding inner feeling of
agitation and tension of the nervous man.

This fits in with what we have said above about the
pure depressive temperaments.   In an adverse situation
the cycloid is either sorrowful or hot-headed, but he is
never in the very least nervous,[1] any more than he experi-

[1] Patients and their relations are apt to describe slight cyclothymic depression, euphemistically and inaccurately, as nervousness.
If one inquires further, one does not come upon what the doctor
understands by nervousness, and what we shall later describe as such,
but upon an indefinite depressive discomfort with feelings of psychic

ences in conflict (whether he be hypomanic or depressive), that tone of feeling which accompanies cool acrimony, sarcastic irritability, or cutting malignity. Naturally we do not mean to say—and this is true mutatis mutandis for all our analyses—that one cannot often enough find nervous circulars ; but only this : on an average, when one takes a survey over a long characterological series, nervousness is not among the outstanding characteristics of the cycloid man.

The majority of cycloids have a particularly well-orientated emotional life, which shades away from the sanguine, quicksilver temperament of the hypomanic, to the deep, warm-hearted feelings of the more melancholic natures, with all possible transitional stages. The temperament of the cycloids alternates between cheerfulness and sadness, in deep, smooth, rounded waves, only more quickly and transitorily with some, more fully and enduringly with others. But the mid-point of these oscillations lies with some nearer the hypomanic, and with others nearer the depressive pole.

Cycloid men have ' hearts '. The word ' heart ', or better, perhaps, ' good-nature ', brings one nearest to an expression of that which is common to the majority of these natures, throughout their various habitual temperamental foundations : the soft, warm, kind-hearted, philanthropic temperament, naturally capable of being moved to joy or sorrow. The word ' humour ' is nearly related to it. We find humour especially in the middle region of the cycloid temperament, where the capacity for laughter from the hypomanic side, and the depth of feeling from the depressive, come together in a successful mixture.

The Social Reactions

The temperamental nature of the cycloids determines also the nature of their social reactions, as we have sketched them in brief above. They feel the necessity

inhibition and inferiority, and the accompanying vegetative neural troubles, disturbance of digestion and sleep, headaches, etc. But it is quite true that a latent nervous disposition, which may be present side by side with the cyclothymia, may be called into simultaneous manifestation by the depressive phase, and may disappear completely after it is passed.

to speak out, to laugh out, and to have a good cry. They seek by the nearest and most natural way, *i.e.*, indulgence in human society, what will bring their spirits into satisfactory motion, rejoice them and lighten them.

Every mood-stimulus finds in them at once its resonance; no inhibition hinders them, and there is no long-thought-out purposefulness with its complicated after-effects ; they are able to give themselves up to the momentary mood of the milieu, and at once to swing with it, to take part, and to identify themselves with it. The least little thing, every object, gets imbued with something of the warm feeling tone. " Lovingly and thankfully " the world is accepted. Naturally only outside the depressive moods. For this reason the average cycloid man, especially in the quiet central region, has a sociable, friendly, realistic and accommodating feel about him. Because his temperament swings with that of the milieu, there is for him no sharp distinction between I and the outside world, no principle of withdrawal, no burning desire to correct according to firmly-held rules, no tragically exacerbated conflict, but a life in things themselves, a giving up of himself to the external world, a capacity for living, feeling and suffering with his surroundings.

What one calls hypomanic egoism has something child-like and naïve about it, which finds its true counterpart in the overwhelming joy in giving presents and causing pleasure to other people. This hypomanic self-love is not an abrupt setting up of the individual's own personality against an outside world, which is regarded with hatred or indifference, but a ' live and let live ', an evenly-balanced swimming in comfort for oneself and the world, an almost ludicrous conviction of the value and ' rightness ' of one's own personality.

This realistic attitude of the cycloid, this natural acceptance of the given—both men and relations—has a somewhat different colouring according as it veers towards the hypomanic or the depressive pole. The hypomanic is the emotional man, the good mixer, who is outspoken, easily moved, and perpetually being influenced afresh. He likes meeting any new person and is at once his friend. A tendency to a certain materialism, to enjoyment, love, eating and drinking, to a natural seizing of all the good gifts of life, is not only unmistakable in the hypomanic character, but may be followed right through the cycloid middle-stages, even down to the depressive region, where we meet it again in a certain type of melancholic, comfort-loving, old wine-bibber. Besides this, the realistic acceptance of their fellow-men is qualified by a deeper ethical sense, as we approach the depressive pole ; we come across it there as a non-moralizing warm understanding of alien peculiarities, as a well-marked good-natured unassumingness, which makes the melancholic cycloid so pleasant in personal relations.

This giving up of themselves, and feeling for reality, has a very close connection with another typical character trait of the cycloids. Cycloids are not men of stubborn logical minds, with well-thought-out systems and schemes. This is true for all variations. When we get to the quick tempo of the hypomanic, this peculiarity becomes chronic, changeable, fickleness. But in the quiet medium stages, and among the melancholics, we find a class of men who talk themselves over in their good-natured way, and who, in spite of their conscientiousness, have a tendency to give in, and make a fair compromise. They are practical men, who first observe the men they have to deal with, and the real possibilities, and then turn to the principle. It is interesting to see how this characteristic comes out in manic and depressive psychoses. The average poverty of obsessional ideas in circulars is well known. Neither the manic nor the depressive, where the case is typical, builds a system of mad ideas with a logical chain of thought running through it, and bound together with logical arguments. The content of their imagination is coloured brightly or sadly, without very much thought, so that a few delusions of impoverishment, or sin, or short-lasting ideas of greatness, are all that emerge. Mood is all important, reflection is reduced to a minimum.

For these reasons, wherever we look we find among cycloids a great deal of fervent joy in work, and floods of practical energy, but in them we do not find to a high degree that hard, all-absorbing power of action of certain schizoid temperaments which remains steadfast to its aim, and inflexible to the end. Only in rare cases do we find strong ambitions in a cycloid. Even hypomanics, on the whole, display rather a dashing impulse to work, and a satisfied self-love and self-sufficiency, than a burning thirst after a high-placed end. In the same way, peculiarities due to strong intra-psychic tensions, straining, over-excitation, fanaticism, are, as a rule, foreign to the cycloid temperament. That is at once their strength and their weakness.

The fact that among the pre-psychotic types of personality in the circular group we very seldom come across a-social peculiarities has undoubtedly something to do with the character - structure which we have described. The descriptions : capable, thrifty, solid, and, above all, diligent, are among the most frequently mentioned characteristics of our material. The more hypomanically-coloured natures are often renowned for their enormous energies. The additional descriptions : industrious, over-burdened with business, enterprising, give one an idea of the nature of these activities ; but it must be expressly mentioned, that an almost naïve disregard for tact and prudence, and daring, not very carefully chosen undertakings, are the rule with the hypomanic temperament. On the other hand criminal behaviour and severe running off the social rails is not often discovered among our material, particularly so long as the psychic peculiarities have not reached the point of a mental disease. To certain individuals an addiction to drink, extravagance, and erotic intemperance are a danger as far as their own personal existences are concerned. And yet it is true, if one does not hold fast to a certain moralizing attitude, that the majority of hypomanic temperaments, in so far as they still remain in the characterological frame, are of great use to society, and that many of the more gifted among them are outstanding and far above the average in their capacities.

In our material there are many excellent examples where hypomanics, who must certainly be reckoned among the buoyant group, have had astonishing and lasting success in certain walks of life, e.g., merchants, speakers, journalists, etc., and are regarded with great respect by their colleagues. Their positive peculiarities are their tireless energy in, and enjoyment of, their work, their temperament, sharpness, élan, daring, lovableness, adaptability, free, unshackled natures, skill in the handling of men, richness of ideas, eloquence, and an astonishingly clear eye for the right moment. Whether the hypomanic is of higher or lower value in the social sense depends above all on the compensating mixture with other characterological peculiarities in his inheritance ; and then, too, it naturally depends on upbringing, and especially on his getting together with suitable fellow-workers, who supplement the cheery whole-hogger in him, and keep in check his tendency to superficiality, tactlessness, over-estimation of himself, and recklessness.

From the middle-region down to the depressive side we find outstanding energetic perseverance. The energetic practical man of the mid-region, we shall describe later. The more depressively coloured temperaments, on account of their cautious, all-too-soft natures, and their tendency to take things too much to heart, are not suitable as leaders and organizers ; on the other hand we find them playing an honourable rôle in more protected situations, as clerks or managers, or even, in times unrocked by the blasts of disorder, placed in situations where a lead has to be given. They can raise themselves from the bottom rung, through their assiduity, conscientiousness, and dependableness, their quiet, practical outlook, and, last but not least, through their goodness of heart, their affable friendliness, and personal fidelity, to the position of a kind of revered, indispensable, true old factotum, beloved of all, of which type I have many among my material. If they are suddenly thrown into violent, unaccustomed, responsible situations, then they easily lose their courage, their wits, and their energy ; indeed, they get a typical repressed depression, as I often saw at the time of the revolution, particularly among manufacturers and clerks. Such was the engine-driver M., a faithful old fellow, who couldn't get on properly because the wretched war-engines had iron, instead of copper, fire-boxes. In spite of all his trouble and precautions there was always something going wrong, or else the trailing-wheel ran itself warm because of the rotten lubricating oil. When such things happened, on account of his exceptional conscientiousness, he could not eat properly, or sleep, for worry; at night it used to wake him, so that he had to get up, and have a look at his engine. When he was put on to shunting, his spirits recovered, until, eventually, he again got a slow train with a bad engine, and at the same time a typical depression. As country clergy too, and honest hand-labourers, these types develop into extraordinarily sympathetic and capable beings.

Among the more depressive temperaments, we often find religious men. Their piety, just like their personality, is soft, very emotional, heartfelt, rousing deep feelings combined with conscientious belief, but without pedantry and bigotry, unassuming and broad-minded towards those who think otherwise, without sentimentality or a pharisaic or sharply moralistic accent.

Psychic Tempo and Psychomotility

The peculiarities of psychic tempo and psychomotility, as they are observed in the circular group, are so well known and so simple to understand, that we only sum them up here for the sake of completeness. Combined with the cheerful disposition of the cycloid, everyone recognizes that in the majority of cases there goes a simple acceleration of psychic tempo. The combination of the two, one calls the hypomanic temperament. The perception is of lightning quickness, and remarkably extensive, not going very deep, but embracing an amazing variety. The train of thought rushes on without the slightest hesitation, its components gliding smoothly into one another—what, in a higher realm of thought, one describes as a ' flight of ideas '. Here come out particularly clearly the hypomanic's lack of system, the way in which he is conditioned by the moment, his childlike abandonment to any impression that is fresh in his mind, to any new idea, the want of judgment, insight, and arrangement, and the consequent lack of construction and absence of guiding ideals : abnormal liveliness of interest combined with very little tenacity. All these peculiarities : the far-reaching many sidedness, the naïve, objective outlook, and the poverty of systematic construction, we shall meet with again in the creative work of the healthy cyclothymic poets and men of science ; while, on the other hand, we shall establish systematic activity, abstraction, and sequences of thought as the distinguishing marks of particular schizothymic groups.

In its salient features, the psychic tempo of the more depressive cycloids is similar to that of the hypomanics as regards the lack of tenacity, system, and sequence, and the absence of complicated inhibitions and complex mechanisms. They also display the close temporal relation between the reaction and the stimulus, and the immediate, soft impressionability. Their tempo, however, is simple, even, and slow. The movements are cautious and economical ; their thoughts take time, their decisions ripen slowly. The combination of simple slowness of psychic tempo with a tendency to depressive moods is what we call the melancholic temperament, which, on the psychotic side, links directly on to the complex of symptoms which indicates an obstructed depression. Between the hypomanic and the melancholic types lies the totality of cycloid temperaments, but only a part is actually a combination of these types ; the majority are to be found in that middle-region of mood and tempo which lies between the two poles.

With regard to the more restrained psychomotility of cycloids, we have not much left to say. Through all phases we can discern here, too, just as with the intra-psychic activities, the absence as a general rule of strong inhibitions, jerkiness, stiffness, and awkwardness. The psychomotility of the cycloid is even, and adequate to the stimulus, and motor expressions and movements are well rounded, fluid, and natural. Only there is a differ-ence of tempo, in that the hypomanic is swift and varied in his movements, while the melancholic is slow and economical. The general impression of the motility and the psychic tempo of the hypomanic is best described by the word ' mercurial ', that of the melancholics by ' com-fortable ', where the word ' comfortable ', in a neat linguistic manner, binds together the pyknic physical impression with the slow tempo and the kind-hearted tenderness of the temperamental disposition.

Cycloid Varieties

A certain anxiousness and shyness is characteristic of many cycloid-depressive natures, but these peculiarities do not appear very frequently in my statistics. This anxiety and shyness seem to be closely connected with the lack of self-assertion, and the tendency to a feeling of inferiority, and are psychologically determined by them ; they generally manifest themselves in these men in moderation, not very strikingly, and they are easily overcome. An abnormal degree of anxiety and shyness in fully-grown persons, where a typical motor stiffness and inhibition of the train of thought makes its appearance frequently, and in daily life, belongs, as far as we have discovered at present, outside the constitutionally depressive frame, in the cycloid sense, and is probably to be referred, where it appears within our character groups, to the intervention of schizoid constitutional components.

The same is true of those cases where the depressive conscientiousness has taken on the character of pedantic narrowness or obsession, where the piety has gone over into systematic gloominess, the richness of the ideas into whimsical invention, and the choleric self-consciousness into systematic querulousness or developments of a paranoiac nature. Schizoid constituents in heredity and physique often go hand in hand with such phenomena, and the psychoses which grow on such constitutional soil, now and then remind one of the symptomatology of the schizophrenes, although they would have to be described in essentials as manic-depressive.

Further, in the make-up of the rarer a-typical forms of manic-depressive madness, such as the nagging, distrustful, seriously hypochondriac, or paranoiac types, and perhaps many cases of agitated melancholia with violent motility symptoms, alien influences in the constitution, whether of a schizoid or some other kind, may be distinguished here and there if one pays careful attention to the details. On this matter we refrain from making decisive assertions, because, although we have plenty of cases which give us a hint in this direction, we have not a sufficiently large series of observations at our command. Hoffmann, how-

ever, on the basis of his investigations into the question
of heredity, has come to quite similar conclusions.

In the sphere of characterology, our frequency statistics, together with a psychological comparison of
individual characteristics, give us certain signposts.
Such peculiarities as we find to be frequent in their
appearance and typical in the schizoid class, while, on
the other hand, their appearance is more isolated and
outside the average among the cycloids, we shall be
inclined to refer conjecturally to schizoid components in
the constitution, even in cases where they make their
appearance within the framework of a cycloid personality.
We shall in this way reach a provisional standpoint for
clinical and hereditary investigations, without our laying
down any dogmatic dictum about every individual
peculiarity, and above all, also, with the consciousness
that not everything characterological must necessarily
be included in the cycloid or schizoid group, or a
mixture of the two, although at first it is heuristically
desirable to make use of these two great classes, which can,
to a certain degree, be firmly grasped, in every possible
contingency.

As regards constitutional depression, we get further
and further away from the essentials of the cycloid group
the more we find among the soft, melancholic characteristics, an admixture of humourless dryness, of a hypochondriacal, hostile attitude towards the world and all
mankind, of sharpness, nervousness, and jerky restless
moodiness (not rhythmic cyclic emotional modifications),
of insufficient affective response, of a grumbling dis-
satisfaction, and of a display of sulky pessimism, or
morose, reserved, ill-humour. This kind of pronounced
depression is not at all the prototype of the constitutional
depression of the cycloid character ; it stands to a certain
extent far nearer the schizoid than the cycloid group,
and indeed I have seen individual cases of this kind go
right over into schizophrenic psychoses. Out of our
material one could form a continuous series leading, in
gradually graded mixtures (as regards the characterology,
physique, and psychoses with which they are connected)
from the typical cycloid over to the typical schizoid.

Our material is far less rich in corresponding hypomanic

transitional forms ; it is quite probable that the rare
instances among hypomanics of types who have gone
to the bad through idleness or neglect, who are described
as outstandingly lazy, arrogant, unsteady, unfriendly,
complaining, and quarrelsome, are based on an analogous
mixed constitution.   The same is the case with the small
group of criminal eccentrics, who, from a characterological
point of view, are right outside the framework of the rest.

All these questions of constitutional mixture will
provide a fruitful and interesting field for the clinical and
hereditary investigation of individual cases.   Before this
detailed work has been done we will abstain from any
final judgment.

Isolated Types

We will spare ourselves and the reader the detailed
arguments on which our description of the types of cycloid
personality rests, but will rather choose, for the sake of
illustration, a few distinctive pictures out of our material.

Cheery Hypomanic Type

The manufacturer Quick, now 40 years old, is the son
of a decidedly circular mother, and a father of a similar
temperament to his own.   In 1911 this active, breezy,
and reckless man of business founded, in collaboration
with another, a small factory starting with a capital of a
few thousand marks, which has since grown into a big
business with seven branches.   His colleague in the business
is a dry, cautious, solid man ; their characters complement
one another extraordinarily well.

With Quick one never gets a word in edgeways.   He
is obliging, always in a good temper, and lovable ; in
his best moods he never ceases talking at a great rate,
and he manages to get in a great deal ; he wanders away
from the subject, comes back again, and there is no end
to his conversation.   As he is closing the door there are
always one or two things which occur to him, and which
he must quickly get off his chest.   He never forgets
anything, except what he wants to ; and this he does
with rapidity.   With one glance round he has taken in
all the decoration of a room, down to a small nail up on

the ceiling, and has figured out the price of every object. His flair for the right moment is astounding. When he has no ready cash he manufactures waggon loads of carbide lamps on credit, causing his colleague to despair. During the next winter, when there is a stoppage in the gas-lighting apparatus, he puts them cheerfully on the market and makes an enormous profit. When he has any end in view that he wishes to attain, he is determined, and refuses to listen to reason. The employees laugh when he is mentioned ; they like him, and all swear by him, but they all look on him as rather a mad fellow.

Quick is a small round gentleman, with a fine fat stomach, upright, stocky, sure of himself, and always at his ease. He is elegantly dressed, and scented ; his tie and the border of his handkerchief are of a somewhat bright cheerful colour, and always match. He washes them himself, and presses them early every morning with the help of a small handkerchief iron ; he has all that he can possibly require ready to hand ; and only ' first class '. His taste in verse and pictures is somewhat loud. He likes to boast, not only that he drinks a great deal, but especially that he eats well at the same time. A pound of caviar is needed to make up a really good breakfast. When he has drunk a great deal of wine he loses his head and becomes coarse and ' Schwabian ' ; in this condition he writes outrageous business-letters to the Jews, whom he cannot bear, which have to be kept back in order to preserve the reputation of the firm. In this state, too, there occur temperamental scenes in the office.

He recently celebrated the birthday of his mother-in-law in the following way : In the morning at 2 o'clock, as soon as he had returned in his car, he went to her bedroom with his congratulations, holding out to her two sacks of fine meal in one hand, and an oil picture in the other. At 6 o'clock in the morning, ten men belonging to the brass band of the state fire brigade (first class !) stepped up to his flat, having been ordered by him in honour of his mother-in-law. They played from 6 to 10 without a pause, " It is the day of the Lord ", " Forget me not ", " Now thank you all your God ", " Mixed Potpourri ", and then " something serious " to finish up with. In the afternoon, because it was raining, and they couldn't earn anything, they had to come round again. They blew, and he regaled them superbly. Quick was in the best of spirits. The people collected below in the square, and joined in the proceedings with their clapping. Quick stepped out on to the balcony and made a speech to the populace. He is now alone at his post ; his ladies are lying on their beds ' suffering from nerves '.

On account of these festivities, which were somewhat compromising for the credit of the firm, he came under our care. His wife and his colleague were very distressed and upset on account of these continuous side - slips. Here, with us, he is delightful, winning, charming, and good-humoured ; he soon became conversant with the whole regime of the house, and here and there found something to occupy himself with. His room was quickly set out with little sofa cushions, hangings, bead fringes, and knick-knacks. Lying about, or standing on his table, or hanging over it, are the following : a small collection of objects of his own manufacture, an electrical apparatus which suddenly gives forth a beam of light, and then grows dark again, a large white porcelain elephant which glows inside, and puffs out smoke producing a delicious smell, and finally a clothes-brush which begins to play a tune when one brushes one's clothes, and, on the wall, a toilet-roll, with a charming musical box arranged inside, which performs a song, " Make hay while the sun shines " whenever one tears off a piece of the paper.

Quick epitomizes his opinion of himself thus : " I am a valuable chap. A man of feeling. My wife hasn't the least idea what she got hold of when she got hold of me."

These bubbling hypomanics are certainly not the most frequent type among the brighter cycloid temperaments, but they are the most accentuated, underlining the distinguishing characteristics of these jolly light-headed creatures, their social advantages and disadvantages. Cases of this nature stand at the extreme pole, where you get the transition from the characterologically hypomanic to the psychotic hypomanic. From here there are all the transitional stages from the flighty to the quietly happy type, which we shall soon be describing. In circular families we find moderate forms, bright, sunny, versatile, and sociable people, who are quite circumspect and unsurprising from a social point of view, far more often than outstanding cases of hypomania. In the case before us the hypomanic characteristics have a favourable constitutional basis, that is to say they are mixed with a trace of energetic tenacity, which in itself is not typically hypomanic. This basis makes possible the great social success of our patient, in spite of the already abnormal grade of his temperamental peculiarities. Of other more frequent bases, especially the troublesome, rough quarreller and complainer, I have no outstanding example. One finds detailed descriptions of them in text-books, often pressed only too far into the foreground. For they do not represent the commonest, nor even the purest type of cycloid hypomanic. The purest type is that of the lovable, sunny, emotional hypomanic, in so far as this type fits in with the general cycloid type, as we conceive it from our study of the pre-psychotic personalities of circulars.

Quiet Contented Type

A retired tax-collector living in D., whose name was Franz Xavier Wurzner, spent the middle years of his life in an almost ceaseless alternation of manic and depressive moods, which occasionally reached a psychotic state. In his healthy periods, Wurzner in many respects resembles his father, who was always satisfied, and busy from morning to night so that his children should have a good education. He did not say much, he was contented within himself, a peaceable man, and everyone liked him. He was a village schoolmaster, used to play beautifully on the organ, possessed a great many books, and occasionally wrote a poem or two, which, however, he kept to himself. He was also a bee fancier. The mother was a good wife, bright and full of life, although she was rather weakly, and always wore a bandage round her head. The house was always full of visitors. There was not a soul whom she did not like to see. She was kind to everyone, and did a great deal of good in the neighbourhood. The beggars streamed in from all the country-side. She had already started singing in the morning when she made the coffee.

When he was 45 years old, Wurzner had to give himself up to rest, because he could not get on any more at the office. He was at this time like " a wild bull, before whom someone waves a red cloth ". He would suddenly become quite enraged. Later on he was repeatedly plunged into melancholy, and in the meantime he spent day and night writing a seven-volume rhymed epic about the Seven Years War.

Now all that is long past. With his small capital he has purchased for himself residence in a home in the country, where he lives quietly as a pensioner in a little room of his own, among old, worn-out folk. He himself is well and lively, he presents a superb corpulent appearance, and his fine face is full of character ; he is calm in his movements, but his eyes are twinkling and never still. Summer and winter alike, he wears a woollen shawl round his neck. He cannot bear open windows. In the morning he puts his room straight, doing everything himself, all the cleaning and scouring, and needing no assistance. " When I can do this no more, then they will all think : ' Now old Wurzner will soon be dying.' " In the morning he goes for an hour's walk, he eats at midday, and then sleeps for an hour " like a rat " ; then again he walks for two or three hours, and after the evening meal he drinks his small flask of wine in a good but not too expensive pub, after which he sleeps nearly the whole night through.

His bottle of beer costs him 45 pfennigs, and beyond that he needs nothing ; that is how he was brought up in his home ; his father was also like that. He likes giving presents ; when anyone does him a favour, he does not leave it at that.

He never allows himself to be put out, and he even gets on with the spiteful old cats of the infirmary. Sometimes he makes an indecent joke, whereupon he is very shocked with himself. It is a long time since he had a row with anyone. Only when old Pfrunder, in the next room, snores or coughs does he get a little waspish. Then he addresses rather drastic protests to the infirmary authorities.

From youth up, everyone has said to him ' If only I had your good temper '. He has always been an excellent musician. He still likes to play the organ and the piano,

K

and he likes playing Beethoven and Mozart best. " Come back again soon, so that we can have some more fun," say the people in his old village, when he has been there again and played them something in the church. He has " read nearly all literature ". Jean Paul is a particular favourite of his. Earlier on, he composed essays on law for his own amusement, but he never published them, and he likes to busy himself with physiology, psychology, and philosophy. His worldly wisdom is of a peasant character. During the war he wrote a little brochure which he sent out to the front at his own expense : " The Golden Fifty ", by Joseph Goodheart, in which he had collected fifty rules for the temperate and prudent conduct of life. This is the sentence with which they begin : " He is and remains happy, who is not a glutton, a tippler, an adulterer, a fornicator, a ' *Boussierer* ' or a fool." " Without a moral foundation and basis one cannot build up a state," that is his view.

When he was still a student, he came home every evening sharp at 10 o'clock. " You can go on the loose quite enough before 10." He never went to a lunch place where they had more than one course. " What more does one want ? Otherwise one will only get led astray into silliness of some sort." " Above all delicacies " he prefers pancakes. Any kind of broth makes him thirsty. He belonged to no societies, and after six terms he did remarkably well in his law examination. He always had a faithful circle of friends round him ; all was gaiety and life whenever he appeared. He joined a chess club, and they wanted to make him president at once.

He had his ' flame ' when he was at the gymnasium. Otherwise he did not pay much attention to the girls ; he was afraid they would want to marry him. Also he was " far too much of an enthusiast for music ", and he had his singing club. That satisfied him. He had an odd anxiety that he might have a diseased wife and sick children ; or one or other might die. That would have made him terribly miserable. He saw daily how much people had to put up with. For this reason he remained single. He used to tell harmless coarse stories in exaggerated terms.

Now he is old and holds no office, but he must do

something, he cannot remain idle. If he has nothing to do he takes a pencil and does a little ' mental work '. Last winter he read through a popular scientific encyclopedia of 12 volumes. For the long winter evenings he always purchases some work of literature ; he also gets hold of illustrated papers, and enjoys looking at pretty pictures. For next winter he is buying the " Speeches of Cicero " ; the Greek classics, Antigone and the tragedians he has not read for a long time. For his 65 years he is still leading an active intellectual life.

Since he has got older and the old friends are no more there, he keeps a great deal to himself. He enjoys being with other people, but he no longer takes pains to seek them out. If he meets anyone on a walk, he addresses a remark to him, and to old women too. Everyone knows him in the neighbourhood. One must not lose one's humour completely. Each spring he takes a joy in every little flower. He likes to call out something to the nice little boys and girls he meets on his way, and then they giggle and say, " Old growler has got out of bed on the right side again this morning."

He has no anxiety about death. He holds fast to his religion. " But I don't wear black cloth, I'm not a saint." Ever since his young days he has been to church every Sunday, as a " God-fearing man ". But outside he does not make much of it. He cannot bear being teased, and this is true about personal matters as well. " What the devil do all these young bloods want to tumble over one another for ? " If a person doesn't believe in anything, then he has nothing against him for it. That is quite as it should be. You can't know for certain which is right.

He for his part takes up this position : " If there is a God, then I have had the luck to come along this road, but if there isn't, then I haven't suffered any damage."

The tendency to optimism, which is, as it were, fundamental in the working out of the cyclothymic temperament, is superbly illustrated by this last remark of Wurzner. But even in this comfortable, cheerful old gentleman we can find clear indications of that depressive element in the background of the emotional character, of which we spoke above, in the characteristic aversion to unpleasant experiences (in his attitude to marriage). From the cyclothymic side, temperaments like Wurzner's form the next transitional stage to that of the artist in life.[1] Wurzner gets his sunny childlike brightness, and his intellectual versatility, from the hypomanic side, but this is already bound up with a certain contemplative calm, and as old age advances, with a tendency to take things to heart, and to this is added an ever stronger preoccupation with the gloomy side of life, inasmuch as all these form the transition to the depressive side. In his social impulses he belongs to the type, which we have already described, of a friendly 'cat that walks by itself', who does not run after other people, but enjoys seeing them when they come to him. A slight tendency to hypochondriacal eccentricity must be included as a constituent in his alloy.

And now, finally, a temperament which must be included in the depressive side.

Melancholic Type

A Justizrat, named Gutle, who had suffered since childhood from slight cyclic fluctuations of mood, fell a victim at the end of his fiftieth year to periodic depression. As a man he has much in common with our old friend the engine-driver. He has a broad peasant's head, a fine specimen of a red nose, and is a man whose pure faithfulness and kind-heartedness stream out of his little eyes, and from every wrinkle of his round trustful face. He himself is certainly of another opinion. He thinks himself a 'clumsy chap', a 'lout' whose peasant descent is still obvious, and at whom people probably laugh behind his back. He feels he has done one or two silly things in his life for which he really should have been punished.

Ever since he was young, books have been his friends ; he was already reading Shakespeare when he was 17, and as a young man he also wrote poetry himself. When he was at school, and in the state examinations, he got

---

[1] One can study the type of life-artist in broad outlines in Goethe and Wilhelm Humboldt. It is an alloy made up of a certain cyclothymic and schizothymic proportion, in which a comfortable enjoyment of life is combined with a hyperæsthetic protection of oneself from wounds. At this point we cannot go further into these complex types.

the best reports ; he was clever, and enjoyed learning, and, in addition, was very industrious and conscientious. As a student he was a member of a good society ; he was already religious then, but he did not wish to study theology.

His external life, which soon led him to a high official position, was quiet and simple. Those above him in rank thought highly of him. In the office he was a good-natured, boisterous fellow, who never meant any harm. He was particular about formalities and conscientious, but he was never petty with those under him. He was not strict with them during office hours, he only wanted to see that the work was being done properly.

In his ordered official life he felt himself in place, only he could not bear a rapid change to new situations, and he felt himself particularly uncomfortable when he was deputizing for someone else, because he was used " to do everything from the beginning ". For that reason the war was a severe blow to him, for he had to jump out of the ministerial office to which he had long been accustomed and act as a representative in the district offices, and he saw himself being suddenly hurled into the difficult and complicated matters of war economy. He was continually feeling himself insecure in his position ; he had the impression that he was being cheated by dealers ; he could no longer get on with things, could not see his way out, and thus he commenced brooding, out of which state his first depression developed.

He has never been an enemy of mankind. He had a particularly deep and lively feeling for joy and sorrow alike. He had his quiet meal in a little wine restaurant, where he sat down comfortably with his good old friends, and even cracked a joke now and again. He is a little embarrassed and difficult when he is in a large gathering of people, or if any stranger comes across his path. If one speaks kindly to him one soon gains his complete confidence.

He is only troubled inside with the feeling that he made mistakes and did wrong at the Ministry. He was, in fact, somewhat limited, but possibly no one would have noticed it.

CHAPTER X

THE SCHIZOID TEMPERAMENT

General Portion

CYCLOID men are simple and uncomplicated beings, whose feelings rise directly, naturally, and undisguised to the surface, so that everyone can soon get a correct judgment of them. Schizoid men have a surface and a depth. Cuttingly brutal, dull and sulky, bitingly sarcastic, or timidly retiring, like a mollusc without a shell—that is the surface. Or else the surface is just nothing ; we see a man who stands in our way like a question mark, we feel that we are in contact with something flavourless, boring, and yet with a certain problematic quality about it. What is there in the deep under all these masks ? Perhaps there is a nothing, a dark, hollow-eyed nothing—affective anæmia. Behind an ever-silent façade, which twitches uncertainly with every expiring whim — nothing but broken pieces, black rubbish heaps, yawning emotional emptiness, or the cold breath of an arctic soullessness. But from the façade we cannot see what lurks behind. Many schizoid folk are like Roman houses and villas, which have closed their shutters before the rays of the burning sun ; perhaps in the subdued interior light there are festivities.

One cannot study the schizophrenic inner life in all its fullness from peasants. Kings and poets are good enough for that.[1] There are schizoid men with whom we can live for ten years and yet not be able to say for certain that we know them. A shy girl, pious and lamb-like serves for months in the town : she is gentle and tractable with everyone. One morning the three children of the house lie murdered. The house is in flames. She has not lost her senses, she understands everything.

[1] Particularly significant are the autobiographies of Hölderlin, Strindberg, and Ludwig II of Bavaria.

She smiles uncertainly when she realizes her act. A young man dreams away the lovely days of his youth. He is so clumsy and loutish that one could shake him. If he is set upon a horse he falls off at once. He smiles in an embarrassed way, rather ironically. He says nothing. One day there appears a volume of poetry that he has written, full of an exquisite feeling for nature, with every blow that some fat lout has given him as he passed by moulded into an inner tragedy, and the polished rhythms flowing on full of quiet.

That is what schizoid men are like. Bleuler calls it ' Autism '—the living inside oneself. One cannot know what they feel ; sometimes they don't know themselves, or only dimly — perhaps three simultaneous things, indistinct and yet with a strong emotional value, inextricably commingled one with the other in a vaguely-grasped mystical relation ; or the most intimate and the most general ideas, forced together into a bizarre scheme with numbers and figures. But what their feeling is, whether it be a banality, a whim, an indecency, or a pearl of fairy lore, that is for no one—that is for them alone.

In the schizophrene group, we are less able than in the circular to separate the healthy from the diseased, the characterological from the psychotic. Circular psychoses flow in waves, which come and go in a fluid manner, compensating one another. What appears before and what after the psychoses we can regard as having the same value. Schizophrenic psychoses come in jerks. Something has got out of order in the inner structure. The whole structure may collapse inside, or perhaps only a few slanting cracks may appear. But in the majority of cases there remains something that never gets patched up. Where the attack has not been severe, we refer to a ' post-psychotic personality ', and in severe cases we speak of a schizophrenic idiocy—between the two no hard-and-fast line can be drawn. But we often are not aware whether the psychosis has disappeared or not. People who for years have performed the duties connected with their calling as merely eccentric and unfriendly personalities, may one day quite by chance disclose to us that the greater part of the time they carry the most fantastic illusions about with them—here, too, no boundaries can be drawn.   And besides, what, after all, is personal eccentricity, and what is to be judged the derangement of a madman ?   Finally, everyone alters particularly clearly at the time of puberty.   Schizophrenia usually manifests itself at this period.   Supposing we take people who have undergone some striking alteration at this time of life, shall we regard them as post-psychotic personalities or as undeveloped schizoids ?   These questions are pertinent when we are dealing with close relatives of schizophrenes.   In the pubertial years the schizoid peculiarities rise to their height ; but with lighter cases at this period, we often do not know (1) whether we see before us the development of a schizophrenic psychosis, or (2) whether we are in the middle of a psychosis, or (3) whether we have already the psychological results of an attack which has worn off, or finally, (4) whether it is all merely the stormy and bizarre pubertial development of a schizoid personality—for the normal effects of puberty, the shyness, the awkwardness, the sentimentality, the pathetic strainings, and the affectation, closely resemble certain traits of the schizoid temperament.

In fine, psychologically speaking, we cannot separate from one another the pre-psychotic, the psychotic, the post-psychotic, and the non-psychotic, or merely schizoid. We only get the right idea of the whole when we see all these together.

In addition there is a further methodological difficulty. The schizoid man always offers us, so long as we have not got the key, only his superficial side, just in the same way as the schizophrenic lunatic does.   For this reason clinicists for a long time saw in dementia præcox nothing but affective disintegration, eccentricity, dull-wittedness, defective mentality, and psychic inferiority.   Those were the necessary preliminary views on which investigation had to rest for a long period.   Bleuler was the first to discover the key to the schizophrene's inner life, and by doing so he opened up the way to astonishing treasures of psychological knowledge, only the least of which has perhaps so far been explored.   For the key to the schizophrene's inner life is at the same time the key, and the only key, to vast spheres of normal human feeling and activity.

It is obvious that, in this connection, we can, even in the case of schizoid characterology, only bring out a part of the total psychic situation by means of our inexact statistics, obtained by serial exploration of the ignorant relatives of psychically undifferentiated schizophrenes of the peasant class. In fact we have to deal primarily with the schizoid surface, and content ourselves with rare, often vague and psychologically inexact indications of the depths below. Of the inner life of the schizoid temperament, however, we can only obtain a coherent account from the autobiographical writings of gifted and educated schizoids, and especially from the objective psychological documents which schizoid and schizothymic men of genius have left behind them. The deeper characterology of the schizoids can, therefore, only become accessible by means of fine sensitive psychological analysis of individuals.

The Career of the Schizoid

Cycloid men keep, through all their manic-depressive vicissitudes, the fundamental symptoms of their temperament as a rule from the cradle to the grave. The biological influence which produces the schizophrene and schizoid personality, on the other hand, is something that is planted inside, that makes its appearance at a certain period of life, and with a certain sequence of phenomena, and then proceeds further. The most common sequence in severe cases is as follows : from earliest childhood there is a recognizable schizoid personality, at puberty a schizophrenic psychosis develops out of it, and this leaves behind it a specific deterioration or a post-psychotic personality, which does not differ in essentials from the pre-psychotic personality, though possibly it may, even apart from gross defects, in the more striking manifestation of other schizoid symptom-groups.

This typical process may, however, vary as to the times at which it makes its appearance. We sometimes find schizoids who look just as if they had already been through a schizophrenic psychosis before they were born ;

from infancy they are as weak in intelligence, and as
obstinate, odd, hostile, and untractable as the majority
of schizoids become later when they have a severe
psychosis behind them.[1]

The congenitally antisocial, weak-minded individual of
the schizoid genre may, in later life, on account of some
katatonic jolt, betray his obvious membership in the
schizophrenic group. All these severely disintegrated, defective conditions, whether they are inborn or acquired,
whether they are tinged with the colour of criminal
hostility to society, or sulky eccentricity, or dull-wittedness, or heboid foolishness, invariably bear the typical
stamp of schizophrenic psychology, but from a characterological point of view they are so unfertile that in
spite of their frequent occurrence we need only make a
short mention of them ; and besides, they are completely
set forth in text-books of psychiatry.

While in the instances we have just mentioned the
schizophrenic influence makes its appearance rather
prematurely, the opposite case of its retardation is not
infrequent. In my material there is a small but note-
worthy number of schizophrenes, in whom no trace of
a pre-psychotic personality was noticeable during the
period of childhood, and who were described as being
fresh, happy, sociable, and cheerful in early life. Here
the pubertial psychosis breaks out suddenly, and without
warning, or the pre-psychotic schizoid appears as it were,
belatedly, in lingering, chronic pubertial alterations of
the personality, which may simply settle down in the
course of life, may persist in the characterological framework, or may turn straight away into a schizophrenic
psychosis. Even from their childhood onwards, schizoids,
as is well known, experience these pubertial modifications
of the personality without psychoses, often after a brief
and glorious flowering of all their psychic endowments. For the psychology of creativeness, this bubbling
out and sudden unexpected drying up of productivity
is very important, particularly in the case of poets
(I would call to mind the poet Uhland, who, though

---

[1] Kraepelin has advanced a similar theoretical view. It is confirmed by the physical examination, which discloses, in these schizoids
who are born weak-minded, bodily stigmata of an advanced degree.

healthy, was physically as well as psychically a typical schizothyme).[1]

Finally, there are a few rare instances in which the schizoid partial components of the hereditary endowment are completely retarded, *e.g.*, until the period of involution, and can still become manifest in the character ; that is to say, where you have individuals who, in early life, were bright, gay, and sociable, and then, after their 40th year, traits of mistrust, hypochondria, sensitive reserve, and sullen hostility towards mankind creep into the picture. We have already touched upon this process of late alternation of dominance when we were dealing with bodily constitutional stigmata.

The Psychæsthetic Proportions

The superficial schizoid peculiarities of character as they appear in our material are as follows, arranged according to their statistical frequencies :

1. Unsociable, quiet, reserved, serious (humourless), eccentric.
2. Timid, shy, with fine feelings, sensitive, nervous, excitable, fond of nature and books.
3. Pliable, kindly, honest, indifferent, dull-witted, silent.

What our statistics reflect in the first place are the pre-psychotic personalities of people who have become psychologically diseased later. We can certainly evolve the fundamental characteristics of the schizoid temperament out of them, but we shall have to fill them in with traits from schizophrenic psychoses, post-psychotic personalities, and the characters of schizoids who are not themselves psychopaths, though related to people who are, without its being possible or necessary to separate out these elements, which are inextricably mixed up with one another.

We have divided the most common schizoid peculiarities again into three groups. The characteristics in group 1 are absolutely the most common, in that they run like

[1] The expressions ' Schizothyme ' and ' Cyclothyme ' refer to constitution concepts of a general character, including both healthy and diseased. (See Chapter XII.)

a scarlet thread through the whole schizoid characterology, as well through group 2 as group 3. Apart from the humourless seriousness, which expresses the weak manifestation of the diathetic (cycloid) temperamental scale, they make up in its essence what Bleuler has described as ' Autism '. Groups 2 and 3 stand in a certain opposition to one another, they form a pair of contrasts similar to that which we find among cycloids in the cheerful-mobile group and the depressive-melancholic group. Group 2 contains, in all the possible shadings, the phenomena of psychic over-sensitivity, from the mimosa-like, timid fineness of feeling to a continual state of passionate excitation. Group 3 on the contrary contains indications of a certain psychic insensitivity, dullness, and lack of spontaneity. It tends, that is to say, to the pole which Kraepelin has called in the severest psychotic cases ' affective imbecility'.

If we want to give a short account of the basis of the schizoid temperament, we must say : the schizoid temperament lies between the extremes of excitability and dullness, in the same way that the cycloid temperament lies between the extremes of cheerfulness and sadness. Besides this, we shall have to lay particular stress on the symptoms of psychic overexcitability, because this has been far too little appreciated as an essential ingredient of the total schizoid psychology, while those symptoms which are to be laid to the score of insensitivity have already had their importance recognized for a long time.

He alone, however, has the key to the schizoid temperament who has clearly recognized that the majority of schizoids are not either over-sensitive or cold, but that they are over-sensitive and cold at the same time, and that in quite different relative proportions. Out of our schizoid material we can form a continuous series, beginning with what I call the ' Hölderlin type '—those extremely sensitive, abnormally tender, constantly wounded, mimosa-like natures, who are ' all nerves '— and winding up with those cold, numbed, almost lifeless ruins left by the ravages of a severe attack of dementia præcox, who hover like shades in a corner of the asylum, dull-witted as cows. And at the same time, even with the most gentle representative of that mimosa group of characteristics, we feel a light, intangible breath of aristocratic frigidity and distance, an autistic narrowing down of affective responses to a strictly limited circle of men and things, and occasionally we hear a harsh, loveless remark passed on men who lie outside this circle, and towards whose behaviour the affective resonance is damped. " There is a pane of glass between me and mankind ", said such a schizoid recently—a remark of extraordinary significance.   We can sense these thin, hard, cold, sharp, splintering panes of glass, when we deal with the later katatonic period of Hölderlin, who was a more than usually lovable representative of the 'mimosa' group, and even more clearly when we come to the later schizophrenic Strindberg, who said of himself, " I am hard as ice, and yet so full of feeling that I am almost sentimental ".[1]   This ' mimosa ' type can best be studied in schizoid men of genius, but one finds it all over the place, and also among the usual asylum material, particularly in intelligent and educated persons, in their pre-psychotic states, or in the initial stages of their psychosis.

The schizoid temperaments, then, as we have said, may be ranged in a continuous ladder from this mimosa-like extreme to the insensitive and cold extreme, as the " hard as ice " (dull as leather) quality becomes ever more prominent, and " the sensitivity to the extent of sentimentality " ever less in evidence.   But even in that half of our material which is primarily cold and poor in affective response, as soon as we come into close personal contact with such schizoids, we find, very frequently, behind the unresponsive, numbed exterior, in the innermost sanctuary, a tender personality-nucleus with the most vulnerable nervous sensitivity, which has withdrawn into itself, and lies there contorted.   " You have no idea how miserable all that makes me ", said a hebephrenic, dried-up schoolboy recently to his parents, a boy from whose external appearance no one could see anything but insuperable hard indolence, psychic paralysis, and complete lack of temperament.   Bleuler was again

[1] Cf. on this point the excellent pathographic study by Storch " Strindberg im Lichte seine Selbstbiographie," *Eine pathographische Studie*, Wiesbaden. (*Grenzfragen des Nerven- und Seelenlebens*), 1921.

the first to show how those mummified old asylum inmates, whom one had been accustomed to regard as the type of affective imbecility, may still have the remains of ' complexes ', isolated, over-sensitive portions of their psychic lives, which have remained intact, and stimulation of which may have sudden and startling results.   And we are constantly coming across cases, where such an individual, who lies there apparently completely insensitive, and turned katatonically into stone, is set free by a jerk, and lets forth from his inner soul almost monumental affective outbursts ; so that, in many sorts of schizophrenic states, we are unable to say straight off how much is a matter of this complete numbing and cramping of affective response, and how much is real affective imbecility.

The mixture in which, in any given schizoid, the hyperæsthetic and the anæsthetic elements are combined with one another, we call his ' psychæsthetic proportion '. And we must remember that we saw quite similar mixtures in the cycloid temperaments with regard to their diathetic or mood-proportions, in that it was only in the rarest cases that we found absolutely cheerful and absolutely miserable men, but much more prevalently combinations and alternations between cheerfulness and sadness : even the sunny, cheerful person often has a clearly depressive background, and traces of humour are to be found far down the line of the melancholic temperaments.

The mood-proportions of cycloids fluctuate in waves. The psychæsthetic proportions of schizoids get jerked out of their equilibrium.   That is to say, the relation between the hyperæsthetic and the anæsthetic temperaments varies spasmodically as life goes on, in the case of many schizoids, without returning again to the position from which it started.   The psychæsthesia of the healthy average man of mixed medium temperament reaches its height in the typical, sentimentally-coloured exuberance and sensitivity of the pubertial period, and then, from the age of 25, it slowly cools off until it reaches a certain quiet solidity of outlook, and often a state of sober, flat, dry immobility. The student song reflects this cooled Philistine feeling of the average man looking back at the days of his adolescence.

The displacement of the psychæsthetic proportions of the schizoids frequently proceeds on parallel lines to this normal development, and forms, as it were, an exaggerated and deepened image of it. The schizophrene, Hölderlin, displays this displacement paradigmatically, if we follow the pattern of his life from the excitable tenderness of his early years as a poet to the twilit dull-wittedness of his decade-long katatonic sickliness. The transition from the hyperæsthetic to the anæsthetic pole is often experienced with terrible vividness by fully-developed personalities as a general inner cooling,[1] and Hölderlin describes it in the following verses :

> " Where art thou ?   But little lived I, and yet breathes cold
> The evening of my life.   And quiet like the shadows
> I still am here ; and already without song,
> Slumbers my cowering heart within my breast."

In this manner a whole group of gifted schizoids develop, even without becoming psychically diseased, men who, having been tender, shy, and nervous in their childhood, experience, in the early stages of puberty, a short hot-house-like flowering of all their capacities and affective capabilities on the basis of an enormously heightened sensitivity of their temperament, in the direction of melancholy sentimentality, or pubertial pathos with an even more exaggerated tension. After a few years, they calm down, still scarcely tolerable as average citizens, but gradually becoming ever duller and cooler, more and more individualistic, silent, and dry. The pubertial wave lifts them higher and plunges them deeper than is the case with the normal man.

Or else it may happen that the psychæsthetic dis-

[1] What, in cases of acute schizophrenia, we call " alteration of the objective consciousness " and " alteration of the consciousness of personality ", rests probably to a certain extent on the psychæsthetic displacement, since alterations in the strength of the sensational qualities and the usual feeling tone towards individual objects (hyper-æsthesia, or anæsthesia) produce completely novel and unheard-of impressions (here strange noises, shrill and meaningful, there a mysterious feeling of something cold and queer, and there, again, inexplicable recognitions).   The delusions of influence and persecution have probably part of their roots in these sudden mysterious modifications of the psychæsthetic illumination.   In the same way, perhaps, the alterations of the internal and external sensations, of which many schizophrenes complain in the early stages, may be biological symptoms running parallel to the psychæsthetic displacements.

placement goes on underground over longer periods, and
without choosing a particular point of time. In all
these various possibilities, however, the alteration of
proportions in schizoids is usually from the hyperæsthetic
to the anæsthetic extreme, from excitement to emotional
paralysis, in such a way that (schematically speaking),
after the first stage of all-round hypersensitivity, those
values which are foreign to the personality lose their
affective resonance, while those values which have to
do with the personality itself, becoming more and more
important for it, retain their accentuation, and only
when those contents which have to do with the personality itself lose their affective value, does the third stage,
that of affective idiocy, set in. The allo-psychic resonance
becomes obliterated before the autopsychic. The half-
dead schizophrene, will, if he is educated, become an
actor or a musician during this transitional stage. The
exhibition of oneself is still an excitement : perhaps he
will even become a futurist painter, an expressionist
poet, an inventor, or a builder of abstract, schematic
philosophical systems. This disproportion caused by the
dying off of the allo-psychic resonance, while the hypersensitivity of the autopsychic remains, produces extraordinary
degrees of self-overvaluation, often proceeding according
to fixed laws. One need go no further to perceive that
a fundamentally false picture of the opposed importance
of the ' I ' and the ' external world ' emerges out of such
a psychæsthetic proportion. We can thus imagine that
many schizoids, during the course of their lives, pass
through a gradual temperamental cooling from without
inwards, so that, side by side with an ever-increasing
numbing of the outer sheath, there remains a tender
hypersensitive inner nucleus which is always withdrawing
into itself. This pictorial mode of expression best corresponds with the remarkable fact that those schizophrenes
who are the most sensitive, and have the finest feelings,
seem to have all over them on the outside a thin icy sheath,
when they are with chance acquaintances ; and on the
other hand, lively reactions of a hypersensitive nature
may occur, even where there is pronounced schizophrenic
petrifaction, if by chance we touch on the innermost
complexes of the personality. " He is a drop of fiery

wine in a bowl of ice ", was Hebbel's admirable remark about the healthy schizothymic Uhland.

We must supplement what we have said with the remark that the stage of absolute hypersensitivity, as also the stage of absolute affective coldness, are, indeed, in the strictest sense of the words only theoretical fictions, which hardly ever occur, to their fullest extent, in real life. What we meet with in practice is almost always certain changing relations in the psychæsthetic proportions of hypersensitivity and coldness. Only a few schizoids pass, in the course of their lives, through the typical process from extreme hyperæsthesia to the preponderatingly anæsthetic pole ; some remain hyperæsthetic, some are already prevailingly torpid when they come into the world. And, finally, there are a few cases, which, after a schizophrenic psychosis, are even more hyperæsthetic than before : such an one was Strindberg.

Social Reactions

Autism, regarded as a symptom of the schizoid temperament, follows in its essence the psychæsthetic scale of the individual schizoid. There are instances where autism is predominantly a symptom of hypersensitivity. Such overexcitable schizoids feel all the harsh, strong colours and tones of everyday life, which to the average man and to the cycloid are welcome and indispensably stimulating elements of existence, as shrill, ugly, and unlovable, even to the extent of being psychically painful. Their autism is a painful cramping of the self into itself. They seek as far as possible to avoid and deaden all stimulation from the outside ; they close the shutters of their houses, in order to lead a dream-life, fantastic, ' poor in deeds and rich in thought' (Hölderlin) in the soft muffled gloom of the interior. They seek loneliness, as Strindberg so beautifully said of himself, in order to " spin themselves into the silk of their own souls ". They have regular preferences for certain forms of milieu which do not hurt or harm : the cold aristocratic world of salons, office work that goes on mechanically, according to fixed rules and regulations, the beautiful loneliness of nature, antiquity, distant times, and the halls of learning.

L

When a schizothyme turns from a blasé, overcivilized, society man into a hermit, like Tolstoi, the revolution inside, regarded from the point of view of the soul of the schizothyme himself, is not so great. The one milieu offers him the same as the other, the one thing that he desires above all else from the outer world : the protection of his hyperæsthesia.

The autism of the predominantly anæsthetic, on the other hand, is unfeelingness, lack of affective response to the world about him, which has no interest for his emotional life, and for whose own rightful interests he has no feeling. He draws himself back into himself because he has no reason to do anything else, because all that is about him can offer him nothing.

The autism of the majority of schizoids and schizophrenes, however, is based on mixtures, in the most varied proportions, of the two temperamental aspects ; it is indolence with a streak of anxiety and animosity ; it is often cold, and yet in the same breath it prays to be left in peace. Crampedness and lameness in one picture.

The nature of the social attitudes of the schizoid man, just as that of the healthy schizothymes whom we shall be describing later, springs from the above-mentioned psychæsthetic relations. Schizoid men are either unsociable or eclectically sociable within a small closed circle, or else superficially sociable, without deeper psychic rapport with their environment. The unsociability of schizoids has the most varied gradations ; it is seldom mere unfeeling dullness, it usually has a clear admixture of distaste, of active turning away, of a more or less defensive or offensive character. This disinclination for human society varies from the gentlest display of anxiety, timidity, and shyness, through ironical coldness, and sulky, distorted dullness, to cutting, brutal, active hostility towards mankind. And the most remarkable thing is that the affective attitude of an individual schizoid to his fellow-men changes colour in a strange rainbow-like fashion : now timidity, irony, sulkiness, now brutality. A particularly good characterological example of this type is the schizothyme, Robespierre. Even with those who are suffering from schizophrenic insanity, the affective attitude towards the outer world has very often this quality of 'insuring' (Adler), of peeping distrustfully sideways out of half-sunken eyelids, and of tentatively projecting feelers and quickly withdrawing them. With a nervous-fingered uncertainty, especially when face to face with a newly-arrived stranger, they run over all the half-tones of the psychæsthetic scale that lies within their registers. This feeling of insecurity is often transferred to the onlooker ; many a schizoid behaves so oddly, vaguely, opaquely, and strangely, or so whimsically, intriguingly, and even maliciously. But for the outside observer, there always remains, behind the 'insuring' oscillations of the schizoid affective attitude, a remnant to which he never comes nearer, which he cannot see through, which never comes to the surface.

Many schizoids among our Schwabian material, perhaps the majority of the pre-psychotics, are characterized as 'good-natured' in their human relations. This schizoid good-nature is something fundamentally different from the corresponding peculiarity of the cycloids. The cycloid good-nature is kind-heartedness, it has always something hearty about it, a participating in, and sharing of, joy and sorrow, an active well-wishing, or a friendly tolerance towards his neighbours, which is of a kind that can be understood. The good-nature of the schizoid child on the other hand is manufactured out of the two components : timidity and affective lameness. It is a giving-in to all the wishes of the outer world through indolence, mixed with a nervous anxiety to set oneself up against them. The cycloid good-nature is friendly participation, in the schizoid it is shy animosity. With suitable constitutional bases, this timid schizoid good-nature may naturally have really good qualities ; there may be something pleasantly soft, tender, and lovable, something clinging about it, and yet there is always a light mournful tinge of painful strangeness and susceptibility. That is Hölderlin's type. More common is the boring wax-like malleability of the schizoid model child who is so often met with, which may be compared with the flexibilitas cerea of the katatonic.

And, similarly, the quality of timidity, an almost universal, and, in extreme forms, a specific characteristic of the schizoid temperament, with its typical foundation in the inhibition of the thought processes, and stiffening of the motility, is the exact translation of certain symptoms of katatonic disease into a rather weaker characterological form. The timidity is, in these cases, a hyperæsthetic affective attitude at the entrance of a stranger into the proscribed autistic area of the schizoid personality. The entrance of a new person is felt in itself as an overwhelming stimulus, as well as an unpleasant one, and this abnormally strong stimulus emits a tetanus-like, laming influence over the thought processes and motility of the body. The helpless feeling of anxiety in new and unaccustomed situations, and the rigid turning away from such changes of environment, is a closely-related hyperæsthetic stigma of schizoid pedants and eccentrics.

We very frequently find quiet lovers of books and nature among the timid, dreamily tender schizoids. The love of books and nature, where it occurs in cycloid personalities, springs from an equal love towards everything that is—first towards mankind, and then towards things ; but the spheres of interest of schizoids do not show this even, affective fixation. Schizoid men, even of lowly origin, are generally lovers of books and nature, but it is with a certain eclectic accentuation. It is due to their flight from humanity, and their preference for all that is peaceful and unharmful. In many instances this preference is something of a compensation. All the sensitive tenderness of which they are capable, and which mankind repels, is poured out extravagantly over the beautiful still objects of nature, and the dead contents of a collection.

Side by side with these quiet enthusiasts we find among those schizoids who are completely antisocial, as a characteristic figure, the sulky eccentric, who broods in a locked, ill-ventilated dungeon over his own ideas, whether they be hypochondriacal meditations about his health, or technical discoveries, or, above all, metaphysical trains of thought. In a more active form, one finds these queer eccentrics and cranks leaving their corners with a sudden jerk, as ' enlightened ' and ' converts ' ; and then, long-haired and sect-founding, they preach the ideals of humanity, raw dieting, gymnastics, and the religions of Mazdazdan, or the Future, or all these at once. Many of these active inventors and prophets have pronounced

constitutional alloys, and they range from extreme schizophrenia at one end to hypomania at the other.   Those
who are preponderatingly schizophrenic are more peculiar,
more exaggerated, more forced, more darkly vague, more
mystical and metaphysical, and have a greater tendency
to systems and schematic formulation, while those who
are rather hypomanic, on the other hand, are unsystematic,
they have the bluster of the itinerant preacher, they are
impulsive, slap-dash, eloquent, and changeable as quicksilver.   Schizophrenic inventors and prophets seem to me,
for the rest, to be far less often pre-psychotic than actuated
by conditions left behind by a psychosis, or even suffering
from flourishing psychoses.

The autistic shutting-away of their fellow-men naturally
tends to a building up of their own world out of thoughts
and favourite pursuits.   And yet this is not necessarily
the case.   Many schizoids are not particularly productive
in thought or activity, they are simply unsociable.   They
growl or run away when anyone comes ; or they sit there
and feel tortured.   Or else they display a monumental
peace of mind, and are simply dumb.   Other schizothymic
peculiarities of character are not wanting in the ' strong
silent men ' (Uhland, Moltke).

Alongside simple unsociability, eclectic sociability within
an exclusive circle is a characteristic, especially of many
highly gifted schizoids.   Many sensitive autists have a
fixed love for certain kinds of social milieux, which fit in
with certain tones of their own psychic atmosphere, and
which they always seek out, again and again, as their
psychic element.   First and foremost comes the circle
bound together by the modes of life of high society, and
aristocratic etiquette.   In the restricted polished formalism
of such a circle, they find all that their delicate feelings
can desire : the exquisite lines of life, which are not
disturbed by painful interruptions, and the damping
down of all affective emphasis in personal relations.   And
thus, this cultivation of impersonal formalities hides what
is so often lacking in the schizoid ; he hides behind his
cool and polite elegance the lack of heartfelt feeling and
direct emotional freshness, which betrays even in these
sensitive natures the beginnings of an emotional coolness.

The aristocratic impulses of certain schizoid natures

manifests itself, even in simple people, in a need for distance, and an expression of the wish that things were otherwise and better, when confronted with their fellow-citizens. The tendency to affect correct hoch-deutsch, in a milieu that does not normally speak like that, may very often betray a schizoid or schizothymic disposition. And the same with an exaggerated care in the tending of the body, or in the choice of clothes. With the gradual further development of the disposition, as the psych-æsthetic proportions become displaced, this painful correctness and punctiliousness may get transformed into exactly the opposite. Indeed we often find—a typical schizophrenic paradox—elegance and neglect, both very striking and exaggerated, existing fragmentarily side by side in the same individual. Moreover, the cold aristo-cratic elegance, which imparts such a delightfully still quality to the faces of many healthy schizothymes, can be traced, in an unbroken line, through all the schizoid transition stages down to the symptomatology of schizo-phrenic psychosis. There we find it in the form of the well-known, artificial, supercilious pomposity in speech and movement.

What is essential to all these characterological tend-encies is their exclusiveness, the striving towards a closed circle—an enlarged autism among people of the same persuasion. The friendship of such schizoids is a sharply discriminating, unique friendship—an inseparable union of two dreamy eccentrics, or a small select band of young men, ethereal, ceremonial, dedicated to each other, and exclusive, keeping apart from ordinary life ; within it an ecstatic cult of the personality, and outside it every-thing is ' common ' and to be put on one side and despised. The point of view of Hölderlin's early poetry is clearly in this direction.

The religious bigot is often to be found in schizophrenic families. Many schizoids are religious. Their religion has a tendency towards the mystical and transcendental. Or else it is pronouncedly pharisaical, pietistic, exaggerated, reminding one of the conventicle, with a tendency to a closed circle, or to personal freakishness.

The same is the case with their eroticism—no warm natural affection, but ecstasy or cynical coldness. They are not out for a pretty girl, but ' Woman ' and ' the Absolute '—wife, religion, and art in one and the same form. Either saint or Magaera—there is nothing in between the two. Strindberg is a superb example of this type.

The third kind of schizoid social attitude is a superficial sociability, without any deep psychic rapport. Such men may be coolly active, calculating, business men, hard masters, or cold strivers, or even indolent, tepid, ironical natures, who move about among people of every kind, without being particularly sensitive to what is going on. We shall describe this type in greater detail when we come to the healthy schizothymes.

In short, the schizoid does not get on in a crowd. The pane of glass is always there. In the hyperæsthetic type, there often develops a sharp antithesis : ' I ' and ' The external world '. There is a constant excited self-analysis and comparison : ' How do I impress people ? Who is doing me an injury ? In what respect have I to forgive myself something ? How shall I get through ? ' This is particularly true of gifted, artistic natures, who have late in life fallen victims of schizophrenia, or who come from families where there is a suspicion of schizo-phrenic disease ; Hölderlin, Strindberg, Ludwig II of Bavaria, Feuerbach, Tasso, Michelangelo, manifest this trait very significantly. They are men who have a con-tinual psychic conflict, whose life is composed of a chain of tragedies, a single thorny path of sorrow. They have, as it were, a genius for the tragic. The pure cyclothyme is not capable of driving a situation to the point where it becomes tragic : he has already adapted himself long ago, and the environment has adapted itself to him, because he comes to meet it with understanding, and in a spirit of conciliation. A healthy individual of this type, out of the pyknic-cyclothymic group was, for example, Hans Thoma, who was as misjudged as Feuerbach, but whose life flowed on like an untroubled, contemplative brook.[1] Rugged, cold egoism, pharisaical self-satisfaction, and overwhelming, hypersensitive self-feeling, are common in all their variations in schizophrene families. But they

---

[1] There is no better introduction to the differences of the cyclo-thymic and schizothymic attitudes towards life, than the comparative reading of the autobiographical sketches in Hans Thoma, *Im Herbst des Lebens,* and Anselm Feuerbach, *Ein Vermächtnis.*

are not the only forms of autism. Another is the striving after the theoretical amelioration of mankind, after schematic, doctrinaire rules of life, after the betterment of the world, or the model education of their own children, often involving a stoic renunciation of all needs on the part of the individuals themselves. Altruistic self-sacrifice in the grandest possible style, especially for general impersonal ideals (socialism, teetotalism), is a specific characteristic of many schizoids. In this way, in gifted schizophrenic families, we sometimes find superb characters, who leave even the most noble schizo-thyme far behind them in impersonal rectitude and objectivity, in unflinching fidelity to convictions, in nobility and purity of disposition, and in stubborn tenacity in the fight for their ideals, while on an average they themselves are surpassed by the cyclothymes in natural warm kind-heartedness towards individual men, and patient understanding of their peculiarities.

Psychæsthetic Variants

So far we have been looking on the hyperæsthesia and anæsthesia of schizoids as if they were single states. But they have very significant variants, about which we do not know whether they are merely quantitatively different, or whether there is a biological qualitative difference between them. At the anæsthetic end we find three important temperamental variants, which, indeed, are often present simultaneously, and which show many transitional variations : dullness (with or without affective lameness), coldness, and " total indifference " (Bleuler) ; while at the hyperæsthetic end the most important variations to distinguish are : sensitivity, sentimentality, and a passionate violence which springs from the presence of complexes.

Here, again, we must bring the pre-psychotics more clearly out of the general schizoid mass. We find statis-tically, at any rate in our Schwabian material, that the types corresponding to those odd eccentrics, cold-blooded, ill-tempered individuals, dry pedants, or scatter-brained wasters, who are so common among the adult relatives of schizophrenes, and among post-psychotics, do not occur nearly so often in the childhood and early pubertial stages of people who eventually become diseased. We certainly find characteristics like rudeness, stubbornness, ill-temperedness, laziness, etc., also mentioned in connection with our pre-psychotic material, in which case one can never be certain whether the relatives have really described the original personality, or its first gradual modification in the early pubertial stages. In frequency, however, they lag far behind the characteristics mentioned at the beginning of the chapter.

The commonest type in our pre-psychotic material is that in which one finds affective lameness ; quiet, timid, tractable, shy people with the predicate ' good-natured '. Striking examples of ' precocious children ' such as Kraepelin has given prominence to, are very common among them. The term ' affective lameness ' has a close connection with popular speech, which describes those people as ' lame (contorted) ' in whose behaviour it is clearly manifest that the most outstanding symptom is a psychomotor one. The expression ' affective lameness ', then, does not coincide with the term ' affective dullness ' which clearly lays the accent on the sensorial side. " One could have wished that he were livelier." " He is a bit tepid." " He is absolutely lacking in life and temperament." Such are the commonest descriptions of young men suffering from affective lameness. This lack of liveliness, of immediately-reacting vivacity of psychomotor expression, is found also in the most gifted members of the group with their hypersensitive inner capacities for reaction.

The quiet cycloid is ' comfortable ', the quiet type of schizoid, which we are describing here, is ' lame '. This ' comfortable ' quality is the characterological expression of the lightest degree of that psychomotor type which we meet with again in the restraint of the depressive. It describes that melancholic something which takes its time for speech and activity, but where we have a warm, immediate emotional participation in every word and deed. ' The lame ' have psychomotor slowness and economy in commo   with the ' comfortable '. But ' lameness ' implies, beyond that, the loss of immediate connection between the emotional stimulus and the motor response. It is for this reason that with the 'comfortable' person we always have the feeling that we are in emotional rapport, even when he says nothing, while the 'lame' appears to us strange, unsympathetic, as we express it in German, 'nicht mitfühlend', because we often cannot read in his face, or in his movements, the expression of what he is feeling, or, above all, the adequate reaction to what we are doing and saying to him. The essential quality of the 'lame' is that he can stand there with a puzzled face and hanging arms, like a note of interrogation, in a situation that would electrify even one of the 'comfortables'.

But when the psychic expression does come to the surface in the 'lame', it is not always precisely adapted to the stimulus, or else it lags behind, until a time when it is no longer suitable. The expression of the 'lame' is very changeable and uncertain, so that one usually takes them for proud, when they are only timid, or for ironical, when they have been most deeply wounded.

In addition to this, there are often irregularities in the actual motor reactions themselves. People whom one would describe as 'lame' are quite often surprisingly reckless in their behaviour, or clumsy in their movements. They do not know what to do with their limbs. Many are also remarkably unpractical, and helpless in the ordinary matters of life, and cut an unfortunate figure when they are doing gymnastic exercises. Pronounced motor inhibitions, due to general timidity or the working of some special complex, play their part here as well. In short, even if one is looking at psychomotility from a narrower standpoint, there is again the lack of immediate working together of the processes concerned in stimulation and reaction. That is lacking which the cycloids possess in such an outstanding degree—smoothness, naturalness, and unconstraint in affective expression and in movement.

In all this nothing has been said about the psychosensorial side of the process. The 'lameness' may be correlated with a real dullness of emotional response to the stimulus before it, or, on the other hand, processes involving the finest sensibilities, and the most extreme intrapsychic tension may be going on behind it. The simple laity, indeed, do not distinguish between these.

They look on the ' lame ' man as stupid, or at all events dull-witted, as an unfeeling, sleepy, boring chap, who has no snap about him, and whom one has got to wake up. He is unsympathetic to them. At school, and certainly in the barracks, the young man who is ' lame ', is the queer bird, at which they all start pecking. In so far as he really has fine feelings inside and is gifted, there lies the real tragedy of such men. For many of them are far more sensitive than the average man.

What we see in a great number of our schizophrenic pre-psychotics, when looked at from the outside, is the appearance of a ' good-natured ' quiet ' cat that walks by itself ', who displays too little temperament, who seems indifferent and indolent, who joins in too little with his comrades, and who puts up with too much. Some of these young people are not very gifted, and then the indolence, the emotional dullness, and the lack of spontaneity come into the foreground of the picture ; they behave ' like idiots '. In the case of precocious children, the special scholastic capacities are good, and yet a great deal of their ability rests on this very emotional defect, on the lack of interest in the rich world of all that which otherwise mainly fills and occupies the lives of young men ; a mildly energetic trait of cold pushfulness may be mixed in with the rest. In the average type of our ' lame ' group, too, we find the qualities of nervousness, excitability, capriciousness, anxiousness, tenderness, and, above all, sensitive susceptibility, frequently mentioned, even by the uneducated relatives of patients ; but such relatives cannot describe these peculiarities more delicately and accurately ; and in the uneducated average schizoid they are, as a matter of fact, psychologically still very undifferentiated. He behaves shyly, or timidly, or distrustfully, or as if he were pushed in to himself. He complains of nerve troubles. He keeps anxiously away from all coarse games and brawls. The more, however, we come into the region of educated and gifted pre-psychotics, the more clearly differentiated become those specific hyperæsthetic qualities behind the ' lame ' exterior, of which we have the extreme case in the Hölderlin type.

In the more highly developed types of the affectively lame, we find frequent indications of nervous distrust, of

occasional obstinacy, of determined excitability, but without their anger having anything brutal or their obstinacy
anything stubborn about them. But most often, perhaps,
in such instances, the hyperæsthesia takes on the character
of tenderness, of inner sensitivity, and that in the form
of extreme vulnerability, with hidden complexes having
long, lasting after - effects and painful, intrapsychic,
emotional tensions ; it may also appear as tenderness for
persons who are not closely connected with the subject,
a tenderness which easily takes on the quality of ex-
aggeratedness, sentimentality, pathos, enthusiasm, or
wistful melancholy ; and, again, in the form of an unwontedly tender impressionability as regards the quiet
stimuli of nature, and the worlds of Art and Literature.
But, even here, the sensitivity remains a selective one,
encircling its object like a belt ; beyond the still, but
rigidly bounded zone of the personal interests, there
remains a vast region of human interests and feelings,
which finds no resonance in these sensitive hyperæsthetics.
In particular, the real feeling for humanity remains limited
towards a few individuals.   To this kind of affective lameness, a partial affective dullness is sometimes also added.

On the negative side, our type of sensitive affectively
lame has a characteristic in common with the whole group
of schizoids. They are, on an average, devoid of humour,
and often serious, without exhibiting either sorrowfulness
or cheerfulness. The diathetic scale, which is the most
important scale among the cycloids, finds on the whole
only a weak expression in their temperament. Schizoids
are very often depressed : but this depression is something quite other than the sorrowfulness of the cycloid.
It has something distrustful, something ill - humoured
and nervous, about it, with a clear quality of internal
excitation and stress, for which reason one finds among
schizoids those constitutionally depressed persons who
are always on the move, while the inhibited depressive
stays at home. Side by side with nervous, strained
depression, we also find, among schizoids, the emotional
attitude of unshakably satisfied, autistic peace of mind,
while their strong positive feelings have less the quality
of free gaiety, than of ecstasy, and exaggerated enthusiasm.

We must regard the type of the sensitive affectively

lame, in its whole range, from the timid, impassive schizoid imbecile up to the highly differentiated Hölderlin natures, as perhaps the most important schizoid type of temperament, at any rate as one of the most frequent pre-psychotic foundations and starting points.   Even among old asylum material, it still may be found in a disintegrated post-psychotic form.   Similarly it occurs among the healthy members of schizophrene families.

We have already considered affective dullness as a component in the ' lame ' temperament.   The expression ' dullness ' denotes passive lack of feeling.   We find emotional dullness, as we have said, very frequently in the schizophrenic group.   The light characterological form in which we often find it among the healthy members of schizophrenic families strikes one as an unshakable peace of mind, as a phlegmatic state, which may be distinguished from the cycloid ' comfortableness ' by the lack of warm, emotional responsiveness towards mankind.   We find the severer degrees of ʰizophrenic insensitivity, generally with a touch of morose brutality, or shy anxiety, congenital in schizoid imbeciles, but it is seen particularly, to a marked degree, in post-psychotics, and also after the equally significant modifications of the personality which occur at puberty.   This inner blunting may betray itself in those who otherwise function perfectly well ; indeed, it may be found in highly gifted individuals, manifesting itself, particularly, in surprising carelessness, and even in neglect of clothes and home. Or else it betrays itself by means of sudden and inexplicable tactlessness, and want of taste, which here and there breaks unexpectedly through the otherwise unaltered façade of good education, appearing particularly grotesque in the previously sensitive aristocratic type of schizoid. Throughout the course of his life, the poet Lenz was an excellent example of such a half-wrecked personality. One can study this disruption of the personality particularly well if one turns to the literary style of the schizophrenically diseased poets, e.g., Hölderlin.   The whole personality level does not sink evenly, but an, if anything, increasing hymnic solemnity and stylistic carefulness will be broken up somewhere, in the middle of a verse, by some outrageous banality.   The psychic

apparatus of such men, in their style, and in their mode
of life, functions like a bad sewing-machine, which keeps
on making a number of fine stitches and then giving a
jump.   Sensitivity and absolute dullness may live here
incredibly closely together : the filthiest shirt beside
polished finger-nails ; chaotic untidiness in a room where
the most valuable and pure works of art are produced.
Such instances are found not only as transitional stages
towards complete schizophrenic idiocy ; they may also
remain intact the whole life long, as baroque types of
personality.   Sense and senselessness, moral suffering and
banal sectarian oddity, one original thought along with
two crazy ones, all in a regular mixture.

At this point we will not go any further into all these
schizophrenic defects, since we have here to do, not only
with affective disturbances, but also with deep-lying disturbances of thought associations : we will rather mark
out only one group from among the affectively insensitive,
which has a certain significance as a temperamental type.
This is the type of the passionate-insensitive, or the
insensitive-brutal.   One usually comes across this type
post-psychotically, after early attacks of schizophrenia,
or as a lingering product of schizoid transformation ;
it may also be congenital.   Temperaments of this kind
are, again, a combination of hyperæsthetic and anæsthetic
components, only, this time, in a very gross form.   If
one observes such characters for a short time in a
protected setting, away from their own milieu, they
generally appear to be of an enviable peace of spirit ;
they give the impression of rather insensitive honest
men, who would do no one any harm.   If one investi-
gates their domestic milieu, it is, as one would expect
from their insensitivity, neglected.   There they are not
restful in spirit, but, under the covering of sulky silence,
there always glimmers a spark of inner tension, which
has the character of a complex, and springs from the
accumulation of all the little everyday unpleasantnesses of
office and family life, which get heaped up inside, which
cannot be overcome, and which cannot be spoken out :
a nervous inner tension, which at times, on the slightest
touching of a complex in an unexpected place, may
unload itself, recklessly, in the most brutal outbursts of

passion, breaking through the insensitive outer covering. This kind of schizophrenic passion, with its psychological mechanism of latent, stored emotion and senseless, eruptive outbursts, has many connections with certain brain-traumatic and epileptic syndromes.   The passionate-insensitive schizoids may be the most brutal and dangerous of tyrants in the home, who misuse their surroundings without a trace of feeling, and direct everything, regardless of everyone else, according to their own pedantic whims.   Many historically famed imperial despots have, at least in externals, a great deal in common with this schizoid type.

' Indifference ' is a common schizoid variant of affective insensibility.   It is an uninterestedness, which is ostentatiously manifested.   That is to say, it is a partial insensitivity embedded in a context of psychic activity. The ' indifferent ' knows that he takes absolutely no interest in many things which are important to other people, and this consciousness gains expression in his behaviour ;   occasionally there are traces of baroque humour or sarcasm mixed in with it.   The ' indifferent ' are very often such half-wrecked creatures as we have described above, in whom certain bits of psychic activity remain intact, immediately surrounded with a mass of insensitive refuse.   Here one must certainly include those cases of divided personality in Bleuler's sense, where the intact portion of the personality may play, half ironically, with the wreckage that surrounds it.   In the realm of psychic disease there is an immediate connection between this and the churlish rudeness of hebephrenes.

From the ranks of the ' indifferent ', just as from among the other half-wrecked insensitives, is recruited a great army of people who are irresistibly sinking down the social scale—the unstable, the extravagant, gamblers and drinkers, rich, well-born young men rendered worthless by women, dissolute students, restless makers of plans, minor criminals, and, particularly, prostitutes and tramps. Many of these connections have been discovered by the Heidelberg school, and in particular by Wilmanns.   A certain group of restless wanderers, too, in whose case indifference is combined with attacks of schizoid depression, is closely related to the schizoid class.   Half uninterested, half internally tormented, hungry for some emotional stimulus to come into the psychic life, which is fast becoming more and more insensitive, they are continually being driven on round the demimonde, from place to place. Occasionally slight schizophrene-symptoms play a part, such as persecution mania, or hallucination. One finds characteristics of this kind in many highly gifted men, *e.g.*, in Platen, and it occurs everywhere down the scale till we reach the simple beggar.

What is the difference between ' affective coldness ' and ' affective insensitivity ' ? In the first place, one describes as cold such natures as are lacking in the heartfelt immediate reaction of man to man, in humour, in unfailing open sympathy for joy and sorrow : in short, natures in which the diathetic temperamental scale plays but little part. One calls another variant of this diathetic defect ' dryness '. Conversely, as we have seen, popular speech describes those people in whom the diathetic scale is predominant, *e.g.*, the cycloids, as warm-hearted. In this general sense, then, the average schizoid is of a cold temperament.

It may be mentioned *en passant*, that sensitive schizoids often seem to have just the opposite reactions. Schiller, who was a healthy schizothyme, says somewhere in his " Essays on Æsthetics ", " When I first got to know Shakespeare I was revolted by his coldness, his unfeelingness, which allowed him to joke in the midst of the deepest tragedy." I have read judgments about Gottfried Keller, which are just like this one about Shakespeare. The fact that schizothymes often cannot enter properly into cyclothymic temperaments. It strikes the sensitive schizothyme as unfeeling, vulgar, and coarse, when the cyclothyme, with a humorous or indulgent smile, or even with something approaching laughter, contemplates and ' fingers ' situations which move the schizothyme to sublime pathos or high-flown melancholy, on account of their melting tenderness, or monstrous vulgarity. What the pronounced schizothyme calls ' feeling ' and ' warmth ' are the strong positive emotions of his psychæsthetic temperamental scale ; while the diathetic uses his own scale as a basis for the same judgments. The average man feels here mostly with the cyclothyme and against the schizoid. We also are here following this prevailing usage of speech.

The expression ' emotionally cold ' has, however, a still narrower meaning. We call a man ' insensitive ' who allows himself to be poked without lifting up his head ; we call a man ' cold ', who can walk over a corpse without feeling anything during the transit. ' Insensitive ' denotes, in popular usage, passivity, whereas ' cold ' implies rather, active unfeelingness. With ' insensitivity ' comes in the notion of a defective psychomotility ; ' coldness ' is pure anæsthesia, which leaves the active capacities unimpaired. With schizoid personalities, it often seems to be only a question of the constitutional mixture, whether they impress one rather as being cold, or as being insensitive, or, what is commoner, as both together. Furthermore, we can directly observe, within the same schizoid life, how insensitivity turns into coldness, or coldness into insensitivity, with the gradual alteration of the psychæsthetic proportions. One can find cases (there is one of them described below) where schizoid pre-psychotics of the sensitive, affectively lame, good-natured type of temperament, on account of a hidden shifting of balance at the age of puberty, have changed, even without a psychosis, into cold, brutal ruffians. How many cold schizoids have subsequently developed as a result of shifts and lurking displacements, cannot be ascertained for certain, particularly among schizoid relatives of patients, because of the superficial nature of the information one has to go on.

It is, however, a fact that traits of active coldness, occasional roughness, and egotistic, irritable lack of consideration are often to be found mingled with the characteristics of the main sensitive affectively lame type. The elegant, aristocratic schizoids, in particular, often seem extraordinarily cold.

Quite generally speaking, in schizophrene families we find frequent traces of active unfeelingingness of all kinds—cutting, cold energy, unkind hardness, mordacity, cynical egoism, despotic whimsicality, senseless sharpness and hatred, right down to brutality, and cruel criminal instincts. Hoffmann gives examples of these types in his book, to which I refer the reader. We should have

M

to parade before his eyes a whole army of poisonous, wizened old maids and household-dragons, of offensive, ironical, sour creatures, of dry, ill-humoured pedants, of brooders, distrustfully watching their own ideas simmer, of cold, sneaking intriguers, mad tyrants, and misers ; indeed, we could fill a whole book with nothing but pictures of all the constitutional variants and social types which, in the sphere of schizophrenic madness, betray anæsthetic components in the form of a weakness, coldness, and dryness of the emotions.

Here, however, we will only point out that a schizoid inheritance may, under favourable conditions, produce plus-variants which are of great social value. That very cutting indifference towards the fate of any given individual, together with the preoccupation with the schematic, with logical sequences, and strict rectitude, which is often rooted in certain schizoid natures, may act as an excellent compensating component of the personality, and turn out men of steely energy and unbending tenacity. Frederick the Great, with his accumulated and inbred schizoid inheritance from the house of Welf, is a superb example of this.

This passionate energy forms the opposite pole to the ' lack of drive ', the complete indolence and weakness of will, which characterize many dried-up schizoid psychopaths and hebephrenes. Here also, on the psychomotor side of the schizoid type, abnormal energy and indolence form a biological pair, exhibiting a contrast between tension and lameness similar to that afforded by psychæsthetic hypersensitivity and insensitivity. The psychæsthetic insensitivity and psychomotor indolence are woven so much into one another, that one can hardly deal with them apart.

Just as it can make for good results, so, in unfavourable alloys, the schizoid emotional coldness can also make for bad ; especially when it is combined with that capricious instability which we have described before, and which is a characteristic of so many schizoids, *e.g.*, in combination with sadistic components. It may here bring about truly bestial criminal natures.

One need only imagine the licentious cruelties which the schizophrene Ludwig II of Bavaria wrote down in dreamy desire in his diary, transferred in reality to a slightly more active nature in a despotically governed state, to obtain some conjectural insight into much that happened in actual fact, in earlier centuries, through the activities of semi-psychopathic emperors.

Expression and Psychomotility

So far we have placed the psychæsthetic qualities of the schizoid temperament in the foreground, because they are the most important foundations on which the personality is built up. But, side by side with their impressionability, we must also take a swift glance at their characterological modes of expression, and the narrower aspects of their psychomotility. We have already said something about the schizoid volitional processes. If we may describe the outward responses and the psychomotility of the cycloids as smooth, natural, and adequate to the stimulus, many schizoids may likewise be recognized by the lack of direct connection between the emotional stimulus and its motor reaction.

In psychopathic schizophrenes, we see the way from psychic stimulus to reaction often so blocked, distorted, and displaced, by inhibitions, secondary impulses, and katatonic mechanisms, that we can no longer recognize it, or only by means of some indirect key. We find this incongruity between stimulus and expression to a lesser degree in many schizoid personalities.

We have already dwelt upon two of the most important symptoms of schizoid psychomotility in their psychæsthetic aspect : affective lameness and timidity. Besides these, there are a whole crowd of variations, which owe their particular colouring only in part to internal differences of proportion and mixture, and in part to simple environmental conditions. One may regard ' affective stiffness ' (Bleuler), as a kind of static counterpart of ' affective lameness '. This stiffness of the movements expressive of emotion comes to view in the schizoid of aristocratic behaviour, as well as in the ' pathetic ' temperament. According to the opportunity and the environment it comes out as pomposity, forcedness, formality, pose, ceremoniousness, or pedantry. Lively schizoids, on the other hand, behave ' hastily ', ' thoughtlessly ', or ' fidgetily ', in which cases the jerkiness of the motor tempo comes out, in contradistinction to the smooth mobility of the hypomanic. The phlegmatic peace of mind is just as much a psychomotor as a psychæsthetic symptom. It may be combined in schizoids with nervous hastiness in the oddest mixtures.

By the side of these cruder stigmata, we find in schizoids a number of minor suppressions and contortions of psychomotor expression which may even have a favourable influence on the personality. We have already mentioned the slightly stylized and restrained quality in gesture and movement, which in combination with hyperæsthetic sensibility makes up the aristocratic symptom-complex, and gives the mode of life of such individuals a peculiarly beautiful line, which we miss when we come to the cycloids. Tact, taste, tender consideration, the avoidance of everything that is gross, vulgar, and ordinary, are the special attractions of this particular schizoid group, and make it the opposite extreme to the hypomanic temperament. You have nothing but sensibility and style on one side, and freshness and naturalness on the other, for which reason these two kinds of men often get on particularly badly together.

One meets with a peculiar military stiffness in expression and movement as an inherited peculiarity in schizoid families, even in circumstances where such things are not brought out by the profession, or are actually discouraged by it. If one describes such men as ' upright ', one has characterized them somatically and psychically alike. One has here frequently to do with masterful personalities, with outstanding tenacity of purpose and strength of character.

From a biological point of view, in Bleuler's opinion, the tendency to psychomotor incongruity goes with the tendency to psychæsthetic hypersensitivity, to intrapsychic inhibitions and spasmodic complex-formations.[1] From a

[1] By a complex we understand an isolated group of ideas bound together by a strong emotion, which, persisting tensely within for a long time, exerts an individual, and often disturbing, influence on the general psychic processes. The term " complex " is often used in a wider sense to mean any emotionally toned system of ideas.

schematic point of view, all three may be regarded as the working of the same agent on different parts of the psychic reflex arc.   Many schizoids, then, are disposed, together with strongly emotional experiences, to have directional disturbances, in the form that we have defined as ' sensitive relation dementia '.   Certain schizoid symptom-groups give that very combination of hyperæsthesia and restraint, which disposes them to sensitive reactions to experience. For this reason we find such sensitive qualities sprinkled very thickly over schizophrenic psychoses as factors in their development.

Psychic Tempo

At this point we will bring our investigation into psychæsthesia and psychomotility to a close, and turn for a moment to the closely-connected question of psychic tempo.   We said that the cycloids have an undulating tempo, an emotional susceptibility which reacts directly to the stimulus in smooth, full, rounded curves, and which swings between gay and sad in deep wavy lines in accordance with the endogenous situation and the environment.   Cycloids have no, or very few complexes, because the incoming affective material works itself off overtly and directly, at once.   Schizoids, however, in so far as they are capable of reacting at all, often have a leaping type of temperament, they have not a rounded, wavy affect-curve, but an abrupt, jagged one.   In the psychoses, one sees this type particularly well manifested in the katatonic patients, in their alternation between sudden crampings of themselves together, and abrupt, incalculable outbursts of emotion.   Schizoids of various shades of temperament are pronounced ' complex subjects ', in whom little, everyday stimuli, just as greater affectively-toned groups of ideas, pile up undischarged, working under cover for a long time in strained tension, and then suddenly spring forth into affective reactions, if anyone unknowingly touches on a sore point.   For this reason, many schizoids often behave oddly, as when they suddenly snap a person's head off at an apparently harmless change of the conversation, or seem hurt, or become perceptibly cooler, or more retiring, or ironical, or cutting in their conversation. On account of this 'complex' mechanism the passage from cause to effect in their affective lives is far more complicated and more obscure than with cycloids.

In this way, if we take a broad view, many schizoid temperaments may be ranged between two poles, i.e., between abnormal inflexibility and abnormal jerkiness. On the one hand, we find people who are toughly energetic, stubborn, mulish, and pedantic, and, on the other, those whose natures are particularly unstable, whimsical, jerky, rash, and incalculable. And we find all possible mixtures and transitions between the two groups. If the cycloid temperaments may be said to vary between fast and slow, then the schizoids vary between tenacious and jerky.[1] The cycloid temperamental curve is a wavy one, the schizoid curve is often jagged.

Certain peculiarities of thought process hang to some extent together with this. Side by side with restless, ragged, literary efforts, characterized by a kind of baroque inconsequence, or an aphoristic obscurity, we find, on the other hand, among highly gifted schizoids, through the group of paranoiac prophets down to the scraps written by severely diseased katatonics, a certain quality of rigidity, a tendency to the enumeration of names and figures, to numbering and schematization, to logical abstraction, and to system-building at all costs. We shall meet with this distinctive peculiarity again in the healthy schizothymic geniuses.

In connection with the jagged affect-curve, we must also mention what Bleuler calls 'Ambivalence', that is to say, the springing backwards and forwards of the emotion and the will between 'yes' and 'no', as an important characteristic of many schizoids. We add here, as nearly related to this, another psychological trait, which often surprises one not only in patients (it may be particularly well observed in many schizophrenes where the psychosis has had a gradual beginning) but also in the biographies of schizoid artists, and in healthy schizothymes, and that is the alternations of affective attitude. While certain cycloid types are perfect representatives of healthy common sense, of conciliatory reasonableness, of

[1] We are not dealing here with those people who are merely indolent, because they are of no great characterological interest.

careful balancing, and of good-natured, affective adjust-
ment, the schizoids, about whom we are talking here, are
marked out by the very fact that they are lacking in
affective moderation.   Such men are either in ecstasies
or shocked, either enthusiastically attracted to a person,
or his mortal enemy, to-day at the highest point of self-
conceit, to-morrow—shattered.   And all this is brought
about by so little—because the person in question once
made use of some indelicate expression, or unknowingly
touched on a sensitive complex.   Either the whole world
or nothing, either, like Schiller, seizing the crown from
his brow, or else a complaining bungler for whom a bullet
in the head is the only way out.   They see no fellow-men
about them who are moderately good or bad, and with
whom one can live, if one only humours them a little ;
no, everyone is either a knight, or a low, common fellow,
an angel or a devil, a saint or a Megaera—there is no
middle course.

These temperamental peculiarities must not be confused with the sanguine exuberance of certain hypomanic
characters.   The cycloid is exuberant, the schizoid is
overstrained.   The temperament of the exuberant goes
in waves, the overstrained temperament leaps up and
then shrinks together.   The sanguine cycloid, however
far his waves rise and fall, always swings in natural,
rounded transitions, right through the middle ranges of
affect, but the schizoid enthusiast leaps over them, from
one pole to the opposite.   We must add here, *en passant*,
that the old temperamental descriptions like ' sanguine '
and ' phlegmatic ' are useless for more accurate psychological purposes because they include, without any sharp
differentiation, both exuberance and overstrainedness,
cycloid comfortableness, as well as schizoid affective
lameness or insensitivity.

This alternating affectivity of many schizoids must be
clearly grasped, because we shall meet with it again among
schizothymes—in normal psychology—and geniuses, as
a tendency to ' pathos ' and high-flown melancholy in
literature and speech, and as a tendency to fanaticism in
behaviour.

We have limited these remarks to a few lines in order
not to step unawares from the analysis of the schizoid

temperament into the region of schizophrenic psycho-
pathology. We repeat that our business here is not to
write a psychology of schizophrenes, but only to throw a
light on the problem of schizophrenia from the point of view
of its connection with a general theory of temperament.
For the advantage of psychiatrists it may be added that
certain fundamental characteristics which are particularly
prominent in many schizoid groups, remind one very
definitely of certain elements in the descriptions which
one finds here and there of the ' nervous character ', or
the ' hysterical character '. There is no doubt whatever
that there are many ' nervous ' and ' hysterical ' individuals,
many psychopaths and degenerates, who are biologically
nothing other than schizoids. Bleuler and his school have
already asserted this. And it may be that many traits
of such schizoids have been incorporated in the current
description of the ' nervous ' or ' hysterical ' character.
For it is very important to insist that ' nervousness ' and
' hysteria ' are merely the names of convenient clinical
classes, and have no constitutional reference, in a deeper
biological sense. There is a ' nervousness ' connected
with the exophthalmic goitre, a ' nervousness ' determined
by brain lesion, and there is schizoid ' nervousness ', etc.
All these are matters into which we cannot enter here ;
they are problems for future investigators, which, as far
as our knowledge goes at present, are still to a certain,
extent, on the whole insoluble. We therefore refrain from
any judgment as to how far schizoidism is involved in the
sphere of nervousness, hysteria, degenerative psychopathia,
congenital idiocy, etc. We only suggest that one must
neither too hastily lump them all together, nor place them
in different compartments. And similarly we deprecate
any attempt to decide at present whether schizophrenia,
or the great schizothymic type of personality, is in itself
a biological unity, *sui generis*, or only a group of types
having some close resemblance to one another. The same
remark must, of course, be made about the cyclothymic
constitution. At first we have the feeling—but that is
not a judgment that can be proved—that the mass of
the cyclothymic group, in their bodily as well as in their
psychic build, make an impression which is simpler and
more narrowly defined than can be said to be the case

with the outwardly very heterogeneous types of physique
and character which make up the schizothymic class ;
and yet this greater external variety is no absolute proof
that there is not an inner unity, at least from certain
points of view.   Our purpose here is only to characterize
as far as possible, both physically and psychologically,
the general features of the schizothymic type, in contradistinction to the general features of the cyclothymic
type, but without saying whether the schizothymic and
cyclothymic types form unities in themselves, or whether,
besides these great groups, there are other fundamental
constitutional classes which we do not know of.

CHAPTER XI

THE SCHIZOID TEMPERAMENT

General Portion

WE are now going to give a selection of a few concrete personalities as illustrations to the theoretical part, in which we laid the stress on the types of temperament, and only spoke of the schizoid imaginative content incidentally (ideas of discovery, and prophecy, etc.). At the same time, we naturally shall not give any particular examples of the great mass of mediocre, simply lame and insensitive schizoids, who are universally known and of no great psychological interest.

Group 1. *Predominantly hyperæsthetic temperament.* *Sensitive affectively lame type (pre-psychotic)*

Young Erich Hanner, the son of a cultured family, underwent a severe attack of katatonia when he was 15 years old. He was a pale, timid youth, who had shot up to a great height, with long ungainly limbs, and a vague dreamy expression on his face, serious, half older than his age, and half movingly childlike. He usually sat huddled up, bashful, and spiritless, so that people thought that he was stupid ; if anyone spoke to him, he would look up surprised, embarrassed, and shy. Everyone was exasperated by his slowness and fussiness. If no one urged him on, he might take three hours to dress in the morning. His parents brought pressure to bear on him for all this, in order to educate him to fresher, quicker movements. He cried a great deal over it, and strained terribly to correct it. He used to work at night up to 12 or 1 o'clock in order to finish his home work. His conscientiousness and punctuality were almost pedantic.

He was very quiet, and easily moved to tears when

anyone upbraided him. He never had any friends at school, and he became less and less able to get on with his brothers and sisters. Whenever he was with other young people he used to smile awkwardly. He never took part in rough games. His school-fellows used to tease him a great deal ; he made no protest, but suffered terribly under it. He quarrelled easily with his brothers and sisters on account of his oddity. He had a bitter feeling that he was different from the others. Speech was always a difficulty to him. He could not get hold of the words. " If I speak a word as soon as it comes into my head," he said, " I have the feeling as if I were shouting insolently into the blue, just like when you spring over stocks and stones." He often drew back after shaking hands, with the same feeling, as if it were an insult to grip a person's hand quickly. He laid great value on good clothes, and could never do enough with his own toilet.

On the emotional side, he was tender, sensitive, and susceptible. When he was older he did not eat meat any more, because it came from slaughtered beasts. He thought it was wicked. He could not look on when animals or men were handled with violence. One ought not to harm the meanest fly. " Two lives for one meal," said he, when his mother wanted to buy two small chickens. When he was away from home, he suffered dreadfully from homesickness. He clung very tenderly to his mother. Later on he developed a religious enthusiasm ; he went every Sunday to church, and wanted to convert his family, and become a missionary.

He had a favourite sister to whom he was very attached, especially in his younger years, and with whom he shared all his thoughts. His prematurely awakened intelligence produced excellent, original ideas, particularly of a technical variety. He liked to think out wildly fantastical inventions ; for example, once he thought out a plan for a carriage which went with paddle-wheels upon the water. He tried a model of it in his bath, worked at it silently and passionately, and sent a copy to the Minister of War. The carriage did, as a matter of fact, go ; it had been well thought out. He also drew and painted very beautifully.

But he preferred to creep into a corner with his sister,

apart from the other children, and build castles in the air with her. They would imagine princedoms in wonderful parts of the world, which they would rule, and there would be hunting, and enchanted animals, a world of magic and an ether ship, that travelled forth to visit all the stars set in the spaces of the universe.

He did not like people to touch him. He often felt as if he were made of glass. . . .

We can see particularly well in the case of this gifted young man how the hyperæsthetic psychic life begins to bloom inwards, as if it were in a hot-house, behind the apparently insensitive exterior ; it flowers into the tenderest devotion for individual persons, into sensitive humanitarian ideals, enthusiastic religiousness, inventions, and dreamy poetic phantasies. The less gifted schizoids of this type are lacking in this delicate productivity, and the ramified inner life that is spun out of it. They seem simply lame, partially insensitive, with a few traits mixed in of excitable timid nervousness.

The two following types, the aristocratic and the idealistic, regarded from the psychæsthetic point of view are not so much independent examples of the schizothymic temperament, as variants of the fundamental type which we have just described. They also are based on a tender inner hyperæsthesia, with a very narrowed capacity for emotional reaction and the autistic self-restriction to a small circle of men and interests which it conditions, together with certain peculiarities of psychomotility and affective expression.

Sensitive cold aristocratic type

Irene Hertel, the 29-year-old daughter of a simple family, whose members worked as clerks, appeared one day at the Institute, accompanied by her brother, suffering from a fairly well-developed schizophrenia with a widely-ramifying delusional system. The brother at once handed us a written account of the disease, composed by himself, strictly in accordance with the regulations, systematically numbered and arranged. He presented a tall elegant appearance, with a very carefully-tended exterior, and a long, pale, cold face ; he was pedantically buttoned up, formal, dry, correct, and very polite.   He held himself upright, sat in his chair without leaning back, had slight, hardly noticeable gestures, and only his lips moved when he spoke ; he never laughed.

As for the younger brother, whom I got to know later, it was possible to come into closer human contact with him ; he was fair, with a clear complexion and soft features, sensitive, obliging, very discrete, restrained in expression, and of a very gentle affectivity.   The mother, who was dead, must have been very similar, gentle, and sensitive ; she could not bear coarser natures, like that of one of her sisters.

" What were you like as a child ? " I once asked the patient herself.   " Idle and overexcitable ", she answered. " Idleness is a weakness, and if one is weak, one is over-excitable."   She found her work very difficult, and racked her brains over it ; in spite of this she was a diligent pupil ; she was severe on herself, and would not give in.   She studied from morning to night.   When she was 16 years old, she remained patiently in a pension in France, where she suffered very much from homesickness and the strangeness of her surroundings.   She would not return home until she had completely mastered the French language.

As a child she was extremely nervous, excitable, and easily tired ; she was also rather quick-tempered.   She often felt she must cry from nothing but overexertion. She used to feel giddy when she climbed mountains. After any slight bodily activity, even after making her bed, her thoughts ' drifted into phantasy '.   She had a strong tendency to day-dreaming.   She saw her fancies, ' like pictures ' in front of her eyes, but it was always after she had exhausted herself.   Her outward appearance was apathetic.   She ' must not go to sleep,' was the remark that was always being addressed to her at school by the teacher, when, as a matter of fact, she was suffering martyrdom in her mind.   She was always peculiar,. reserved, and had no girl friends in the school.

Even when she was still very young, she gave the impression of being a ' serious, quiet character '.   The direction of her taste and of her ethical outlook were very decided. She had her feelings completely under control, and one would never gather anything about her from her external behaviour, even her depression. She never spoke to anyone about her apprehensions and thoughts, although internally she was very susceptible, and had a tendency to distrustfulness. Her external behaviour manifested a satisfied, almost cheerful quietness, which made her seem very serious. She was unsociable, and liked being by herself ; it was only with great trouble that one could persuade her to go to balls and parties ; once there, however, she controlled herself completely, danced, joined in everything that was going on, and betrayed no nervousness. She was never in love, and never showed any warm feelings for any man. Her family considered it unthinkable that she should ever have thought of marriage ; it would be impossible to imagine anything like that of her. If any indelicacy was let fall when she was in a company, she would give a quick little smile and hurry away.

She had a pronounced taste for refinement, flowers, and *de luxe* editions. She had a peculiar preference for descriptions of society life—of the court, fine ladies, and fashionable sport. She enthused about aristocrats and well-dressed people. Her personal appearance had something about it that was distinctly stylish, well-bred, and sensitive.

As to her own person, she was absolutely unassuming, and so considerate that she would beg a person's pardon a hundred times if she thought she had injured him by any word she had spoken. When she shared a room for some time with a sister, she hardly dared to breathe, so as to be certain of not disturbing her. In all her dealings she displayed a sensitive, gentle tact ; she was very kind to everybody, but all the same, with the exception of her mother, she never became intimate with any-one. However friendly one might be, one could never be cordial with her.

Her mother was the only person with whom she had any intimate psychic relations. Her mother had always protected her, even within her own home ; she had kept her from all unpleasantness, and from any contact with household affairs. She, alone, saw into her psychic life ;

no one else knew anything about her erotic thoughts, which later became pathological. "Since mother went, everything makes a far deeper impression on her," reported her brother. "Since then, everything is at once incorporated into her delusions. After mother's death, a few years ago, a deep gulf appeared, and she has never been able to find the bridge over, to get to her father and brothers."

The psychosis developed quite gradually, more or less from the pubertial period, without any distinct beginning, hidden behind, and springing out of the external personality; after the death of her mother the disturbance became noticeable. She believed that she had fixed indelicate eyes on a young professor, whom she had idealized from a distance, and that now she had fallen a victim to his revenge. A systematic persecution, instigated by him, with the help of neighbours and relatives, was now directed against her. Distrust and outbursts of emotion followed. A feeling of hostile coldness sometimes came over her, a destructive impulse, "The thoughts rush rapidly through one's head : destroy, pull down the curtain, hit someone." She became more and more peculiar, colder, and more reserved ; her expressions were vague and rather unnatural, an involuntary laugh would sometimes come over her. She was no longer able to concentrate, and all her thoughts seemed as if they had 'flown away'.

In this condition she came to us. She hardly ate anything, she scarcely spoke; her room was fresh and neat. One could hardly hear her walking up and down. She is very fair, and looks ethereally transparent, with a thin nose, and blue-veined temples. There is an atmosphere of 'distance' about her. Her movements are slow, refined, and aristocratic, with a few awkwardnesses here and there. If anyone speaks to her, she draws herself slightly back, and leans against the cupboard. There is something strange and very dreamy about her. Her hand is thin, long, and very flexible. When she is greeting you she reaches out the tips of her fingers, which are cold and quite transparent. She smiles distantly, confusedly, and uncertainly.

The psychæsthetic relations are here throughout the same as they were in the case of the young man, only that the coldness and 'remoteness' are altogether more strongly accentuated. On the other hand, the emotional expression and the psychomotility have a different quality. The subject is not awkward, lame, and timid, but polished, quiet, even, and completely under control—delicate tact and taste. One sees not the slightest indication of the sensitive inner feelings in the superficial motor behaviour. It is that that we call aristocratic. There hangs closely together with this the indication of a cool, tenacious will, with which we have so often met in the schizoid class. The elder brother is a very good example of a variant of this cold aristocratic type, the tender susceptibility rather more in the background, the quiet restfulness, on the other hand, raised to poverty of emotional expression, cold correctness, pedanticism, so that the result is almost mechanical. There is an immediate transition from this to what Bleuler, when dealing with schizophrenic psychopaths, calls " emotional stiffness ".

Type of pathetic idealist

Franz Blau, a young artist, a student at the Conservatory, came to us one day by himself, completely confused, full of burning emotional obsessions within, with an empty smile, an exaggerated politeness without, behind which was a strained, almost hostile distrust. His manner was abrupt and patronizingly cordial, with a certain stiffness in his expression. He was much given to grimacing, and his movements were exaggerated, unnatural, and rhetorical. He always made use of the most general expressions, and abstractions, and he got round concrete questions with a great deal of verbal bombast. He was ' tragic,' and quite vague. " Relations were entered into with other men ", he said, when he wanted to recount how he was acquainted with someone in M. Music, sexuality, religion, all are spoken of with one breath, and as if they all had the same value. Spiritual bankruptcy, ruin—" I am lost ! " He is suddenly raised to a height of exaltation. " If only I could find peace—peace at last ! "

After a few days of quietude and waiting, he had summoned up enough confidence to speak out. I immediately wrote down in the form of pencilled notes, giving a verbatim report of his expressions, all that he poured forth in many hours of conversation, quite of his own accord, and almost without being asked any questions at all. They are given in what follows. He spoke fragmentarily, in a melancholy voice, tired yet full of passion, but with natural expression as soon as he came to his own terrible experience ; his account was subjective in the highest degree, but quite other than it was in the first few days ; the affected grimaces and drawlings only seldom interrupted the train of his conversation.

' " More reality ! " That's my error. Realism ought to have come in to the idealism. " You are sentimental, and like loneliness " says the girl. Yes, I love music, nature . . . all that is higher !—I find no happiness in music —Father banged the door : " The whole thing is your fault, all due to your rotten mode of life ! " Then we come down to fighting with knives, that's what it's like at home. Father tyrannizes over everything, Mother doesn't count ; when he is not there everything goes smoothly enough, and when he comes, then everything in the whole house is cramped. He is a strict pedant. " Take off your shoes at once "—that was what greeted me when I used to come home, when I was a child. I ought to have been treated gently. Mother had no sense, no tact, and no feeling.

' " He's a miserable creature " cries my father, " he ought never to marry, and that's an end of it ! "— " Marry ? " That's a hard word, doctor—" Partner for life ! "

' Melancholy. Complete exhaustion. . . . I see, ever before me, the streets of M.—the little girl who would have been good for me. It storms over me. It completely oppresses me. It comes through my body and up my spine, it travels over me like a fear. I have a tender soul. Everyone treated me at home in such a way that I always felt : " You are a rotter."

' I am an idealist, and the world looks different to me. . . .

' When I was a child,' he told me on one of the next few days, ' When I was a child, immediately after dinner I had a piano lesson from 1 to 2. If I did not play

N

properly I was severely punished. A 2 o'clock I had to go back again to school. At first I was to be a musician, but then father forced me to go for a time into business. During the business hours I often ran off secretly up to the Girls' Home, and gave music lessons there. There was a kind-hearted Sister who had a great influence on me. She was over 40 years old. When she was transferred after three years, I felt horribly homesick and miserable. I was never in love with her. But I had clung to her with my very soul. For the first time I felt that someone liked me. I confessed everything to her.

'When she had gone, a terrible agitation broke out in me. For two days I went into the asylum. After that, I never got over the fact that the Sister was no longer there. I was entirely overwhelmed by it.

'One day I appeared at her place in a distant town, to say good-bye to her. I was completely under her sway. "Francis," she said, "if you can't possibly get on without me, then I will come too." She ran away from the convent, and went with me. From February to July we lived together in a quiet corner of the mountains. At first, when she was with me, they were the quietest days of my life. Then I kissed her, and was fearfully excited physically, but I did not touch her. This older person took the place of my mother, who she ought to have been. "Sister, you must stay with me now," I cried, "I can't face it any longer!" I had completely lost my head, and knew no longer what I was doing. The loveliness of nature made me drunk—I saw that everything was a terrible mistake. . . .

'With her I went home. My father met me at the station. I was suddenly seized by some men, and bound; I was to be taken to the asylum. "You can go," he said coldly to the Sister. I raved. My entrance into the asylum was terrible. I was so much off my head, that I destroyed everything in the house—everything on to the floor!

'A few months in the asylum, then again into the mountains to recoup, but quite alone this time. Melancholy. I did not know where the Sister was; I wanted to go, myself, into a monastery. A complete loss of spiritual contact with mankind, with my family—that was what it was. Besides music—nothing. Everything was so upside down. At that time I did not understand properly about sexual matters. I have been ill since then, in continual unrest and melancholy, I have never come out of a state of excitement. I had learnt for the first time that love plays a rôle in the life of man.

' I was now to study music. If only the Sister had been there I should have got on with music. I was entirely under her influence, I could not bring myself to break the bonds. She lived another quarter of a year with me at the music academy in M.—we kept up a little ménage together ; she cooked for me. I did well in my examinations ; music was the one and only thing that interested me. The great town troubled me ; I had to watch myself whenever I met people.

' Then it all collapsed. In the town I got a completely new view of life. I realized that, spiritually, she was too simple for me. She was not very intelligent, but she was kind-hearted, the child of quite simple people. She had never been used to anyone but nuns. I had always called her " auntie ". " We must part ", I said to her. That ought never to have happened. But I was in the most awful state at Christmas, at first, when she went away. After we had parted, I wrote her letters of twenty-eight pages, all of them pointing out that I needed someone to whom I could be spiritually bound.

' Two months after she had gone away, I began a new liaison. I got to know a singer in the Peterskirche, a treasure, who led me by the hand like an angel, a sincere creature.'

Now the psychosis began again. He had the feeling that the Sister knew all about his new affair, he had no guarantee that she could not have discovered it. People began to spy on him through the landlady, through the doctor. ' I suffered like a person who is haunted by a persecution mania, only with this difference, that I was really being persecuted.' One day he told the girl all about the Sister, he told her the story perfectly frankly.

' I did not know what I was doing for restlessness. I had to break off my studies. I went to a nerve specialist in the sanatorium. I had so much weighing on my mind that I had to get hold of some man to whom I could unburden myself. The girl was allowed to visit me at the Sanatorium, and the Sister came too, at the request of the doctor. I thought that the Sister must have had a hand in the game, and I was furious with her, so that at first I wouldn't speak to her. The situation was horribly strained. She saw how attached I was to the girl, and she talked kindly to me. I ought never to have gone to the girl . . . nor to the Sister . . . nor to the doctor. I saw no way out. The Sister said she would never see me again, and went away into a convent in the South.

'If the girl leaves me too, then I am lost. "You don't understand me", I said to the girl. If the girl doesn't understand me any more, the Sister must come back again. I wandered eight or nine hours over the pass, covered with snow, until I came to the convent of the Good Shepherd. "I am in need of spiritual help", I said, "the Sister must come out". "Francis, you must leave me now", said the Sister, "you have got someone else now!" Then I couldn't speak to her any more. Three times I forced my way into the Convent, and was repulsed, having accomplished nothing. And so I went home alone.'

We repeat that the whole of this verbatim protocol [1] is made up of the actual words of a psychopath suffering from severe schizophrenia, and were spoken when his psychosis was at its full height. We have restricted our part as far as possible to putting in order the sentences, which were often muddled up with each other, and to omitting a great deal that is unimportant; only in a few places are the original words of the patient not used, and in such places a long series of remarks has been compressed into one short sentence which gives their meaning. The general outlines of his life history have been confirmed by his relatives. We have known the family for some time, because a sister of the patient previously came under our treatment for a simple imbecile hebephrenia. The family is more or less what the patient has described. How far reality and phantasy mingle with

[1] The telegraphic nature of the style in many places is due to the fact that in the transcript the most important phrases have been selected, and not whole sentences.

one another in the details, it is neither possible nor profitable to discover. We are using it as a psychological protocol, not concerning the history of his life, but concerning the way he feels towards life in general. Even if the whole were a dream or a poem, which is not, in point of fact, the case, it would be just as useful to us.

And the attitude towards life of this schizophrene is, through and through, tragic, and full of pathos. We have the sensitive idealist on the one hand, and the coarse natural world on the other. More reality, love, contact with mankind ! A chain of hopeless attempts to orientate himself to reality. A tentative projection of his feelers, and an immediate cramped, wounded withdrawal into himself, and into loneliness. Never quiet observation, weighing of pros and cons, no gradual adaptation of himself. But all or nothing, ecstatic enthusiasm at one moment, and extreme coldness and hostility at the next. A violent rush forwards, and a violent catastrophe, again and again—but never a journeying quietly down the paved middle way. Franz Blau belongs to the class of men, of whom we said that they had a natural talent for tragic experiences, and whom we find so often among schizoid geniuses. According to the strength of the emotion which is hidden behind the grand distorted gestures, such men seem to the healthy to be either really tragic, or ' hysterical ', overstrained and affected. We can see exactly the same sort of thing in Strindberg. We can find the most typical examples of this schizoid type only among gifted persons ; and only those gifted men whose art is of a literary nature can really describe this kind of schizoid attitude to life. The average schizophrene is incapable of putting the conflict properly into words, even when he has a dim awareness of it.

In its psychæsthetic proportions this pathetic type is like the two which we have described before : hyperæsthesia with a narrowed circle of emotions, and, springing from that, the autistic incapacity for objective registration of reality, and the determined turning away to the unreal, to the ideal, to abstractions, to the beautiful and the realms of thought, to the building up of a shut-away, tender, inner world. We find an exaggerated,

elective attraction to a few people, and an abrupt recoil-
ing from others. Further, the schizophrenic method of
thought, through which that affective tendency is
realized, is clear in the case of Franz Blau : mystical-
romantic, a vague turning aside from concrete questions.
What is his ideal ? 'The Higher'.   A ringing word
without any content at all, but filled with a burning
affective value.   This abstract ideal comes about by *condensation*, a schizophrenic association-mechanism which
is very closely related to dream psychology ; sex, religion,
and art are conglobulated into a composite of ideas,
vaguely contoured, but with enormous emotional strength,
and when Blau says ' the higher', elements of all three
groups swim together in a dim mist before him.   This
confusion of sex and religion is well known to be a chronic
characteristic of the schizophrenic content of thought.
But this is by the way.

The difference between the pathetic type and the
other two, therefore, lies not on the psychæsthetic side,
but in the strength of their impulses, their ' intrapsychic
activity', the pressure which leads to emotional expression.   Those tender, but at the same time weakly-impulsed
natures, like Fräulein Hertel and young Hanner, if they
escape destruction through the endogenous psychosis,
find the only way out which remains for pronounced
hyperæsthetic cases, in a compromise with real life : a
slight cautious withdrawal into themselves, as into a
capsule, and a retirement into a quiet restrained milieu
which does them no harm.   Such resignation is only
possible to weakly-impulsed natures—and, indeed, these
are very common among schizoids.   The tragedy of
such people as Franz Blau lies in the fact that they have
strong characters, an impulse to emotional expression, to
psychic movement, to seek love and contact with mankind. " More reality ! Music alone does not make me
happy !" And this impulse drives them mercilessly into
all the thorn-bushes on the path of life, thorns for which
their tender hands were never made.   They are always
being wounded anew, always being pricked again.

There is no doubt that the biological background of
the sexual disposition plays a decisive rôle here.   Those
who, like our first patient, remain tied, with childlike

tenderness, to their mother's apron strings, or those who, like Fräulein Hertel, without the need or the capacity for a real love affair, can satisfy themselves in a distant dreamy love for a stranger passing by, to whom they have never spoken a word, can let life stream by them without fights and conflicts, in a kind of twilight satisfaction. I know of people who have carried a quiet erotic obsession round in their hearts for years, and who, all the same, have never become acutely diseased. But men like Franz Blau, in whose schizoid basis some whimsical inheritance has planted a burning, aggressive eroticism, cannot resign themselves, much less actually find happiness in reality. Their lack of moderation, set about with psychæsthetic prickles, kills every beautiful, binding human relation as soon as it makes its appearance.

In schizoids with such strongly marked temperaments, one is able to see particularly well the jerky alternating character of the emotional response. This abrupt, convulsive tossing to and fro, this passionate, contorted, cramped withdrawal into oneself, these loud and sudden outbursts of extreme psychæsthetic emotionality—this is what we call ' pathos '.

Group 2. *Predominantly cold and insensitive temperaments.*
Cold despotic type (moral idiot)

Ernest Katt, a 23-year-old student, persecutes his parents with fanatic hatred, and the most brutal insults ; he calls his father a ' dishonourable lout ', and his mother a whore, threatens to beat them with a riding-whip, and steals and forces money from them whenever he can. Their whole life is made a continual martyrdom, during which they are never, for one moment, free from the danger of bodily harm. His mother has her purse lying before her on the table ; with a nonchalant air, a cigarette in the corner of his mouth, he reaches for the purse, takes out all the house-keeping money, sticks the notes quietly into his pocket, and gives the purse back to her. His father refuses to pay his debts. He takes up a pair of silver spoons, has a careful look at their hall-mark, and puts them in his pocket. He pawns all the movable objects of value in the house, until his demands are acceded to. When he is threatened with the police, he just shrugs his shoulders ; he knows that his father won't make a scandal. He misbehaves himself promiscuously with waitresses and well-educated young ladies, whom he smuggles by night into his room in his parents' house. If anyone is indignant about his morals he merely gives a cold laugh. It is only when he is required to do some work that he becomes quivering with rage ; after such an episode he leaves the room bathed in perspiration.

His studies have gone completely astray ; without having any end in view, he has already made several starts in all the faculties, idled, and then done nothing in the end—philosophy, psychology, æsthetics, all muddled up with one another. He usually sleeps the whole morning away. Eventually he came to the conclusion : I am an exceptional man, the usual mode of life is not suitable for me. Now he wants to be an actor.

Outside his own home he is quite different. He is completely under control, behaves in the most charming manner, passes as a young man of good breeding and social ability, is a great favourite among his comrades wherever he goes, and in good society he plays a certain part as *maître de plaisir*. He is rather fascinating with young ladies, and with many he enters into tender relations. He always wears a monocle, has a surprising weakness for the nobility, and tries to give the impression in his own person of noble descent. " I cannot move in the circle in which my parents live." His political views are ultra-conservative, harsh, and arrogant. Sometimes the sudden whim takes him to play the part of the proletarian, who would have a good mind to ' shoot off ' the whole bourgeoisie.

One day Ernest Katt came to us alone. He had a thin, nervous frame. His face was very long and pale, cold, still, and, as it were, petrified—hardly a gesture. His bearing was rather nonchalant, drooping, aristocratic. He spoke lifelessly, and in an undertone, with no emphasis whatever. Occasionally there came out something stiff or affected in his speech, or else some strange, disconcerting expression. If he speaks for any length of time, the thought processes become quite confused. One has the feeling that his thoughts are escaping him while he is forming the sentence. He cannot be tied down to concrete questions, and he always escapes into general abstractions ; idealistic speeches about personality, views about life, psychology, art, race through his mind, leading nowhere, almost chaotically mixed up, now obliquely joined on to one another, now passed over in unfinished sentences. " I have given up the struggle." " I stand fixed upon a spiritual basis." " Spiritually, I am completely conscious."

There is a coldness of feeling, and a sophistication about his behaviour, that cannot be surpassed. And yet, between-whiles, one catches glimpses of psychic devastation and confusion, with echoes of despair and misery. " Inner hopelessness and conflict," as he says. He has a leaning towards " sport, theatres, and psychology"; only nothing that savours of a livelihood, nothing that " anyone else can do as well." His parents are always getting in the way of the unfolding of his personality. They have only to give him the means which he needs to live in " his sphere ", that is to say, to satisfy his artistic craving to live in a pampered aristocratic milieu. He never gets anywhere. He can never feel himself. It would be far better if he could only creep away. He has " an impulse to express himself, a desire for beauty, for contact with human beings." He writes a great many letters. But all his feeling has died in him. He leads a " purely artificial life "—" in order to squeeze myself forcibly into the social machine, in order to experience myself, in order to gain self-expression." He bursts into a convulsive fit of weeping. " I want humanity, I want society."

He has never had any sense of humour ; he feels that himself, and he has never been able to get over his preoccupation with his own personality. " The world is a stage to me, on which I only play myself." He has never had any friends, and he has no interest in youth. He has never been seriously in love with a woman. He has had a great deal of sexual intercourse, but has always been emotionally cold. " For me it is only a convulsive attempt to get away from myself." Everything else in life is " technique ", " scene-shifting ", a cold external

show, theatrically unreal. He still has left a strong
æsthetic feeling, especially for the drama and music.
Beautiful music " is great fun ".

He plays the part of the interesting, bewitched spirit
of beauty, which hovers over life. Sometimes he will
say suddenly, " I am a sausage."

Earlier in life, Ernest Katt was quite different : a
weak, silent, spoilt child. His father spoke of him as
follows : He was always among the best of the school-
,boys. There was in his character, side by side with a
pronounced conscientiousness, a seriousness beyond his
years, an abnormal solidity and an extraordinary energy
for work. His laconic, joyless, reserved temperament
was even then a cause of anxiety.

For the rest he was a good-natured, tractable, and
lovable young man, and especially gentle to his mother.
The entrance into puberty was delayed ; for a long time
he took not the slightest interest in girls. At this period,
while he was in the top forms at the gymnasium, a remarkable gradual change of his nature set in. He became
shy, very nervous, and remarkably hypochondriacal.
There was a noticeable decrease in his capacity for perseverance and his general mentality. Superficial reading
took the place of concentrated study, and he went in for
vaguely defined philosophizing and unsatisfactory attempts
at poetry. Faustian moodiness set in. His appearance
suffered on that account ; he had to be forced to wash
himself and do his hair. He sat about for hours broody
and stupid. The result of the standard leaving examination was a bitter disappointment of the hopes to which
his earlier efforts had given rise.

At the same time his whole character changed. The
good-natured quiet boy became dissatisfied, morose,
stubborn, and incalculable. He hated his father. He
still remained very affectionate and gentle to his mother,
and also to his sister, until the latter married and died
shortly afterwards of tuberculosis. He then set himself
against his brother-in-law, actuated by obsessional
jealousy, and got it into his head that his parents were
guilty of her death, and he began to persecute even his
mother with almost fanatical hatred. At intervals traces
of the old gentleness came to the surface, and they come

back even now in a spasmodic way. " His love for his mother was the last prop that he had."

It is worth while to glance at the father's family. One of his father's sisters fell a victim at puberty to psychic disorders with a high degree of excitability ; since then she has been excitable, misanthropic, and an affliction to her whole neighbourhood. One of the father's brothers was a remarkably good scholar ; at the ' High School ' he suddenly lost all his energy for work, obtained no employment, became hostile towards his parents, and eventually lived, harmless and professionless, a preposterous eccentric. A nephew of the father (father's sister's son) was not normal, and never achieved anything.

When we come across a case like this, and compare it with the one before, we cannot help asking ourselves : do all these kinds of personality form a biological unity, or only a group of personalities linked together by the possession of a few common characteristics. What has this completely shameless, cold cynic, this brutal, dangerous tyrant over his own parents, to do with those gentle good-natured idealistic creatures whom we have described so far ? Now, of course, we should be the last to say definitely that the schizophrenic group—or the schizoids —must form a biological unity. We are only going into the question as to whether, as critical empirical investigators, we ought to place the dividing line between the individual psychological types exactly at that point where we are most tempted to put it if we follow our feelings.

It is not without a purpose that I have placed the two last cases next to one another. They give us pause to wonder : How is it that the gentle idealist Franz Blau, is the son of a cold despot ? And how is it that the insensitive tyrant Ernest Katt, was as tender and gentle as a lamb when he was a child ? Such is the odd connection in heredity and personality with which we are constantly meeting in the schizophrenic group. We must pay special attention to this connection precisely because it is so unexpected, because investigation alone has shown it us, and because one would never have come upon it by means of speculative psychological deduction—any more than one would suppose, *a priori*, that a mania and a melancholia had any internal relation with one another.

The picture of our patient before puberty corresponds in all its essentials to the chief schizoid pre-psychotic type of sensitive, emotionally-lame, precocious child. What went on in him at puberty was no severe schizophrenic psychosis, but it must certainly be regarded as the biological equivalent of a schizophrenic process, particularly when we take his heredity into consideration. The personality which emerged after that, is, from a strictly theoretical point of view, to be looked on as a post-psychotic personality.

The personality before and after puberty seems as if it had been divided by a gulf. And yet this pubertial change does not signify a break with the former personality, but only a modification of it. It is a typical example of what we mean by the "*displacement of the psychæsthetic proportions*." When we look more closely into the last case, and also into the picture which follows of the brutal cynical despot, we find a number of characteristics which we have noticed in the more sensitive prepsychotics—the pronounced taste for the aristocratic, the tendency to build up a sensitive, artistic musical inner life apart from the rough agitations of ordinary men, and even up to the last, indications of sentimental elective affection for individuals breaking through, and in particular the characteristic clinging to the mother-ideal. Even in this soul, which is already almost icy cold, we find the last tremblings of the same tragic conflict which we saw in our pathetic idealist—the bitterly disappointed "impulse to self-expression, love of beauty, and desire for contact with mankind," the tearful recognition always coming to the fore ; "I lack humanity!" With his ever-diminishing remains of sensibility he still feels, without being able to protect himself, the ceaselessly oncoming process of emotional freezing. "All feeling is dead," he is leading an existence which he calls "a purely artificial life." At intervals he rouses himself convulsively and tries to live violently, to satisfy the cravings of his youth, and to burst away from the iron mould into which he is vanishing. And then he sinks back into

" inner hopelessness and conflict", or joylessly smiling, attempts once again to build up an elegant personality out of the emptiness and the remnants of sensitivity that are left. At the end the tragic grimace : " I am a sausage."

Hölderlin died the spiritual death of a schizophrene more beautifully, but otherwise no differently. His verses, which we quoted above, come again into our minds. He had the more fortunate fate ; he sank, after a short transitional period, into the deep twilight of complete insensitivity. Ernest Katt, on the other hand, has remained standing half-way along the road to katatonia. At first, at any rate ; perhaps permanently. Such schizoids are the most unfortunate, to whom just enough sensitivity remains to enable them to feel how cold and empty they are. If we look at such a frozen emotionless monster genetically and from the inside, then we see quite a different picture from that which appears when we only note down his social behaviour. Then it is that we not only see the family connection between the gentle artist and the brutal despot, but we feel it, too.

The psychæsthetic proportions have been displaced, the centre of gravity of the temperament has passed from the hyperæsthetic over to the anæsthetic pole. The psychic tempo has also experienced a similar derangement : from tenacious, hyper-conscientious pedantry to jerky eccentric caprice. If this latter displacement does not occur with the former, then we do not get the type of the erratic despot we have been dealing with, but that of the pedantic tyrant and cold fanatic, which we shall describe later when we come to such historical figures as Robespierre, Savonarola, and Calvin. Schizoids like Ernest Katt, on the other hand, remind us forcibly of those Neronic figures—those grotesque imperial incarnations of bestiality —with their mixture of jerky capriciousness and trembling rage, of blasé theatricality and cold calculating cruelty. But we still lack biological material which has been sufficiently examined to enable us to decide whether we have here to do with mere external analogies, or with biological connections.

Passionate Insensitive Type

Dr Graber, who has been a practising medical man for over fifty years, has lived for a long time as a widower with a crowd of young children. He comes from a non-conformist family. His father, a gifted man, brought up his children with a rod of iron ; he was very fanatical, a religious enthusiast, and very pedantic. Since the views of the orthodox Baptists did not satisfy him, he founded a more exclusive sect about his own person, over which he had complete control.

Graber himself was also decidedly gifted, he was always at the top of his class in the school, and was very self-conscious. From the time he was at the ' High School ' at the latest, he was noticeable on account of many eccentricities. Then he went to the tropics as a missionary, where, on principle, he always went without a hat, even in the broiling sun. Now he has been living for some time in the country.

After the death of his first wife, a sensitive well-educated woman, about ten years ago, his practice and his home-life began to go to wreck and ruin. For some unintelligible reason he married, soon afterwards, a coarse, completely uneducated person with a doubtful past. The married life which ensued, a chain of outrageous circumstances, had to be brought to a close after a year.

During the war, when he was engaged in quiet military training, he was found one morning on top of his official quarters, where he had castrated himself with an old knife he had picked up. He remarked that he had had to suffer under a strong sexual drive which ran counter to his moral and religious feelings.

His children never loved him. People were always frightened of him, they hid all their thoughts anxiously from him, and had nothing in common with him. He lived isolated in the midst of his family. He was remarkably silent, and hardly spoke a word at meals. Though people saw that he was internally very upset and agitated, *e.g.*, about his practice, no one ever heard a word of what it was that troubled him. But supposing something quite trivial capped the climax, then he suddenly flew into a frenzy of rage, shouted, beat and struck at his children until they were all lying about the floor. He usually seemed depressed, unfriendly, and weighed down, hardly ever in a comfortable frame of mind. Quite recently, on a Monday, the son of his housekeeper came on a visit; this annoyed him, but he hardly said anything about it until the Saturday, when the young man happened to stay a little longer in bed in the morning. Then followed on that Saturday morning quite suddenly and without any explanation, the wildest scene. When the housekeeper came into the room, he screamed at her, " he leaves the house within an hour ! "—repeating this without ceasing until they had hurried the young man off to an inn.

He was singularly unpractical ; his bicycle was always going wrong, and he took an endless time repairing it. And in spite of the fact that his practice had dwindled until it was very small indeed, it occupied him from early to late, because he was always putting himself out unnecessarily about it.

As far as his external appearance went, he was completely indifferent ; his suit was neglected and untidy, his hands dirty. He took no trouble over his food.

He was a mixture of pedantry and caprice. One never knew whether one was doing the right thing. His was economical even to avarice. He held the view that when children are very small they must eat a great deal. He always forced one of his daughters, who was nervous and weakly, to eat enormous helpings. She often was secretly sick from fear of him, and then had to eat again at once, as soon as she came back into the room. At any hour of the day or night he might call his children to do some job in the house or garden.

A man who knew him well writes as follows about him : " In early days he showed indications of a high degree of psychic excitability, he was easily influenced by other people's wills, and he had a tendency to eccentricity in many ways ; at times one would be surprised at his indifference—amounting to complete apathy—even in difficult situations, *e.g.*, when his practice went wrong, and when his financial position became perceptibly more and more tenuous, and then again there would be frenzied outbursts of passionate excitement on the occurrence of small mishaps, and contradiction."

A little time ago he was occupied with the baptism of two of his children who had not yet been baptized according to the Baptist ritual. At that time he was very festive, quite different from his usual gloomy absent-minded self. All the week he wore a black frock-coat, had all the lamps lighted, and at night walked sleepless up and down as if he were expecting someone. In the mornings he read an unwontedly long extract from the Bible, but otherwise he said nothing. On Sunday morning he had all his children drawn up in front of his house. "Anyone who isn't there, never enters my house again." They had to stand there without umbrellas; it was pouring with rain. Then he gave, in military wise, the command to march, and he walked before them himself, without hat or umbrella, in white trousers to the church.

On the day after the morrow, when he was taking a walk with his two unbaptized children, it began to rain. Then the thought came to him: here is water enough for baptism. Immediately, while he prepared them with an instructive address, they had to set out with him, bare-headed and without umbrellas, for a three-hour tramp to the nearest large town, where he delivered them, dripping from head to foot, over to a family of Jews. In this way he considered their baptism as accomplished.

He backed up this behaviour with texts, which occurred to him *en route*: " He did not spare his only begotten son," and " Here are the children whom I have delivered unto the Lord."

This last act was the immediate cause of his being taken into our Institute. Here he was completely changed. No trace of excitability. He displayed the picture of a comfortable worthy gentleman of an incredible peace of spirit. His speech and movement were very slow, and almost ceremonious. He went for walks, played music, and was satisfied to sit in the corner of a sofa and smoke a pipe of tobacco.

That is the picture of Graber's personality, looked at from without. Inside he was harboured, and probably for years, a phantastic schizophrenic system of delusions of a religious nature, which he left behind for me in writing, a detailed scheme, full of ciphers, and symbolic figures ; usually he would not talk about it. During the last few years, two psychotic attacks, lasting for a few weeks, made their appearance, with detailed anamnesia, of which the first had to do with the castration, while the second went back to the time of the baptismal ceremony described above. That he had similar attacks earlier in life is probable, but cannot be proved specifically.

What, now, shall we say of this picture ? If we take away the sensitivity from the account we gave above of Ernest Katt and give it a little more insensitivity, then he will no longer be fundamentally different from Dr Graber. The displacement of the psychæsthetic proportions is here still further in the direction of the anæsthetic pole, and at the same time the whole form of the personality is very coarsened, and crumbled into ruins ; and then the psychic façade, too, which had remained intact with Katt in a kind of deceptive polish, has, in the case of Graber, suffered seriously. We no longer find sensitive artistic feelings, aristocratic manners, social dexterity, and attention paid to personal appearance. The early indications of indifference to personal appearance which we met with in the case of Katt, appear here palpably in the shape of dirt and actual neglect. Even in the former case we saw frenzied rage appearing threateningly from among a few remnants of sensitivity. Here, in Graber's case, we find only brutal passion, and in place of sensitivity a very much coarsened kind of inner hyperæsthesia ; a sulking inner state of excitation, which may relieve itself at any time in senseless outbursts of temper, after the manner of people suffering from severe brain traumata. When there is complete absence of external irritation, there is also complete absence of internal depression, and we are left with the picture of perfect peace and dullness. If the disposition may be described as the living together of dullness and passion, the psychic tempo results from a mixture of pedantry and tenaciousness on the one hand, and unsteadiness, and baroque, jerky capriciousness on the other ; thus we have a junction of the two typical extremes of the schizoid temperament.

Graber is a representative of a particularly large group of temperaments found among average schizoids,

Q

which is perhaps the most common next to the group of the sensitive, emotionally-lamed like Erich Hanner, and which may be found in particular among post-psychotics and congenitally defectives.   Only of course with these sulky-dull creatures the psychic content is far poorer when one is dealing with simple country-folk, and the various sides of their temperaments are less clearly differentiated from one another.   On the whole the Graber type is the limit at which one can still speak of a personality in the face of growing schizophrenic disturbance.   When the displacement has gone still further, we can no longer talk of a post-psychotic personality, but only of a ruin, a schizophrenic idiocy.

In Graber's personality, and, in a still more unified form, in that of his father, traits of the cold fanatic come to the front, characteristics of a man who gazes with passionate tenacity on his idealistic guiding thought (*e.g.*, his Baptist baptismal ceremony), displaying complete emotional coldness towards living men, even towards his own children, whom he maltreats.

Unsteady Loafer ("*Indifference*")

Karl Hanner, a blood relation of Erich Hanner, was from childhood upwards very gifted and very naughty. From the time when he was a student he was regarded as being no longer quite normal mentally.   First he went through a complete theological course, was for a short time in an office, then went over to philology ; for this he used up the last savings of his poverty-stricken family. Before the state examination he was seized with examination fright, suddenly ran away and disappeared to America.

There he sank lower and lower down the social ladder, and finished up in a hopeless position.   He was so clumsy that he could only have taken employment in a factory with machines at the risk of his life.   An attempt to recommend him as a tutor was shattered by his complete nonchalance, his untended, dirty hands, and bad manners. So he was for a long time out of work, and lounged about by himself ; what he lived on, no one knows to this day. All day long he read old books in a public library, and by night he slept in the open air on benches. And yet he needed nothing, he lived like an ascetic, drank nothing, smoked nothing, stole nothing, and did nothing he ought not to have done.

In this condition he was discovered after some time by a young nephew who had emigrated : lean as a skeleton, dirty and disreputable, with his clothes hanging down about his body. He would inquire unconstrainedly of his nephew, how he was getting on, he was always drily amused, swung his stick, and sang student songs, interspersed with Greek and Latin quotations. A complete philosopher and stoic. He was incredibly well-read. He was at home in all philosophical systems. He was not of the opinion that it went ill with him.

His nephew bought him a ticket, gave him some travelling money and a good overcoat, and put him on a steamer in New York. By Bremen he had already sold the coat ; what became of the money, no one knows. Thus he appeared one day, on foot, looking like a wandering labourer, in a tattered suit of clothes, before the door of his old parents' house.

The further history of his life offers nothing new. Long-suffering friends of his youth occasionally got him into some small post. He was of the greatest use in systematic office work. And yet he came and went when he pleased, had shocking manners, would not answer, made cutting remarks, and picked a quarrel with everyone he met. His freedom he valued more highly than anything, and he hardly needed anything to live on. Gold or any good thing never remained long in his hands, he gave away or exchanged everything. Sometimes he would appear uninvited, after years of absence, at the homes of old acquaintances and relatives ; he would run into the room, walk up and down with great strides, his hands behind his back, and say not a word. If he did say anything, it was a sarcastic *bon mot*. He had an old sister with as sharp a tongue as his own. When he came in sight of her, the fiercest quarrels took place. He threatened her with a stick, abused her coarsely, and finally called her a " parson's daughter ". That was the most insulting thing he could say.

I have often seen him—a spindle-shanked little man,

singularly clumsy, stiff and ungraceful in his manner and movement, angular and awkward, when with anyone else. He did not know what to do with himself. Even if they dressed him up in a perfectly good coat, he always looked like a scarecrow. Everything hung about him. He would always be mistaken for a tramp.

As he grew older he became more and more peculiar and more and more neglected ; he was incapable of taking up any employment ; and children used to run after him in the street. He became noticeably confused, dull, and childish, and at an advanced age he died in an asylum.

The schizoid symptom of " Indifference " comes out particularly well in this case, seen through a slightly humorous veneer. The humorousness itself is due to some admixture and is not a schizoid characteristic. What is fundamental in such loiterers is that they are rather dull than cold emotionally, and rather incalculably capricious than pedantic. They are fairly good-natured, but incorrigible. The incapacity for orientation to reality, and the leaning towards the abstract and metaphysical comes out very clearly in our instance. He links up on one side with the gifted restless wanderers like the poet Platen, and on the other side with the army of harmless weak-minded tramps and loafers.

CHAPTER XII

AVERAGE MEN : CYCLOTHYMES AND SCHIZOTHYMES

At this point we shall relinquish our position on the boundary of psychiatristic research. It is only when we have boldly followed up the notions which we have so far obtained into the realm of normal psychology, that the problem of the constitution will unroll itself to its fullest extent. With this advance into normal psychology we are not making a jump, but, as we spin out the threads which connect physique and psychic disposition, passing step by step from the psychotic through all the variants of psychopathic personality, and as, in the process, we leave farther and farther behind the serious psychic disturbances which were the point from which our investigation started, we find ourselves, unexpectedly, in the midst of healthy humanity, where no face is strange. We recognize as normal familiar manifestations those same characteristics which we came across before in a distorted form. We find the same type of face, the same physical peculiarities, and we find that behind the same external architecture dwell the same psychic impulses. The same disposition works here as the sensitive, delicate, regulative mechanism of the healthy psychic inhibitive processes, which there breaks violently through the equilibrium, rushes on to its own destruction, and ruins the whole psychic structure.

In this way we shall best escape from the narrowness of the psychiatristic outlook. We shall no longer look at the world through asylum spectacles, trying at every turn to pick out minute peculiarities and abnormal traits from the healthy personality, but we shall be able to stand free in a wider circle, we shall learn to make a correct valuation and analysis of health, or better, of the biological norm as such, and from this wider circle we shall form a better judgment of the true proportions of the smaller group of the mentally diseased. We shall no longer look on certain types of personality as psychopathic abortive forms of certain psychoses, but vice versa, certain psychoses will figure as caricatures of certain normal types of personality. The psychoses are thus only rare exaggerated editions of large and wide-spread groups of healthy constitutions.

For this reason it is advisable to change the nomenclature also. We call the members of that large constitution-class from which the schizophrenes are recruited, " *schizothymes* ", and those corresponding to the circular psychotics are called " *cyclothymes* ".[1] One may for convenience call the transitional stages between illness and health, or the abortive pathological forms, " schizoid " and " cycloid ", as we have already done. We must, accordingly, make it clear from the outset, that the notions " schizothyme " and " cyclothyme " have nothing to do with the question : pathological or healthy ; but that they are inclusive terms for large general bio-types, which include the great mass of healthy individuals with the few cases of corresponding psychoses which are scattered among them. The words do not indicate that the majority of schizothymes must have psychic clefts, and that the majority of cyclothymes must have periodical emotional disturbances ; we are only using for the sake of convenience a designation for the healthy corresponding to that which is already applied to psychopaths of the same type.

The method employed for the following investigation was as follows : Out of a few hundred healthy persons, who were very well known to me as regards both their bodily and psychic natures, I picked out about 150 whose physique was characterized by significant and unmistakable marks of the asthenic, athletic, or pyknic types.[2] Of the majority I possess photographs. Corresponding, then, to the schizophrene group, were found

---

[1] To have two expressions for lighter and more severe degrees of the same disturbance, " Circular " and " Cyclothyme ", as is the case at present, is a verbal luxury, which seems no longer compatible with scientific progress. Instead, therefore, of inventing a third expression, we take the word " Cyclothyme " to indicate the general constitution, a function which it admirably fulfils.

[2] Severe dysplasias of the physique play a very small rôle among normal healthy individuals, and, as we shall see later, among geniuses. For this reason we make no special mention of them.

people with long noses, angular profiles, abnormally high
middle faces, long-oval and egg-shaped, narrow facial
contours, and figures which were either thin and slender,
or wiry and lanky, or having marked muscular and bony
relief ; over against these we have in the circular group
the well-known pyknic figures, with their full smooth faces,
having broad, shield-shaped or five-cornered contours and
a harmonious construction of the profile, their short necks,
rounded limbs, and characteristic tendency to fatness.

Thus there emerged two large classes of temperament,
of which the one is encased in all essentials in the pyknic
form, while the other has a physique corresponding to
the schizophrene group ; here, again, there is also a small
number of partial or complete crossings.

The class of temperaments which have been found to
predominate among pyknics may be subdivided into the
following minor classes, which are joined to one another
by a broad band of transitional groups, and are often
present in the same individual as different phases or
aspects of his nature ; we are only describing here the
male representatives of the groups, as they are met with
often enough when they are young among students, or
later on in the world of business ; it is quite easy to fill
in the female variations for oneself.

1. *The Gay Chatter-box*

One hears them from afar off ; they are always in the
vanguard, when everything is going well and smoothly ;
in every conversation they are there with their loud
remarks, and wherever there is festivity on hand, there
they may be found pouring out some long speech, or
engineering some noisy joke. They like play and drink
more than deep thought or severe dangerous hardships.
They are a lively fresh element which swims merrily
about over the surface without any ambitions ; we like
to see them, they are likable, comfortable, mobile, good-
natured, though sometimes tiresome on account of their
lack of tact and sensibility, on account of their blustering
heartiness, naïve egoism, and wearying propensity for
chattering.

2. *The Quiet Humorist*

They sit and watch and do not say much. They only
need warmth. Here and there they make some superb
comment. They are born story-tellers ; in their mouths
the simplest occurrence becomes homely, delightful, and
droll. They speak broadly, comfortably, and without
any artificial phrases. They light up in society and
when there is activity going forward, becoming lively,
witty, resolute, and drastic. They are satisfied with the
world, and have a natural good-will towards humanity,
especially children ; only unkindness and " principles " are
contrary to their nature. They are firm friends, they live
and let live, and they know exactly how to handle men ;
they like honesty and homeliness better than anything else.

3. *The Silent Good-tempered Man*

He is a good fellow, a bit phlegmatic, he has a heart.
He moves with caution, and does not like to commit
himself. He seems sympathetic, without his saying
anything. He is on good terms and at peace with all
mankind. He has his permanent club and his evening
when he plays at nine-pins. When he can manage it he likes
to withdraw to the country in some small post, in which
he does his work faithfully and conscientiously. His duties
do not weigh lightly upon him, and he has too little self-
confidence. He does not accomplish very much for himself.

If we turn to the special attitudes to life, in business,
and in general dealings with their fellow-creatures, which
are characteristic of such temperaments in middle age,
we find, besides those which we have already mentioned,
two large main groups, which one can take either as
types *sui generis*, or as merely developmental phases or
later stages of the temperaments with which we have
already dealt, or of their transitional forms.

4. *The Happy Enjoyer of Life*

This type develops particularly well where the intelligence which goes with the temperament in question is

meagre, and the spiritual education not very far advanced. It is found, that is to say, among simple folk, and also among educated persons who are of peasant descent. In the upper strata of society it is tinged with a more æsthetic feeling for the " art of life ", without losing its broad material basis. But the type is most frequently incarnated in the middle-class man who has his corner at the inn, where he is as it were a reproduction of the humorist and the good-tempered man (types 2 and 3) on a trivial scale. Here again in the foreground is the tendency to philanthropic good-nature, the liking for a jolly joke without much thought or depth in it, but along with this goes a general love of comfort, an undisguised preference for all that is material, for what can be appreciated by the senses, and for such concrete good things of life as lie nearest to hand. In Schwabia these people are called " Vesperer " [afternoon-tea-ers], inasmuch as their lives are made up of as many little daintily prepared " between-meals " as possible, with suitable drinks to go with them, for which reason the pyknic physical tendencies which have characterized them from childhood, emerge into full bloom.[1] Their business activities form a modest appendix to their main occupations.

Mörike in a short comic poem has described a pyknic-cyclothymic type which closely resembles this one as " Summer-waist-coats ":

> Dear cousin! He is one
> Of those *friendly creatures*,
> *To whom I give the name of summer-waist-coats.*
> For they really have a something
> Like sunshine in their being.
> They are the worldly officials,
> Financiers and auditors,
> Or financial administrators,
> Or even sometimes lords of merchandise,
> By no means *petit maîtres*
> They often have fat round bellies,
> And the country of their birth is Schwabia.

---

[1] We would call to mind again at this juncture that the diagnosis of the pyknic type is not merely made from the unreliable symptom of layers of fat, but from the general build of the skeleton. An athletic or an asthenic who has been fattened by artificial over-feeding always presents an appearance quite different from that of the corpulent pyknic.

> Recently upon a journey
> I met a summer-waist-coat
> Posting off to Besighein
> And we took a meal together.
> First we had a little soup
> With red crayfish swimming in it,
> Some beef with mustard from the French,
> And lovely little radishes,
> And with it we had veg. and much besides:
> Snippets from the latest papers,
> And that at many places
> Yesterday the rain came down in sheets.
> And while he chatters on, the good old fellow
> Pulls a little silver box from out his pocket
> So that he can pick his teeth a bit,
> And finally he fills his meerschaum pipe
> To help along the drinking of his coffee,
> And smoking thus he punctuates his speech
> With a glance out of the window for the horses.
>
> And as I looked upon him from behind
> I fell to thinking : ' Ah, that such as these,
> These dear, bright, smiling summer-waist-coats,
> These comfortable pourers-out of comfort,
> Eventually must die the death of all men.'

The expression " summer-waist-coat " delightfully combines the suggestion of the pyknic physical appearance with that of the pyknic qualities of sunnyness and comfortableness. The poem contains, in a humorously veiled and indirect character sketch, a whole series of temperamental peculiarities which characterize the less gifted average cyclothyme of moderate emotionality : goodheartedness, sunny-friendliness, knack of getting on easily with people, sociability, with a tendency to love of comfort, an emotional restfulness, and an absence of hastiness and nervousness ; and behind it all is concealed a certain Philistine quality, a satisfaction with the more modest pleasures of life and the most banal topics of conversation, a life of superfluous epic breadth and prolixity, a lack of tension, of pathos and idealism, and of high purpose.

5. *The Energetic Practical Man*

This is a mid-type, which unites the fresh mobile liveliness of type 1 with the faithfulness to duty and sound understanding of men of types 2 and 3. They are people who have their hearts in the right place, and of whom one can make use whenever one is in need. They are always sitting on committees, always overburdened with work, and enjoy being overburdened. They work untiringly. They always like to have a great deal to do, and above all a great many little jobs, and occasionally something new, and they have a pronounced tendency to concrete practical activities : medicine, politics, social welfare. Whatever they do has hands and feet ; they move skilfully, are prepared to compromise, but yet are resolute ; they speak out their opinion once and for all, and yet are ever in a good temper. A few of them are ambitious, but more have a sure comfortable feeling of their own value, finding their worth in themselves, and being less interested in rank and distinction than in the refreshing feeling of activity. They do not care for abnormal exalted enthusiasm and loud idealistic ardour.

This type tends towards the hypomanic side, flowing over into the quicksilver temperament of the ever dilettante Jack-of-all-trades. What is called in common speech a " Pasha "—people who govern their environment with a certain naïve magnificence of manner, and get all the practical advantages they can out of it—is very closely related to this type, and there is a continuous series leading over to the corresponding schizothymic group of cold masterful men and egoists.

Thus we come to the end of the series of cyclothymic temperaments, having contented ourselves with portraying directly from life only a few of the most significant personalities of this type. We believe ourselves to have been of more service to the reader in this way, than if we had enumerated every single peculiarity and all the many mixtures and shades which lie between the types we have taken. We gave up such an idea for the sake of clear delineation as opposed to completeness, and we only add that for the same reason we have picked on these individual types after a careful comparison of all the others in respect of their fundamental characteristics.

We may now proceed to the pictures of those men of everyday life who in their physique are most like the schizophrenes.

1. *The Polite Sensitive Man*

His whole nervous system is tender ; he flies from all that is common ; he takes an æsthetic interest in tea, and is affected by the scent of the hay. In society he prefers a carefully chosen circle. *Odi profanum vulgus.* Painful care is lavished on tending his body. Such men may easily be upset by a bad ironing-crease, they cannot get over æsthetic details, and they have a tendency to little vanities, and social pedantries. They like to cultivate their own personalities, and observe their own psychic refinements. They are very subject to subtle changes of mood and depressions. They are readily put out, and are ' touchy ' in personal relations, they can easily be deeply wounded without anyone's knowing it, one word is sufficient to make them fundamentally colder in their feeling towards their old friends. They have no moderate tones. They are either sentimentally ecstatic or bitingly cool and abruptly retiring. Their feeling for art is delicate and civilized and there is a tendency to decadence. Their taste is magnetically drawn in the direction of polite social circles. Theirs is not a straightforward, robust, vigorous temperament, with strong natural roots ; their inner feelings are frequently rather broken up, internally insecure ; they cast a confused and sometimes ironical light, and when expressed they are either vague or logically formal. In the faintly toned milieu where they feel at home, they are charming, lovable, sensitive, obliging, attentive, tenderly sympathetic, and all behind a hardly perceptible atmosphere of distance. They are capable of a deeply intimate feeling for very few of the people who stand near to them. They have pure and lofty characters, and a refined charm, and their only fault is their violent antipathies towards individual objects.

This valuable type passes on the degenerative side, without a break, over into the region of the blasé and decadent, of those people who are pretentious outside and hollow within, who over-indulge their emotions and

PLATE 27

GOTTFRIED KELLER
Etching by Stauffer-Bern
(By permission of the Kunsthandlung Amsler u. Ruthardt, Berlin)
Cf. also the portrait by A. Böcklin, 1889, in G. Keller, *Gesammelte Gedichte* Stuttgart

[*face p.* 220

are yet emotionally-lame inside, the empty society
marionettes off the top shelf, the æsthetes, and the cold
" intellectuals ".

2. *The World-hostile Idealist*

They build themselves apart a kingdom of philosophical
ideas. They labour at the construction of certain favourite
ideals, or they have a " mission " which is undertaken
with sacrifice. They prefer the abstract, the airy, or lonely
nature. In their rare dealings with mankind they suffer
from shyness, awkward unskilfulness and stiff formality ;
only with a few very old friends are they intimate, where
" the idea " can be discoursed of with warmth and understanding sympathy. Their internal disposition varies
between abnormally exaggerated self-confidence and a
feeling of inferiority which springs from their insecurity
in the face of real life. Their contempt for the decorations
and external comforts of life may reach a deplorable
stage of asceticism, or even serious neglect. In many
instances the outer man is sharply sarcastic, nervously
irritable or sulkily retiring, others again have something
touching and even great in their childlike apartness from
the world, their truly stoic freedom from all ordinary
requirements, and their self-abnegation. Yet others are
always prepared to stand up in public for their convictions, to hold forth on them, and collect disciples
about them.

Side by side with this rather more intellectual aspect,
there is often to be found a closely related moral idealism
and rigour, which refuses all compromise with the possibilities of everyday life, which upholds abstract, *a priori*,
principles of virtue, now enthusiastically, with the sweeping
exaggerated zeal of one " called ", now with pharisaic self-
satisfaction, now with unflinching devotion to a rule of life
which gradually turns into brazen inflexibility.

We have already mentioned that under favourable
conditions this type may produce well-developed, fine
characters with through-going moral energy, greatness,
and purity of outlook.

3. *Cold Masterful Natures and Egoists*

A few energetic figures of officers and officials are to be found in this group. Insensitive to danger, rigid, cold, and born to rule. Their sphere of interest is sharply circumscribed and narrow, they have a pronounced consciousness of their calling and position. They are always very correct in their attitudes and they have an exaggerated notion of honour. Their self-love may easily be quickly and lastingly wounded ; they are subject to overwhelming momentary depressions when touched on any tender spot (" snappy " is the students' inimitable description of this kind of affective behaviour). They find it hard to forgive. When there is an open struggle for right and equity they are decisive and take sides. It is always " either—or " for them. When anyone thinks differently from them, particularly in political matters, they always look on him as a vulgar fellow. To their own kind they are polite and correct. Of other callings they have no understanding, but they may easily be impressed by productivity. They feel at home in an atmosphere of commands, and stiff bureaucratic discipline, but they do not understand how to handle individual men. Their passion for rights and discipline borders on stupidity and painful misanthropic coldness. In other milieux we find the same men again, hard, avaricious, inflexibly obstinate, power-seeking landed proprietors, and domestic tyrants.

A variant of this type may be found particularly in the official walk of life ; he is not stiff and rigid, but rather coldly clever, mildly ironical, tractable, unscrupulous, and cautious, temperate through and through, with a pettifogging, sharp, formal intellect, ambitious, successful, and somewhat of an intriguer.

4. *The Emotionally Dry and Lame*

No wit and no fire. Their laugh is weak ; they are oppressed into silence. They have ungainly gestures. They are astonishingly silent, almost dumb, but a few are dully babbling. Partly friendly, and partly misanthropic. Dry. Constitutionally subaltern. Or quiet fools. Or else moss-grown members of the underworld, full of hypochondriacal whimsies.

It is easily seen that these types, picked as they are from among average healthy men on the basis of their physique, differ, as far as their most pronounced representatives go, in no fundamental respect from those whose portraits were drawn above with the help of psychiatristic pathology. Both signposts, physique as well as endogenous psychosis, point more or less to the same goal in the investigation of general human characterology; they correct and complete one another. By combining both methods it is quite possible to set the general psychological theory of temperaments on a firm basis.

CHAPTER XIII

GENIUSES

GIFTED individuals are so rare that it is impossible to submit them to serial statistic investigation, but, for that very reason, the class is more productive of well-defined, characteristic, individual personalities. In this chapter we intend, not to point out anything fundamentally new, but to apply the notions which we have obtained after investigating a great mass of material to a few great personalities, bringing out still more finely discriminated particular traits. We hope, later on, to be able to publish the individual analyses of certain geniuses, of which we have already made use in many respects in the last chapters, and therefore we only give here a compressed general account. Our method was first to investigate the individual psychology of such highly-gifted persons as later fell victims to circular or schizophrenic psychoses, or came from families which were disposed in that direction. After that, with the additional help of physical investigation,[1] a larger number of geniuses could be differentiated, or rather, the groups which had already been established by means of comparative psychology could be confirmed and completed by a glance at their physique.

[1] It must be mentioned with regard to the illustrations in this section, that we have deliberately chosen less known and more out of the way pictures, which for that reason are from a historico-critical standpoint in some ways not the most suitable for comparison, and not the best authenticated. The portraits on which our demonstration is based are historically so established, well known, and easily obtainable that there is no need for them to be reproduced. We have also ignored the problems of nationality and race, on purpose, because so far, among European peoples, more or less analogous relations have emerged from a comparison of portraits and individual psychologies. Of course it would be perfectly easy to fill out the whole of this chapter by referring only to German personalities.—We are not blind to the important part, which, besides the individual psychology of the great leaders, has been played by the spirit of the age and the people, but we have here purposely set it on one side.

When we make use of a combination of all methods—comparative individual psychology, the investigation of psycho - pathological geniuses, and a comparison of physiques—then we shall arrive at groups which are fairly well established empirically.

First and foremost is this true of poets and authors, who lend themselves best to individual psychological investigation in every direction. Here we have material made up of pictures and biographical data which is at once rich and easily get-at-able, here, above all, we have the self-revelation of the individual temperament in the whole mass of poetical output, an objective psychological document of incredible value, and of such a nature that it cannot be obtained from any other kind of genius. For this reason we shall give a more detailed treatment of poetry, because such objective indications of temperament help us to a scientific picture of the general mode of feeling of highly-gifted personalities, even in those respects in which they are not artistically active.

Cyclothymic Artistic Temperament

Corresponding to the cyclothymic temperament the two groups of Realists and Humorists stand out quite unmistakably. In order to indicate the type in its most important variations we mention the following names (only having regard to their temperaments, and not to their greater or less spiritual significance) : Luther, Lieselotte von der Pfalz, Goethe's mother, Gottfried Keller, Jeremias Gotthelf, Fritz Reuter, Hermann Kurz, Heinrich Seidel.

All the personalities which we have named have either a typical pyknic physique, or else outstanding pyknic components. The following points are to be noted from the psychiatristic point of view. Hermann Kurz was a circular with typical manic fits ; Fritz Reuter suffered from periodical depressions, of a partially dipsomaniac, and partially manic - depressive symptom - colouring ; Goethe's mother, herself a healthy hypomanic, had a daughter who suffered from occasional melancholia, and a son, the poet, who had slight periodic mental disturbances ; Luther had severe, and to a certain extent

P

endogenous, emotional disturbances, and certain attacks of melancholia of a definitely pathological nature, with striking bodily symptoms accompanying them (*e.g.*, in 1527) ; the maternal family of Gottfried Keller was apparently manic-depressive.

In the group of realists and humorists, therefore, we find numerous biological connections on the one side with the pyknic physique, and on the other side with the manic-depressive class, in the widest sense of the word.

The realists and humorists of the cyclothymic type of temperament are so closely linked together, that it is hardly possible to separate them out into two groups. The works of the realists, like Gottfried Keller, Jeremias Gotthelf and Hermann Kurz are sprinkled through and through with humorous touches, while, on the other hand, in the humorists, like Fritz Reuter, the tendency to broad, drastic, realistic representation makes up a large part of their natures ; from such psychological documents as the letters of Lieselotte or Goethe's mother it is impossible to make up one's mind whether to reckon them among the realists or among the humorists. It is particularly significant that where we have the exposition of reality without humour, as with the naturalists, or clever, witty epigrams without any affectionate painting of the truth, as with the Heine-Voltaire group, the psychic and physical stigmata of the cyclothymic constitution is very much modified or else vanishes completely.

Now what marks out the realists and humorists as a literary group, is at bottom the same collection of characteristics which we have already underlined as being essential to the cycloids and cyclothymes : homely humanity and naturalness, true-hearted nobility, the affirmative attitude to life, love for all things that are, because they are as they are, but especially for mankind itself, and its homeliest manifestations, sound understanding of human beings, and a home-made moral judgment which values virtue, but is still able to laugh good-naturedly at the grossest scamp. They have a relieving laugh, and a relieving anger. They have the capacity to give anyone a good dressing down, but they are incapable of bitterness and sharp irony.

One significant literary characteristic of our group is

PLATE 28

TORQUATO TASSO
Engraving by P. Caronni, after the drawing by Longhi
From Scherr, *Geschichte der Weltliteratur*

face p. 226

that on an average there is very little lyric and dramatic talent, but on the other hand, there is a preferential tendency to unstylized prose and discursive epic narration. The material-impulse, to use Schiller's terminology, outweighs the form-impulse. With the cyclothymes, the poetical beauty lies in the superb colouring, richness, and emotional warmth of individual descriptions, and not in the construction. (" Der Grüne Heinrich " is a typical example.) Herein lies their strength and their weakness. Beside a cyclothymic-realistic narrative, the novel of a schizothyme is colourless, but on the other hand, if one measures the cyclothymic method of narration by schizothymic standards it is formless. There is little sifting of the important and unimportant, there is no restraint, there is lack of form and construction, of excitement, of the penetrating delineation of problems, of dramatic design, of pathos, and of grandeur. A quality of good-humoured home-made " *Banausentum* " comes ever clearer to the surface the more we descend in the cyclothymic-realistic temperamental middle-region from the important figures to the region of more mediocre activities.

In individual cases we find again the diathetic variation from the hypomanic to the meditative, while simple melancholic types are hardly to be found among productive men, even apart from poets. At the extreme hypermanic pole stands the epistolary style of Lieselotte with its bubbling humorous naturalness, in its crude, unbridled robustness often overstepping the bounds of decency and good taste. Goethe's mother, quieter, sunnily hypomanic, appears in her letters as a milder, refined edition of Lieselotte. In Luther too a simple naturalness is to be observed, a robust vitality, a tendency to quick bursts of laughter and outspoken abuse, and his literary productions betray a lack of form and system. The picturesque, sensuous, country speech reaches its highest point in his works. All three are born letter-writers and anecdotists with a direct and untutored feeling for their mother-tongue ; no ingenious seeking after effect, no thought of dignity or the structure of sentences. So long as they are in a good humour, every word has a droll, lively quality in their mouths, and one story tumbles out after another.

At the other end of the cyclothymic series stand the

meditative artists of the Gottfried Keller type [1] (Goethe, too, as regards the cyclothymic aspect of his temperament, had much of this characteristic) who accept things as they are, who gaze lovingly about them, poke and touch, collect untiringly, and create out of their store a friendly, accurate representation, in natural clear colours, word for word and picture for picture like the original.

A certain preference for simple men, and for minute delineation on a large scale is unmistakable in Gottfried Keller, and it is even more evident in the humble, quietly contented pleasures of Seidel's " *Leberecht Hühnchen* " ,figures, or the home-spun honesty of Gotthelf's peasantry.

The personalities we have described must serve us as the most typical group of the cyclothymic poetic temperament. Now for the variations and border-line cases. We may indicate a very closely related group with the names of J. P. Hebel and Wilhelm Busch. [2] They are both of very mixed physique ; in Hebel the pyknic quality comes out particularly clearly (especially in the frontal view of his face), while it comes out fairly distinctly in Busch in the pictures of him in advanced years. In their literary styles they both show the typical realistic, humorous, philanthropic, smiling emotional warmth. But in both the epic prolixity and formlessness are lacking. They have on the contrary a pronounced flair for what is fundamental, and a feeling for the compression of their matter into a few characteristic strokes of the pen, while Busch has also a sense for polished verse form. Their style has an anecdotal or epigrammatic snap, it is taut, pointed and finished, with graceful phrases. [3] In Busch it is important to notice, from a diagnostic point of view, a clear tendency to philosophic reflexion, and a dash of eccentricity.

They, therefore, may be regarded as transition-forms

---

[1] We cannot here go further into the schizoid streaks in Gottfried Keller's temperament.

[2] The humorist Busch also had circular depressive emotional disturbances.

[3] The " graceful " must on no account be confused with the hypomanic. The pure hypomanic individual is broad, luxuriant, vigorous, but certainly not graceful. The psychically graceful individuals whom I know personally have a prevailingly asthenic physique, but of course it is true that there are occasionally periodic-hypomanic traits to be seen. It is therefore probable that gracefulness manifests an alloy of hypomanic tendencies and hyperæsthetic acuteness.

between the real cyclothymes with their broad anecdotal humour after the manner of Fritz Reuter, and the group of wits, sarcastics, ironists and satirists whose nature is indicated by the names, Heine, Voltaire, Frederick the Great, Nietzsche. This group belongs quite decidedly to the schizothymic side. Their physique points very definitely in that direction in the case of the first three, and to a certain extent in the case of Nietzsche (skull sharply curving inwards at the base, excessive growth of beard and brows, just as in the case of the abnormally developed tower-skull, Chapter V). In Heine and Frederick the Great we still find traits which are at least closely related to cyclothymic humour. For the rest, however, one can see clearly the connection of the witty-ironists with the schizothymic group in their individual psychological affinities ; in Heine we find romantic sentimentality, in Voltaire a tragic quality, and in old Fritz a distrustful hostility towards mankind, and at bottom a cuttingly cold personality. Nietzsche may very well stand as the prototype of humourless brilliance. A brilliant idea is never with him the fruit of enjoyment, but always of bitterness. In the construction of his personality he is a classic example of a psychæsthetic with the typical mixture of tender sensitivity and cold consciousness of superiority. We cannot go any further into the psychological analysis of this witty-ironical group here, we will only call attention to the fact that its essential connection with the schizothymic mode of feeling comes on the witty side from the antithetical tension, and the abnormal refinement of the feelings, and on the ironic-sarcastic side, from the autistic, misanthropic, hyperæsthetic affective attitude. To that extent the empirically established biological connection with the schizothymic temperaments is also explicable. We can look on the witty-ironical class as an exact schizothymic correlate to the cyclothymic humorous group.

In the kindly humorous authors who show strong indications of ' sentimentality ' as Schiller uses this word in his æsthetic doctrine, that is, for example, of self-conscious childishness, contemplation, pathos, and mournful affectivity, the physiques are very mixed ; as in the case of M. Claudius and Jean Paul (the latter, however, with

striking pyknic components). In Raabe, with his tendency to reflexion and pathos, the anatomy of the face is
prevailingly that of a schizothyme. One must be carefully on the lookout for all such varieties and partial
components, even though nothing decisive can be said
about them from the few examples we have at our disposal.

Among the variations of poetic realism, we find a
rarer form, which is not very warm-hearted, but rather
coldly and drily observant, and with a slight touch of
sarcasm in its humour ; that is more or less what
Fontanes is like. In many individual psychological
traits he comes near the cyclothymic group, and physically
there is much that is pyknic about him. Critics, too,
with the fresh temperamental naturalness, the humour,
and the sound understanding of human nature of Lessing
and Fr. Th. Vischer, are, in spite of much admixture,
closely related to the cyclothymic group, in which direction
their physiques also seem to point. Where, on the other
hand, the realism is pronouncedly bitter and humourless,
we come again very near to the schizothymic class both
psychologically and as regards physique as well, as in the
case of Droste-Hülshoff (typical asthenic physique) where
the realism is mixed with a strong flavour of romanticism
and love of the loneliness of nature, or in the case of
Hebbel, where it is modified by a torturing preoccupation
with the problematic and by a tragic tone in his feeling.

But the best transitional form in the direction of the
schizothymic class is displayed by the type which is usually
called ' Naturalism '. Realistic observation is still present
in many respects, but it is no longer rooted in quiet contemplation, in a simple directness which goes out to meet
the object, in a generous love of everything that exists,
or even in humour ; on the contrary it springs from
pathos, from the tendency to passionate discord, to a
negational attitude culminating in a caricature which is
a subjective distortion of the truth—an art which does
not spring from warm diathetic middle-tones, but from
a harsh psychæsthetic antithesis. We can here build a
series stretching from the cyclothymes over to the schizothymes, beginning with, say, Zola with his marked propensity for pure observation, breadth, and epic objectivity,
passing through Ibsen and Gerhard Hauptmann and leading

to Strindberg and Tolstoi, becoming more and more dramatic, antithetical, and subjective and ending finally among the mystics, transcendentalists, direct deniers of the truth, and the class of psychæsthetic autists and pronounced schizoids, to which Tolstoi was very nearly related, and of which Strindberg was a member. When one makes a comparison of portraits from Zola to Tolstoi one can follow a correlative transition from the more pyknic countenances to the long faces of the schizothymes.

Schizothymic Artistic Temperament

Schiller, in his essays on æsthetics and particularly in his differentiation of " naïve " and " sentimental " poetry, of " material-impulse " and " form-impulse ", has worked out with sure intuition and the use of precise concepts, a number of characteristics which divide the cyclothymic and the schizothymic artistic temperaments from one another. On the whole biological investigation affords a superb confirmation of his æsthetic analyses, which only require to be rectified in a few points, such as, for example, his classification of the comic (where Schiller, being to all intents and purposes a schizothyme, is characteristically lacking in full capacity for sympathy). However we had better not turn, as he does, to the highest peaks for our examples, because the most complete geniuses, like Goethe, Shakespeare, or Rousseau, are usually complex constructs and syntheses, and are inferior in constitutional purity to many of the smaller fry.

To indicate the most typical group of schizothymic poetic temperaments, we mention the following names : Schiller, Körner, Uhland ; Tasso, Hölderlin, Novalis ; Platen.

They represent in essentials the three groups of ' pathetics', romantics, and formal stylists, with a common tendency to the idealistic in form and content.

The physique of the above-mentioned artists is unmistakably on the schizothymic side. They are all lanky, or thin and meagre. Uhland, Tasso, Novalis, and Platen [1] have fine examples of the angular profile.

---

[1] The ubiquitous outline drawing of Platen's face is highly stylized and useless. When dealing with portraits it should be a rule to compare all the known pictures at different ages and in various artistic styles,

Körner, in those pictures which do not idealize him, is of an altogether asthenic type, with a long nose and hypoplastic pointed chin. Schiller's strikingly tall meagre appearance, with the abnormally long limbs, tender skin, steep oval face with its disproportionate length of middle face and chin, and great sharp-hooked nose, is well known.

As far as psycho-pathology goes, Hölderlin was a victim, and probably Tasso too, of schizophrenic psychosis ; Platen had perverse impulses and was a pronounced schizoid psychopath ; Schiller and Novalis died of tuberculosis, of the constitutional connection of which with the schizophrenic group we have already spoken.

The pathetics represent the more highly-coloured, impulsive, and active natures, while the romantics include rather the psychæsthetic types, the tender, feminine, retiring individuals of the schizothymic group. Tragic pathos is the sign of the battle of the autistic soul with reality, elegiac romanticism is its flight from it. Whatever else may be said about it has already been said in the section on the schizoid personalities. Pathos and tender sentimentality, while superficially opposed to one another, have the most intimate connection from the individual-psychological point of view. The heroic and the idyllic are complementary schizothymic moods. The middle-tones—the quiet, simple acceptance and enjoyment of life—fall right outside the hyperæsthetic temperament. The heroic and the idyllic are both extreme, tense moods,

otherwise we shall run the risk of serious errors. The portraits of well-known masters are not always the best ; for example, under the bold free strokes of Dürer, the schizothymes easily come out too rounded in appearance ; while on the other hand the often very clumsy popular wood-cuts from the time of the Reformation frequently show a strong feeling for what is anatomically characteristic. Portraits from the German classic-romantic period are to be evaluated with the greatest care, and as far as possible compared with verbal delineation. The tendency to idealization at the expense of what is anatomically correct is very great at this time. Photographs are on an average more reliable than paintings, yet even here the lighting and the effect of perspective may often lead one astray. On the whole, however, by comparing a series of portraits of famous men it is possible to arrive at some data which can be used for scientific purposes ; and after all, many have their temperaments so marked upon their faces and physique, that even the worst portrait cannot blur them. This chapter is based on a detailed comparison of hundreds of pictures of famous men, taken from all the civilized peoples of Europe.

between which the emotion jumps, alternating from one to the other. The schizothymic soul, worn out by the noisy drama of the heroic battle, suddenly feels the need for something diametrically opposed, for tearful tenderness, and dreamy bucolic stillness. In Schiller's temperament, which is distinguished for its tenacity, its overwhelming energy, and its amazing courage, the heroic gestures are again and again interrupted by fits of tenderness. He has no great political drama without a few sentimental love scenes here and there, which never have the quality of natural passion as is the case with cyclothymes, but always have a sentimentally exaggerated character. Exactly the same mood-colouring comes into all these interludes, whether he is describing Karl and Amalia, or Max and Thekla, or Marie Stuart and the beauty of nature. Or look at Schiller's lyrical poetry, where to our astonishment we find the Hercules of idealistic apotheosis sitting by a fountain like a Rousseau shepherd, looking after his lambs, and twining a wreath of flowers.

In Rousseau himself the pathetic and idyllic elements were fairly evenly balanced. But even in such a case as Hölderlin, where the idyllic, romantic tenderness, and the tendency to withdrawal into himself, has decidedly the upper hand, we still hear the restrained pathos, or even the loud tragic passion of the heroic youth Hyperion, breaking through over and over again.

The heroic and idyllic are as closely bound up with one another on the psychæsthetic temperamental scale as the realistic and the humorous are with regard to diathetic proportions.

Just as among cyclothymics there is a preponderance of diffuse, objective, prose narration, so with the schizothymes we find a decided preference for the lyric and the drama. This is an exceedingly important characteristic which is reflected by the collected works of both groups of poets with the precision of a legal document, or a scientific experiment. With the cyclothymes we find an objective, calm, self-identification with the external world. The poet in autobiography (" Grüner Heinrich" " Ut mine Festungstid ") displays himself with a smile, an object among objects, modelled with the same affectionate touch, with the same regard for the facts, and on the same scale of dimension as the rest of his figures. But with the schizothyme there is always present the autistic contrast : here am I, and there is the world. The ' I ' either occupies itself with itself and the observation of its own emotional states, dreaming lyrical dreams, or it views itself as the antithesis of all that lies round it, as the tragic hero in a fight against gigantic odds, battling with the despicable breed of hostile and evil forces, either victorious or crushed ; there is no middle path such as the cyclothyme chooses. If the schizothyme writes stories, they are never objective, but lyrical through and through, exalted, like ' Hyperion ' or 'Heinrich von Ofterdingen', rich in emotion and feeling for nature, poor in humanity and action ; or else they are full of conflict, tragic or ironical, obsessed with problems, passionate indictments like those of Strindberg and Tolstoi, brutally naturalistic, or expressionistic and symbolic—something flung in one's face.

A tragic dramatist without striking schizothymic components in his personality is unthinkable. The important German dramatists after Schiller : Grillparzer, Hebbel, Kleist, Otto Ludwig, Grabbe, have these schizothymic traits in their characters to a very marked degree as the predominating factors ; in the cases of Grillparzer, Hebbel, Ludwig, and Grabbe, the physique also is quite unmistakable, and Kleist's odd, undifferentiated, almost hypoplastic childish face seems quite clearly to point in this direction. In Hebbel as in Kleist, and particularly clearly in Schiller, we find the attempt, which never quite comes off (except perhaps in ' Wallenstein ') to make use of the weaker realistic-humorous components of the constitution in order to increase the effect of the dramatic ' pathos '. In Schiller's sketches of and letters about Wallenstein this problem is clearly expressed in the consciously deliberative manner of the artist ; while in his later works he tended just as consciously towards the Graeco-French[1] construction, to purely schizothymic stylistic tragedies with a rigid elimination of anything of a realistic-humorous nature.

[1] It is well known that Schiller fought against the extreme tendencies of the French drama. But it was for the reason that he was psychologically in sympathy with this formal style. He struggled against a disposition which was very strong in himself.

This fundamental biologically-determined dilemma in the drama has never found a satisfactory solution. As soon as the cyclothymic, realistic, humorous element becomes the most important factor, as with Shakespeare, the construction of the tragedy threatens to break down into formlessness, while on the other hand, when it is completely eliminated after the manner of French high tragedy, the drama begins to rigidify into typical schizothymic schematism, a kind of emotional mathematics with stringent rules, types, and dialectical antitheses. A strong light is thrown on the complicated questions of æsthetics, when one can deal with them from a biological point of view. The humorous and the passionate are opposed constitutional elements, which cannot successfully be blended together. It is for this reason that in the drama of all cultivated peoples tragedy is far more successful than stylistic comedy, and that comedy remains only a modest offshoot of the main dramatic activity, however much it has been furthered by theorists of all ages as the noblest goal of poetic art, and however eagerly it has been sought after and demanded. It is because the cyclothyme has the humorous vein, but no sense of the dramatic, while the schizothyme has dramatic passion and feeling for form, but no humour.

Next to the 'pathetics' we have mentioned the romantics as the most important schizothymic type of literary style. Romanticism has for us a quite precise meaning, which is different from the ambiguous, vague, traditional reference of the word, or rather our meaning only includes what is fundamental in the other. The pathetic is the struggling autist. The romantic in our sense is the autist who flies without a struggle into a world of phantasy. Many things which are different from a literary point of view are now seen to have almost the same psychological significance. Hölderlin takes flight to the noble purity of classic Greek style, Tasso and Novalis to the mystical devotional darkness of the Christian Middle Ages, Rousseau to the bucolic tranquillity of imaginary nature, and imaginary primitive man, and others again to the free play of their phantasies in a fairy world. The one we call a classicist, the other a romantic, in the conventional sense, and the third a pastoralist or idyllist.[1] But if we compare the individual psychologies of the artists who make up these classes, then as far as their schizothymic aspect is concerned, they are as like one another as eggs. They are always tender hyper-æsthetics, of but little vitality, little resistance and driving power.

We have already analysed their psychic mechanism in earlier sections, the way in which they are constantly wounded and repelled by reality and their immediate surroundings, their sentimental taking refuge in an environment which will not harm them, and the hot-house-like blooming of an inner world of dreams and desires which is foreign to the truth. It is interesting from a characterological point of view to see how such pronounced schizothymic romantics as Novalis and Hölderlin worship the quite differently constituted schizothymic Schiller with sentimental reverence, while the strongly-alloyed, constitutionally ambiguous personalities of the Tieck-Schlegel group have a decided preference again for synthetic, complicated natures like Goethe and Shakespeare.

And in ordinary usage the word ' romantic ' has another meaning, which we must not omit. It signifies the attraction for everything ' folk ', for simple folk-tunes, primitive customs, and all that belongs to the past. At this point again there is a bridge leading to the cyclothymic side, to the sensuously concrete, simple, empirical and realistic. This aspect has already been indicated in romantics who are preponderatingly schizothymic, like Uhland and Eichendorff. In the kindred temperaments of Mörike and Moritz Schwind (and to a great extent Justinus Kerner) we find a peculiarly favourable compromise between sensitive phantasy, and folk-tale humour. In all these there is evidence of pyknic components in the physique. This diathetic-psychæsthetic compound is far more satisfactorily welded together in the fairy atmosphere

[1] A broad bridge leads from the idyllism of the schizothymic order to a kind of idyllic poetic style with a strong cyclothymic colouring— a style in connection with which we mention the names of Gessner, Mörike, Stifter. Gessner was physically a pronounced pyknic, and both the others have marked pyknic features. In this type the close connection with the cyclothymic temperament is betrayed either by the broadly realistic miniature-painting (Stifter) or, as in the case of Gessner, by the kindly, bright, sensuous placidity.

PLATE 29

ALEXANDER VON HUMBOLDT
Engraving by F. Bolt after F. Krüger
(Cf. also the engraving by Meyer in Klencke, *A. V. Humboldts Leben*, Leipzig, 1876)

[*face p.* 236

PLATE 30

JOHN LOCKE
Engraving by Dean, after the painting by Kneller
(From *Works of J. Locke*, London, 1824)

of Schwind and Mörike, than in the combination of humour
and tragic pathos, which is always a brittle structure, apart
from a few happy exceptions.

So much for the emotional colouring. Now as to the
schizothymic artistic form, the style hovers, as we have
already said in general, between two polar opposites : the
most refined, subtle feeling for style and the most rigid
formalism on the one hand, and completely indifferent
carelessness, Bohemian slovenliness, even deliberate, grat-
ing ugliness, and a cynical trampling on and rending of
all sense of form and grace, on the other. Or else it
oscillates between affected pomposity and sudden taste-
less abandonment of all attempt at style. If the cyclothyme
is more or less weak as far as form is concerned, the schizothyme is either a virtuoso in form, or else he falls into
crass formlessness. It is just the same as in the case of
their private lives, where the cyclothyme likes what is
pleasant and comfortable, while the pure schizothyme
often has no choice between the life of a knight and the
life of a tramp.

We need pay no closer attention here to schizothymic
formlessness. It has episodic outbreaks in little artistic
revolutions among the ' moderns ', as ' Sturm und Drang ',
as passionately individualistic, naturalistic, or expressionistic hostility to any form at all. It may manifest
itself as with Grabbe in ruinous collapse, or as with the
poet Lenz in a schizophrenic psychosis, or, again, as with
Schiller, it may remain a pubertial phase, a transition to
the sphere of aristocratic formalism. It is in the development of Schiller himself that we can see best how radical
hostility to form and classical worship of it may be
biologically connected, as phases of the same personality,
and may develop one out of the other. The same developmental stages are observable in the evolution of Goethe
in his schizothymic aspect, from the ' Sturm und Drang '
phase to that of the pompous reserved *Geheimrat* and
the superb, pure classical style of the ' Iphigenia ' and
' Tasso ' period, only that with him the Sturm und Drang
period is very much modified by cyclothymic elements,
as is apparent in the style of " Götz v. Berlichingen ".
An excellent example from modern literature is Gerhard
Hauptmann : first crude naturalism, then, to everyone's

astonishment, fairy-tale romanticism of exquisitely beautiful poetic form. The opposite development, also, is not rare
among schizothymes : empty formalism at puberty, later
developing into an extreme hatred of form. The autobiographical works of Tolstoi are typical illustrations of
this change. In more pronounced degrees, it is usually
brought about by psychotic attacks, or their equivalents.
The youthful development of the typical cyclothyme contains no sharp contrasts which can be compared with this,
and even the manic-depressive alternation of mood only
produces, in artistic style, a moderate, undulating change
of atmosphere, because at the height of the depressive
phase, artistic production is immediately prevented by
melancholic inhibitions. The chronic ' Weltschmerz ' poet
is usually a hyperæsthetic schizoid ; at any rate he is never
a pure cyclothyme (Lenau).

In the dramatist the schizothymic artistic formalism
is shown in the strong systematic construction of a work
as a whole : in details, it manifests itself in the preference
for well-sounding verse, pure rhythms, and choice expressions. This tendency to formalism in language runs
through all the types, Schiller, Hölderlin, and Platen.
We have picked Platen out specially because he is an
almost perfect example of the hardening of schizothymic
formal beauty into cold, marble-like smoothness through
the lack of diathetic components. Goethe refers to this
defect of all cyclothymic emotional warmth, when he
says of Platen : " He was lacking in love. He loved his
readers and fellow-poets as little as himself."

Another manifestation of schizothymic formalism which
differs from Hölderlin's sonorous outpourings of broad
hymnic solemnity, is the style of Uhland, which lies in
the region between romanticism and the tragic pathos of
Schiller, and has developed a form which may also be
found among other schizothymes—a lyric which compresses a very strong emotional content into quite short,
transparent, smooth-running quatrains, which sound as
simple as a naïve little folk-song. This form is obviously
closely related to the gift which certain schizothymes have
for the epigrammatic, for pithy, polished, witty remarks,
and also to their scientific passion for effective condensation.

Of the average schizothymic poet it may be said that

his particular artistic gifts lie rather in the realm of acoustics, in the music of words, where they bear wonderful fruit, while the artistic strength of the cyclothyme lies in the sphere of vision, in the capacity for vivid description,[1] and in the graphic quality of their language. We never find this naïve visual objectivity among the pure schizothymes. And yet they may be very rich in picturesque expression. But either their expressions have been chosen with a certain logical consciousness, as with Schiller, or they are dreamily coloured, merging into one another with no fixed scenic objectivity, vaguely symbolic, and chosen for their sound, as with Hölderlin. These significant differences of style may easily be seen if one compares the two groups : Luther, Gottfried Keller, Fritz Reuter, and Schiller, Hölderlin, Platen.

With such as are less artistically gifted the schizothymic formalism may degenerate into toying " artiness ", or pedantic dryness, and everywhere we shall find logical reflexion intruding itself.

The Plastic Arts

In the plastic arts we observe here and there differences of style which are more or less analogous to those we noticed among the poets, only far vaguer, because of the technical education involved and the influence of artistic schools. We find much simple objectivity among pyknic cyclothymes like Hans Thoma, and a hearty, impetuous, zestful feeling for the living world in the pictures of Franz Hals, who was thick-set and " rather lusty of life " ; while on the other hand among the typical schizothymes we find the tendency to classical beauty of form, as with Feuerbach, and extreme tragic pathos, as with Michelangelo and Grünewald.[2]

[1] The combination of painter and poet among pronounced cyclothymic artists of the first order is remarkable : Goethe, G. Keller, Fr. Reuter, Wilhelm Busch.

[2] As far as their physique goes, the three last-named artists are distinctly schizothymic (the unfortunately not very well-authenticated self-portraits of Grünewald manifest an extreme angular profile). From the psychiatristic point of view the following is of interest : A brother of Feuerbach's father suffered from some incurable mental· disease in his youth (probably schizophrenia), and his father from hyperæsthetic nervous depression. Feuerbach himself suffered occasionally

Special mention need only be made of what is now called " expressionism ", a thoroughly schizothymic form of art, which agrees in all its fundamental tendencies with those artistic feelings which we find again exhibited in the pictures of highly-gifted mentally-diseased schizophrenes. From the æsthetic point of view the analogy conveys neither praise nor blame, merely a simple fact to which only the prejudiced would close their eyes. Psychologically the movement is of the greatest interest. What we call by the collective name of expressionism, has various psychological components, all of which, as we have seen, are typically schizothymic : 1. A tendency to extreme formalism, the cubist element. 2. A tendency to dramatic conflict, to the most extreme exploitation of the expressive powers of colour and gesture, even consciously verging on caricature. This is the essence of expressionism in the narrower sense of the word, the sense which brings out the close connection of our modern art movements with their patron of the Middle Ages, M. Grünewald. Something of this tendency is concealed in the greatest schizothymic masters throughout the history of Art, even behind styles which are outwardly quite different, behind the Renaissance forms of Michelangelo, as behind the gothic manner of Grünewald (it is only necessary to compare the closely-related expressions of tragic pathos in the gestures and contrasted movement of the representation of the Resurrection of Christ on Grünewald's Isenheimer Altar, and of Michelangelo's drawings). 3. An autistic component, a rebellious turning away from real forms, a refusal to draw things as they really are, even where the deviation from actuality is not strongly motivated by the expressionist requirements of formal or dramatic representation. 4. Finally a component which is based on a well - known schizophrene thought mechanism. This is the dream-component, the pronounced tendency towards displacement, condensation, and symbolism in the Freudian sense. Such mechanisms as for example the depiction of a number of obviously heterogeneous pictorial fragments on the

from persecution-mania. In Michelangelo, and still more clearly in his father, there are attacks of persecution-mania, which at any rate are closely related to the schizophrenic type. Hardly anything is known of Grünewald's life, only that in later life he became a melancholic eccentric, which points in the schizoid direction.

same piece of canvas (a peasant's face which represents an agricultural landscape at the same time, etc.) are very common in modern expressionist works of art.

Suitable points of vantage are lacking for the analysis of the corresponding types of temperament in music, because the well-known great composers usually had complex biological bases, and only a musical specialist could collect sufficient material about the less important figures.

Scholars

The scholars, as we shall see to be the case with men who have devoted their lives to activity, have usually left far less objective material which is of use from the point of view of individual psychology than the poets, and can therefore be dealt with briefly, inasmuch as many points which are already well known to us are again illustrated in them. And also, apart from the few men at the top of the tree, there is a great dearth of easily-obtainable pictures, and especially of biographic material which has been compiled with reference to individual psychological factors ; what does exist is made up rather of enumerations of what they have done and their controversies, or else of panegyrical fragments put together for popular edification.

It is interesting to notice how the physical type of the scholar has shifted on the average during the last century. In the old days, theology, philosophy, and law in particular, were dominated by long, narrow, sharply-cut features, by figures like Erasmus, Melanchthon, Spinoza, and Kant, while now, since the beginning of the nineteenth century the pyknic type of figure has got the upper hand, particularly in science. A comparative glance at large collections of portraits will give a rough scale. For example, I have looked through a representative collection of portrait engravings of 1802, theologians, philosophers, and lawyers, and out of approximately 60 pictures about 35 had schizothymic physiques, about 15 were very mixed and indefinite, and only about 9 were pyknics. In an illustrated medical lexicon containing famous doctors of the nineteenth century, under well-known names I found about

Q

68 pyknics, 39 mixed or indefinite, and 11 divided between the physiques corresponding to the schizothymic class.

However great the risk of error in such a summary examination must necessarily be, the differences are in favour of the schizothymic physique among the representatives of intellectual activity of earlier centuries, whose work was prevailingly abstract, metaphysical, and devoted to systematic reasoning, and on the other hand, of the pyknic physique among that group of scientists who are occupied in describing what they have observed ; and this distinction is so marked that we cannot pass it by in complete silence.

It is not easy to pick out good individual examples, particularly of the cyclothymic scholarly temperament, because the few great personalities are very complicated, while for the less important there is not enough biographic material. Modern empirical medicine was founded by three prevailingly pyknic figures : Boerhaave, Svieten, and Albrecht Haller. A typical pyknic of the same period is the versatile, active, well-travelled J. G. Gmelin, famous as a botanist and geographer, and, as a pioneer in Siberia, the forerunner of A. Humboldt. Among the famous scientists and doctors of more recent times, many are of the pyknic type, or have well-marked pyknic components ; for example we mention Gall, Darwin, Robert Mayer (circular psychoses), Werner Siemens (energetic practical man), Bunsen (sunny, humorous, active temperament), Pasteur, and Robert Koch.

One can give a fairly clear idea of the cyclothymic type of scholar, if one mentions the names of Albrecht Haller, Goethe, and Alexander Humboldt ; although in each case we must allow for the weaker schizothymic streaks in their constitutions. From a biological point of view we may mention that Haller suffered from abnormal obesity and passed through a melancholic attack of a circular nature about which there can be no dispute ; that Goethe was the son of a typically cyclothymic-pyknic mother, and was himself prone to slight periodic emotional disturbances and periodic corpulence ; and that A. Humboldt in the latter years of his life had a face of a pronounced pyknic shape, and a decidedly cyclothymic

PLATE 31

H. G. R. DE MIRABEAU

(From *Mirabeau's Letters*, London, 1832)

[*face p.* 242

PLATE 32

J. CALVIN

Late engraving

From the monograph by Prof. D. Benrath, " Calvin und das Genfer Reforma-
tionswerk " in Werkshagen's *Der Protestantismus,* which also contains
numerous other portraits of Calvin for comparison

personal temperament with very sociable, active, kind-hearted, lovable, humorous traits.

These scholars have the following characteristics in common : 1. The extraordinarily extensive nature of their investigations, ever spreading out into wider fields of inquiry, a versatility and fluid intellectual activity which stretches over almost all provinces of human knowledge, and yet has a strong artistic feeling for the general co-ordination of the whole. 2. The direction of their work throughout to empiricism and observation, the tendency to the collection of concrete elements of knowledge, and observable objects connected with natural history, and the piling up of masses of written data, the naïve joy in the senses, in the direct observation, and handling of the objects themselves. " He fingers too much," says Schiller of Goethe, a remark which is characteristic of both men. The sciences which they all three preferred are, significantly enough, ones which lend themselves to observation and description : botany, anatomy, and physiology, the theory of colour-vision, geology, and ethnology. 3. On the negative side, it is at any rate true of Goethe[1] and Humboldt that they had an instinctive dislike for all rigid systematization, all theoretical construction and metaphysics, for all philosophical and theological pronouncements which do not stand " firm with marrowy bones " on the floor of the earth, on the evidence of the senses. " You must trust your senses, and never let them perceive anything false " was Goethe's scientific motto to the end, while all the rest is the " unfathomable " to him, which may only be reverenced humbly and in ignorance. When Humboldt was an old man, he said even more decisively, with his light humorous composure, that he was not going to meddle with " the blue objects beyond the grave ". Goethe was only able to patronize Kant's philosophy *faute de mieux* and superficially, in spite of Schiller's efforts, while Humboldt with instinctive certainty turned his back on the philosopher Hegel, who stood then at the height of his fame.

This all-embracing, observant, empirical, active, collect-

[1] Goethe, however, varied in his taste, which is accounted for by the pronounced schizothymic streaks in his nature. At times he has a feeling for mysticism and metaphysics. It may be clearly observed how the two emotional tendencies conflict within him.

ing and describing, unsystematic kind of science, with its passion for this earth, seems to be that which lies nearest to the cyclothymic temperament, so far as we can judge under the material difficulties which we have mentioned. At any rate it is what we should expect from that type of temperament as we have got to know it among cyclothymic individuals in general, and as it is clearly manifest in the discursive, epic realism of the cyclothymic artist.

Side by side with this particular inquiring disposition there often comes to the fore among practical active cyclothymic scholars an inclination to the easy popularization of knowledge in the form of libraries of hand-books for the masses, essays, and popular lectures ; it is very clear in the case of Alexander Humboldt for example. It hangs together with the easy fluid mobility, alertness, verbal dexterity, and many-sided activity of the cyclothymic temperament. It is at once an advantage and a disadvantage, just as the cyclothymic habit of observant, collecting, empiricism is accompanied by a certain lack of concentration, system, and deep thinking. It lacks that very quality which the schizothymic Schiller regarded as the most important principle of work : bringing the greatest strength to bear on the smallest points.

When we pass over in the natural sciences from the observant descriptive side to the exact theoretical wing, the class of mathematical physicists, it seems to us that the more schizothymically coloured personalities both as regards physique and psychology become more numerous. There is no disputing that very pronounced schizothymics are to be found among mathematicians. Among the living there are many examples, as also among the great ones of the past. The following among the most famous mathematicians of history manifest among other things marked schizoid physical symptoms : Copernicus, Kepler, Leibnitz, Newton, and Faraday. Good examples of pyknics are very rare among them. Möbius says, on the basis of his careful investigations,[1] that the majority of mathematicians are nervous, that peculiar characters, and original eccentrics are common among them. Ampère very probably underwent an attack of schizophrenic

[1] P. J. Möbius, *Über die Anlage zur Mathematik*, Leipzig, Barth, 1907.

mental disturbance, and the obscure psychosis of Newton is most easily understood as a light schizophrenia occurring late in life. The psychoses of Cardanus and Pascal are described by Möbius as "hysterical". The elder Bolyai was a schizoid psychopath, and the younger fairly certainly suffered from some schizophrenic mental disease. Möbius draws attention to the rarity of a simultaneous propensity for medicine and mathematics, which exactly fits in with our own investigations; while, on the other hand, the combined gift for mathematics and philosophy is quite common.

This preponderance of schizothymes among philosophers, rigid systematists, and metaphysicians is significant. It points to the predominance of the "form-impulse" over the "stuff-impulse", the preference for rigid construction, for formalism, the taste for the intangible and unreal, all of which is analogous to what we have seen when dealing with the schizothymic poets. Here again we can differentiate two in many ways interpenetrating groups: 1. The accurate, clear logicians and system builders of the Kantian type, who correspond roughly to the stylistic formal artists and dramatists in poetry; and 2. the emotional, romantic metaphysicians like Schelling, who correspond to the romantic poets. In less distinguished theosophical minds this schizothymic mode of thought may attain, by virtue of katathymic mechanisms, a quite extraordinary degree of logical vagueness and eccentricity, which latter may sometimes be capricious, sometimes manifest itself in schematic constructions.

Both intellectual dispositions, in spite of their apparent differences, are closely related to one another. Even in the exact epistemological critics of the Kantian type, we find marked metaphysical leanings, a tendency to turn their gaze to "the starry heavens above", a seeking after *a priori*, supernatural, religio-moral postulates. While on the other hand the intellectual romantics, the least important and quite vague among them often in the most pronounced degree, have an unmistakable inclination to a constructive conceptual presentation of their ideas. Thus one is always being surprised by coming across the well-known "mystical corner" in the background of the emotional life of even the most accurate thinkers, a corner which one will seek for in vain in the exquisitely observant empiricists like Alexander Humboldt.

This connection between systematic exactitude and mystical unreality in thought is one of those things which one would never have guessed *a priori*, and which one gets to know by experience almost against one's will. The connection comes out far more clearly than in the case of healthy schizothymics, when one turns to the intellectual thought-structures of mentally-diseased schizophrenes, where a content which is *par excellence* irrational, *e.g.*, of a mystical religious nature, is constantly found to be written out in the most systematic form, as a tidy scheme of concepts, ciphers, numbers, and geometrical figures, with the greatest possible show of exactitude.

As regards the biological foundation, from among those important philosophers of whom we were able to obtain a sufficient number of good portraits and good biographical material, we have secured a series of excellent examples of the combination of schizothymic physique and private personality. The pyknics, on the other hand, are surprisingly rare ; among the 27 classical philosophers whom we have investigated up to the present, we have no good unmistakable example of the pyknic physique, and distinctive pyknic components are very much in the minority.[1] Kant, Spinoza, Jakobi, and M. Mendelssohn among others are pronounced asthenics. Spinoza also suffered from tuberculosis. Besides those named, other fine schizothymic faces and occasional athletic ones are found, *e.g.*, in Locke, Voltaire, Lotze, Schiller, Hegel (remarkably long middle-face), D. F. Strauss, Hamann, Herder, W. Humboldt, Fénélon, Hemsterhuis, and Kierkegaard. Fichte had pronounced schizothymic bodily symptoms (large nose), and such are also displayed in youthful portraits of Schleiermacher (tendency to angular profile, shortened egg-shaped face, asthenic physique) ; in both instances pyknic components seem to have made their appearance in later years, with parallel modifications in their individual psychology. Of the old humanists, Erasmus and Melanchthon have typical schizothymic physiques and characters. According to the portraits, which do not altogether agree

[1] In facial formation we have so far found pyknic traits most conspicuously in Rousseau, Schelling, and Schopenhauer.

with one another, and from verbal descriptive evidence, Schelling seems to have been physically mixed; psychically he was decidedly schizothymic; "too much character", very shy and irritable in his personal relations, altogether lacking in humour and gaiety, in conversation generally " in a kind of knot which is difficult to untie " ; he had abrupt alternations of mood, and an inclination to para-noiac attacks of the nature of complexes. A peculiar contrasting trait in his character is indicated by the fact that in earlier stages of his development he inclined to Goethe's attitude to nature, and had a leaning towards a critical, anti-romantic, " epicurean " view of life. It is quite possible that these characteristics, which rather hint at a cyclothymic component, run parallel to the pyknic strains in the physique. Kant, on the other hand, in his private personality, displays the schizothymic type of " world-hostile idealist " in its highest and purest form, with Spartan freedom from desires, childlike simplicity, and the most genuine idealistic morality.[1] Leibnitz, with his optimistic, polypragmatic nature, is both physically and psychically an excellent transitional type lying between the schizothymic and cyclothymic groups, but physically he was more of an asthenic.

In the private lives of schizothymic scholars we find in many quarters a tendency to speculative cloistered, thinking which turns its attention away from real life (Kant-Newton type), in others again, rather the heroic-fanatic side of the schizothymic nature (Fichte-Schelling type), in contradistinction to the conciliating, active, cyclothymic nature of the Humboldt-Goethe group, with its widely-travelled experience, and its capacity for delving sympathetically into the fullness and breadth of human life from all sides.

The suggestions we have here outlined with regard to the scholarly disposition must be received and looked into with great care, in consideration of the difficulties we have mentioned in collecting a sufficiently large amount of empirical material. They are certainly only to be applied to those with a pronounced congenital gift for research, while it must be remembered that with the

---

[1] Curiously contrasted with an occasional inclination for society, eating, and enjoyment.

average scholar, just as in the case of any profession, the fortuitous circumstances of the particular scientific interest then predominant, the education which has been received, and the general environment, are often more decisive factors in the choice of research and its direction than is the constitutional factor. For only a few men (and of course, this is true of other groups) are so one-sidedly schizothymically or cyclothymically disposed, that if they wish, and have good endowments, they cannot also do something requiring the opposite qualities of thought and feeling, if external conditions demand it. And only a few scientific fields of specialization are so one-sidedly dependent on either observation or accurate systematization that they cannot offer any attraction to the opposite type.

Leaders and Heroes

Both the cyclothymic and the schizothymic temperaments offer, when present in certain proportions, favourable bases for practical activity ; while in other proportions, e.g., cyclothymic melancholia, and, on the schizothymic side, pronounced degrees of hyperæsthesia and emotional lameness, advanced insensitivity, and " ragged " defective types, they are on the whole decided failures when they are placed in responsible posts which demand practical ability, and they may even actually do definite harm, after the manner of schizoid criminals suffering from " imperial obsession ".

We are only concerned here with the productive practical aspect of the temperaments as manifested in geniuses. On the cyclothymic side we find a number of advantageous qualities in the hypomanic temperament : cheerful animation, optimism, daring, a quick grasp of situations, a mobility, and a bubbling practical energy. In the moderate cyclothymic natures we have also : sound understanding of mankind, homeliness, practical instinct, kindliness, friendly conciliatory skill in the handling of men. On the other hand the pure cyclothymic is as a rule lacking in firmness of character, idealistic ardour, and tenacious, logical principles of action and method. The cyclothymic metal is, in itself, somewhat too soft. In great leaders of a prevailingly cyclothymic temperament, we always find, in so far as we have been able to get a general view, important schizothymic characteristics.

The following types of leaders of a cyclothymic nature' may be distinguished when we examine the few historical examples which are accessible by means of biography :

1. The bold whole-hogger and tough, simple, fighter.
2. The confident organizer on a grand scale.
3. The conciliatory diplomatist.

The last group stands in closer connection with the moderate cyclothymes, while the two first owe their personal energy in the main to their hypomanic components.

A wonderful example of a leader of genius who unites these two sides of the cyclothymic character in himself, is Mirabeau, the great leader in the first outbursts of the French Revolution. Physically he seems to have had a round short-limbed figure, full of temperament, flexible, soft, and mobile : a typical pyknic.

He possessed in equal perfection the élan of the daring whole-hogger, as well as the foresight and skill of the diplomat : he was a fiery spirit, full of oratorical force and brilliant perception, full of wit and self-confidence ; and with all this he was nevertheless always just and conciliatory ; a man of reckless life, a glutton, a gambler, and a debtor, with a past which would not have shamed any young gallant, he yet was as good-natured as a child, one who lived and let live, a friend to mankind who pressed a coin into the hand of every beggar. He was easy and indulgent with his inferiors, his homeliness could not be beaten in the obscurest corner of the provinces, and he took a delight in this quality of simplicity. He was a master of popular, moving oratory, he had sure control of the most heated debate, skilfully smoothing and guiding it in his delicate, politely-humorous manner ; in the dryest documents he would find a way to bring in some witty conceit or graceful turn of phrase. He was unscrupulous, and not of the purest morals, but through and through he was a great figure ; he was resolute, had a sound understanding of men, and was free from fanaticism and doctrine.

In recent German history we have often seen skilful diplomatists of a pyknic-cyclothymic constitution, sometimes warm-hearted, co-operative, working on a grand scale, active, tireless organizers like Friedrich Naumann, sometimes lovable, obliging, and adaptable like Prince Bülow, and sometimes naïvely self-confident, poly-pragmatic dilettantes.

As an example of the group of great organizers we mention the great engineer and inventor Werner Siemens, a superb character, with a sharply-curved nose, twinkling eyes, and a wide, full, pyknic-shaped countenance. He had a dominating nature, full of spirit, joy of life, and energy, he was untroubled, fresh, manly, and elastic ; a creator who was ever bringing forward new plans and ideas in overwhelming numbers, to the point almost of ruining himself ; he was one of the great modern masters of industry, of diabolically clever business daring, who, starting from home penniless, conquered the world in his " almost giddy flight " and stamped on the face of the earth gigantic undertakings in Russia and overseas. An abounding, fundamentally gay personality, a great optimist, genuine, proud, spirited, and altogether un-sentimental. As an example of a rather weaker edition of this type we have Bodelschwingh, well known as a psychotherapeutist and social organizer on a large scale, with a fundamentally optimistic, courageous, philanthropic, original, humorous nature. His constitution displays still more clearly the essential pyknic-hypomanic character-istics. Though we call men of this type " organizers ", the strong point of their organizing powers lies far more in their hypomanic love of initiative, in their power of laying foundations and overcoming difficulties, than in their capacity for systematic construction.

As representatives of the type of blunt heroes, whole-hoggers and fighters, we mention Blücher and Luther, though with regard to the complex personality of Luther, we can only throw light on an important part of his nature by allowing for his melancholic and schizothymic characteristics. Both display, with pronounced cyclo-thymic - hypomanic traits, a tendency to congenital emotional disturbances (and, in the case of Blücher, depressive psychoses), and, with Luther there is also a pyknic physique. But besides that there are well-defined schizothymic streaks in their constitutions : Blücher had an a-typical physique, and a mentally-diseased—probably schizophrenic—son ; in Luther the schizothymic characteristics are explained by the portraits and characterology of his parents, and pictures of himself when he was young (tendency to angular profile). These heterogeneous components explain in both the tenacity of will, and the indications of fanaticism.

Their type is lacking in the flexible, conciliatory quality of the one, and the talent for organization of the other, of the two last-named groups. Their greatness lies in their blazing fiery nature, which—in real hypomanic fashion —in its first onslaught sets on fire, tears down, tugs forward and sweeps together everything that lies in the path, while construction is left for others. The un-systematic emotional politics of Luther (Peasant War !) and the good-humoured obesity of the equally pyknic rulers who were on his side, stamp the beginning of the German Reformation, as far as its organization goes, with a cyclothymic character. Blücher and Luther were men of unparalleled homeliness. The masses loved both their heroic and their childlike qualities, their direct, noble, storminess, their boisterous passion and defiance, their moving, rough speech, their fidelity and their coarse-grained mother-wit.

The heroes of the schizothymic temperament are made quite differently. Their success rests in the main on the following aspects of schizothymic characterology : their tenacity and systematic logical minds, their freedom from desires, their Spartan toughness, and stoic powers of resistance against all difficulties, their coldness towards the fate of individual human beings on the one hand, and on the other, their delicate ethical sensitivity and fanatical integrity, especially the readiness of their ears to catch the sigh of the weak and oppressed, their hyper-æsthetic pity, disgust, and indignation in the presence of suffering and waste caused by disregard of moral laws, of epidemics of disease, cruelty to animals, and oppressed classes of human beings, and above all their tendency to idealism. The reverse side of these advantages is a certain love of the rigid and doctrinaire, a narrow one-sidedness and fanaticism, usually a lack of charity, of comfortable, natural, human tolerance, of the understanding of concrete situations and the peculiarities of individual strangers.

The following groups may be distinguished :

1. Pure idealists and moralists.

2. Despots and fanatics.

3. Cold calculators.

We will deal briefly with the last class as being the least important. In the diplomatic qualities of Prince Metternich, a man of a pronounced schizothymic countenance, many of these characteristics may be recognized. In Schiller's presentation of the general Wallenstein this foreseeing, unscrupulous, cold, calculating method of getting the better of men and situations comes out particularly clearly, in paradoxical combination with the mystical-metaphysical aspect of the schizothymic nature, a combination which is quite correct from a biological standpoint. A rather more passive, timid variant of such shifting, cold, diplomatic, emotionless tactics is, e.g., the behaviour of Erasmus in the conflicts of the Reformation. One may, for our purpose, compare his portrait by Holbein, which speaks volumes in anatomical build and psychic expression. Voltaire is a meagre, cunning, sarcastic little man : " Be virtuous " he writes to a friend, " Mentez, mentez ! Il faut mentir comme un diable, non pas timidement, non pas pour un temps, mais hardiment et toujours."

Inasmuch as the schizothymic class is full of antitheses, containing all the extremes, and only missing out the means, so we find abruptly set up against this cold, flexible, to a certain extent a-moral type, the high-minded passion and iron firmness of the pure idealists and moralists. The names of Kant, Schiller, and Rousseau will indicate this group.

What is peculiar about these natures is that although they did not play a part in practical life, and—with the exception of Schiller—were unsuited for it, yet they have brought about gigantic practical results, simply by means of the utterance of their ideas, undertakings which in magnitude and permanence far outweigh the historical performances of those practical calculators of whom we have spoken. The restless, timid hyperæsthetic Rousseau, a recluse, shy of the world, with a sensitive persecution-mania at his heart, from his forest retreat set the soul of the French people surging with ideas, which were the immediate factors in bringing about the great revolution. "Nature", "the Rights of Man", "the State Covenant". He gave the catchwords for which the time, already pregnant with action, was waiting.

The Kantian 'categorical imperative', and, indeed, the whole Kant-Schiller idealism is connected, though not quite so immediately, with the world-important events of the war of freedom, and it is even connected with the permanent development of a certain aspect of classical Prussianism.

The influences which these and other less important schizothymes have on their time is due to the rigidly exclusive nature of their emotions and logical formulations. They are not men who see everywhere more or less goodness and badness, who find practical possibilities and ways out. They see no possibilities, only sheer impossibility, deadlock, no compromise, the abrupt halt ! "So far and no further." They do not see ways, but only the one way, the one narrow way ! Either . . . or. This way to paradise, that way to hell. Hot hate is mingled with moving dreams and hopes ; the harsh caricatures of Schiller's early dramas, the Utopian idealism of Rousseau, the one categorical imperative, " Thou canst, then thou oughtest ! " So they draw the one line, which looks so straight and simple, crosswise through the whole of reality. So they coin the burning or cutting catchwords, the few strong phrases which go to the very bones and marrow of an imperfect, rotten, heavily-foreboding, fearful generation. They are the heroes for the great periods of upheaval, when there is no longer any use for realists, for ages when the impossible is the sole possibility.

The autistic mode of thought turns here—not to reality, for that is impossible—but to stirring up an effective ferment for the conversion of one historical reality into another. In certain acute historical situations such ferments are more effectually brought about by means

of autistic battle-cries, even of mediocre fanatics and
Utopians, than by all manner of practical political efforts
and deliberations. We may observe this ferment-pro-
ducing quality of the autistic intellect, of the one-sided,
rigorous, sharply and antithetically defined idea, in the
ethical doctrine of the great lonely thinker Kant, where it
masquerades in a dry scholarly style, with no dramatic
pathos, and no side-glance after its popular effect. Often
and often has such a harmless catchword from the quiet
study of a scholar resounded threateningly in the struggle
of everyday life, and the sudden explosive kindling of
the heavily-charged atmosphere of an age has had results
before which the instigator himself has recoiled horrified.

Herein lies the internal relation between the idealist
and the revolutionary, that quality which leads us on to
the schizothymic type of fanatic and despot. All the
elements of highly-strained moral idealism are to be found
in the members of the group, Savonarola, Calvin, and
Robespierre,[1] a rigidly uncompromising ethical attitude,
an autistic appropriation of and self-identification with
the idea of their age, a fanatical hatred for reality, for
beauty, for enjoyment, for all that seems to laugh, or
bloom, or bubble.

There is nothing left but pure, barren, religio-ethical
schematism—a world that has become virtuous through
pallid fear, hedged about with railings. Wherever anything shows itself which might in the slightest degree
encroach upon, cover up, or push aside the categorical
imperative, wherever any living thing sprouts, it is at
once nipped in the bud. And at the head of them all,
Robespierre. The bloodhound ? No, the disciple of
Rousseau and tender mother nature, the timid, gentle
sentimentalist—a pale virtuous ghost, a monstrous kind
of schoolmaster without any taste for monstrosity. He
is well up in the literature of the *contrat social*, his favourite
reading, and with pedantic exactitude he translates it into
reality. He has no idea what he is perpetrating. He goes
on lopping away with righteous integrity. He has no
idea of anything but—virtue and the ideal. He has no

[1] The student-union figure Karl Follen is an excellent parallel
from German revolutionary history. Cf. the monograph by R.
Pregizer, *Die politischen Ideen des Karl Follen*, Tübingen, 1912.
(" Beitr. 2. Parteigeschichte," No. 4.)

idea—that he is hurting anyone. And meanwhile he writes poems like Hölderlin, and is bathed in tears of emotion when he speaks. Unpretentious, bourgeois, respectable, modest, a gentle sympathetic companion, who fears nothing so much as a public ovation and the ladies.

There are few personalities in history who present such a classical example of schizothymic characteristics in their most bizarre contrasts as Robespierre : the most icy emotional coldness, together with overstrained emotions, heroic pathos, and idyllic sentimentalism ; the highest idealism and the greatest brutality, fanatical tenacity and sudden jibbing at decisions, the impression of close reserve side by side with the most open devotion to principles. Sulkiness, distrust, affectation, pedantry, and timidity are all found in certain degrees. A virtuous murderer, an inhuman product of humanity, " A fanatic of cold reflexion gone mad."

A singular idealist. Mirabeau, his cyclothymic antipode, said, shaking his head over him : " This man believes everything he says."

We find the same schizothymic triad : idealism, fanaticism, and despotism, in the greater and more far-seeing personality of Calvin. Robespierre moves like his ghostly caricature in another century. The idealistic-theocratic revolutionary leadership of Savonarola in Florence, Calvin in Geneva, and Robespierre in Paris have characteristics in common which are of great historical significance. And out of the cowl of Savonarola peers the angular profile,[1] a threatening indication of what lies behind.

The spasmodic creations of lesser schizothymic figures crumble after a short time, while the Calvinistic ecclesiastical structure has remained for centuries, having

[1] The following facts may be noted from a biological point of view : Calvin's face is of an extreme schizothymic form, as one may easily see from the historical portraits of him (haggard, very long face, abnormal length of the middle-face, long sharp nose, and, in many pictures, a hypoplastic under-jaw). Robespierre was the son of a consumptive mother, and a father who eventually became mentally diseased (depressive, with restless impulse to travel). He himself was slim, his face yellowish, pale, thin, with sharply-cut features and a sickly look, his forehead was low, and his nose jutted out from his face, free, and curved ; he suffered from tic-like shruggings of his shoulders, his laugh was like a grimace, and the movements of his body were stiff and mechanical.

gradually become more and more human, as a petrified monument of a great schizothymic soul : the soul of a born organizer, stern, cold, systematic, with a strict code of ethics, fanatical convictions, aggressive, impatient, pure in thought, pure in speech—without imagination, without smiles, without feeling, without humour, and devoid of any conciliatory quality. The sworn enemy of all diathetic emotions.

It is less well known that in four years Calvin condemned more than 50 people to death, and banished a still larger number, mostly on theological grounds. The cyclothymic Luther animadverts in this connection that " Hangmen would not make the best doctors of divinity."

And, finally, the schizothymic strength of character produces its masterpiece in the heroic tenacity of Frederick the Great.[1] The enlightened absolutism of the state which reflects his personality in every detail, is a masterpiece of schizothymic mechanism, based on a categorical sense of abstract duty, a Spartan simplicity and hardness, a rigid automatic obedience to command, monumental pedantry, and exact logical systematization, which the king himself tried to direct towards an ideal of reason and virtue of an abstract philosophical nature—which accounts for the fact that here and there in the strict judicial code we find evidences of despotic caprice starting up, and hundreds of indications of withering sarcasm. This schematic scaffolding of Frederick the Great's political theories is modified by the not insignificant realistic-humorous components of his nature, and so made practicable on a large scale. It is to this cyclothymic admixture that he owes the predicate " great ".

" An excessive amount of character," " a piece of granite," says Rawlins about Schelling.

Nobility of spirit, greatness of conception, tenacity

---

[1] The following biological facts are to be noticed : Old Fritz had a notoriously small thin body, with a classical angular face. Three of his grand-parents were Guelphs. In Frederick's nearest blood-relations and elsewhere, the house of Guelph provides us with a typical collection of pronouncedly schizoid eccentrics, with a few suspiciously schizophrenic psychoses scattered here and there ; this schizoid inheritance goes on manifesting itself until we reach the schizophrenic psychopath Ludwig II of Bavaria and his brother Otto. (Cf. Strohmayer and Sommer.)

in contrary fortunes, hardness, purity and integrity of
personality, heroism, such is the nature of great schizothymes. Such was Schiller. The incomplete and broken
he hurled without a second thought behind him. Away
with Bürger, away with Schlegel, away with everyone
who cannot live and die. One kick at the ink-spattering
of his age. And then ever purer, freer, and nobler :
Hercules. The apotheosis of the virtuous personality.
This alone remains : the ideal and the will. " He was
rocky," says Jean Paul, still somewhat frozen after his
visit, " he was rocky, and of iron determination, full of
precious stones, full of sharp, cutting powers—but without love." Goethe, however, when as an old man, he
thought back on his friend, repeated with solemnity :
" He was like Christ, and so ought every man to be." [1]

---

[1] The remark is a construct embodying the substance of various
sayings of the older Goethe.

R

CHAPTER XIV

THE THEORY OF TEMPERAMENTS

In the course of our inquiry the three expressions, " constitution, character, and temperament " have come to have the following meanings :

By ' constitution '[1] we understand the totality of all individual peculiarities which are referable to heredity, *i.e.*, which have a genetic basis.

We have only based our investigations on one class of constitutional factors, namely the mutual relations between physical structure, psychological disposition, and psychiatristic and internal morbidity. The notion of constitution is essentially psychophysical, and general-biological, and has to do with the interrelations of body and mind. The concept of character, however, is a purely psychological one.

By ' character ' we understand the totality of all possibilities of affective and voluntary reaction of any given individual, as they come out in the course of his development, that is to say what he inherits plus the following exogenous factors : bodily influences, psychic education, milieu, and experience.[2]

The expression ' character ' lays the accent on the affective side of the total personality, without, of course, the intelligence being separated from it at any point. The notion of ' character ' has a great deal in common with the notion of constitution, namely, such psychic qualities as are inherited ; it eliminates, however, the bodily correlates, which the notion of constitution includes, while on the other hand it includes exogenous factors, the results of education and environment in particular, as important elements, which are left out of

---

[1] We are here in fundamental agreement with the excellent differentiation of Kahn on the subject of " Constitution, biological-heredity, and Psychiatry." (*Zeitschr. f. d. ges. Neurol. u. Psychiatr.*, 45, 1920.)

[2] This is dealt with in greater detail in my book on *Sensational Influence-Obsessions*.

the notion of constitution.   Moreover, so far it has not been usual to include conditions of severe pathological mental disturbance under ' character '.

Outside this exactly defined sphere of reference one can use the expression ' character ' for the general structure of the personality, without laying any particular stress on the differences between constitutional factors and those which are exogenously developed.

And finally, the expression ' temperament ' has for us no well-defined meaning, but it is a heuristic notion the breadth of whose field of reference we have not yet determined, but which should be a landmark for an important fundamental differentiation in biological psychology.   Let us provisionally picture two main inter-acting systems :

1. The psychic apparatus, which is more or less what one calls the system of psychic reflex-arcs, that is to say the factors which, by means of a train of happenings which probably has some phylogenetic foundation, bring about the perceptual and imaginal digestion of psychic stimulation, from the moment of sense-impression to the effective motor impulse.   Their bodily correlates are the brain-centres and paths in inseparable combination with the sense organs and motor events, that is to say the ' sense-brain-motor apparatus '.

2. The temperament.   It is, as we know certainly from empirical observation, co-determinated by the chemistry of the blood, and the humours of the body. Its physical correlate is the brain-glandular apparatus. The temperament is that group of mental events which is correlated with the physical structure, probably through the secretions.   The temperament works in with the activity of the ' psychic apparatus ', providing feeling tone, inhibiting, and pushing forward.   The temperament, so far as our empirical investigations go, has a clear influence on the following psychic qualities : (1) On the psych-æsthesia, abnormal sensitivity or insensitivity to psychic stimulation ; (2) on the mood-colouring, the pleasure or pain colouring of the psychic content, particularly on the scale which lies between gay and sorrowful ; (3) on the psychic tempo, the acceleration or retardation of the psychic processes in general, as regards their particular

rhythm (tenaciously holding back, suddenly darting forward, inhibition, formation of complexes) ; (4) on the psychomotility ; on the general movement-tempo (mobile or comfortable) as well as on the special character of psychic - activity (lame, stiff, hasty, vigorous, smooth, rounded, etc.).

In addition it may be empirically established that the forces which influence all these factors play an important part in the determination of the types of perception and imagination, in what is called intelligence or mental disposition, as we have so often pointed out in the illustrative chapters, particularly regarding scholars and artists. As to the way in which temperamental influences and structural peculiarities of individual brains work in with one another, e.g., in what is called abstract and concrete thinking, optical and acoustic imagery, we cannot yet say. At any rate the possibility must be left open that the activities of internal secretions are spread over the anatomical structure of the brain as well as over the rest of the body, so that the question assumes an almost dizzy complexity. We shall therefore do well to sum up under the notion of temperament such psychic elements as experience teaches us to be particularly readily and frequently responsive to acute chemical influences of an exogenous (alcohol, morphine) as well as of an endocrine nature, that is to say affectivity and general psychic tempo.

The following details may be noticed with respect to the biological foundation of our notion of the temperaments : the brain is at least the effective organ for all such activities as have an influence on the temperament even in so far as they proceed from the chemistry of the blood. That direct action on the brain can cause modifications of the temperament of a most decisive order, is shown by observation of brain trauma. It is very necessary to underline this obvious circumstance, so that we shall not fall from the extremist brain-anatomy theory into a one-sided view about secretions, which is the fashionable danger of to-day. How far, besides this rôle of effective organ, the brain also has an active part in the conditions of such psychic qualities as the mood-colouring and general psychic tempo, we cannot as yet say for certain.   As regards the various sensory and psycho-motor function types, the types of perception and imagination, we shall not yet attempt any answer to the question : How much of these various types of psychic function is represented in the anatomical variations of the brain-apparatus, and how much depends on the modification of that apparatus by various chemical secretory influences ?   We shall, however, regard it as a step forward, that we have at least formulated the question.   The one-sided theory which would tend to reduce all psychic events to changes in the brain centres, will thereby be fundamentally modified.   And in any case it is no question that has been invented out of the blue in our leisure time, it has been forced upon us as we have proceeded with our empirical investigations in the course of this book.

And now for the internal secretions.   It is an empirical fact that the endocrine system has a fundamental influence on the mentality, and especially on the temperamental qualities, and it has been demonstrated with reference to the thyroid gland by the medical examination of cretinism, myxœdema, cachexia strumipriva, and exophthalmic goitre, and with reference to the genital glands by experiments in castration.

We now see again, in the great schizothymic and cyclothymic temperamental groups, the correlation between physique and temperament, that is to say, that very biological relation which also forces itself so much on our attention in gross glandular disturbances, when we observe the parallelism between psychic malformation and hypoplastic physique among cretins, and between abnormal length of the extremity bones and dislocation of the psychic temperament among people who have been castrated young and eunuchoids, phenomena, indeed, which can be seen occurring under fixed biological laws even among higher animals.   In hypophysis the influence on the bodily growth in the direction of acromegaly is particularly startling, and there can be no doubt that parallel influences on the temperament can be detected in acromegalics, only they are not yet sufficiently worked out clinically.   And to an even greater degree where there is a polyglandular syndrome can one observe the massive influence of glandular disturbance on the physique, on the growth of tissue, and also on the psychic functional capacity.

It is not a great step to the suggestion that the chief normal types of temperament, cyclothymes and schizothymes, are determined, with regard to their physical correlates, by similar parallel activity on the part of the secretions, by which we naturally do not mean merely the internal secretions in the narrow sense, but the whole chemistry of the blood, in so far as it is also conditioned to a very important degree, *e.g.*, by the great intestinal glands, and ultimately by every tissue of the body. We shall therefore, instead of the one-sided parallel : Brain and mind, put once and for all the other : soma and psyche—a way of looking at things which is being more and more adopted in clinical investigation.

To back up the secretional approach to the temperaments comes the following empirical material from the field of the endogenous psychoses as the extreme exaggeration of the normal types of temperament. In the first place there is the fact that in manic-depressive madness, and also in schizophrenia, the brain disturbances, in spite of careful examination, have not hitherto proved of importance ; indeed, in circulars the examinations actually had a negative result, and in so far as here and there brain conditions were found they can very well have been caused indirectly by secretional poisoning. For this reason the clinical attitude towards these psychoses leans more and more in the direction of a secretional explanation.

In the second place we have set out, as occurring in schizophrenia, a series of particular phenomena of physique, sexual impulse, and clinical developments (see Chapter VI), which taken all together are at any rate very deleterious to the generative glands—in which connection we must not think of any massive monosymptomatic disturbances of the generative glands, which are known not to involve schizophrenia, but we must rather picture a complex mal-functioning of the generative glands in combination with the whole endocrine apparatus and the brain. But for the present we must recommend caution, because we cannot arrive at any certain conclusions on the ground of our empirical material, and in particular we cannot go so far as to say that the generative glands must be involved in every case ; moreover it is quite conceivable that different endocrine-chemical combinations may have the same psychotic effect. Besides these numerous facts which lead us to suspect the influence of the generative glands, we also meet, in isolated instances, physical conditions which seem to point to massive polyglandular disturbances (see Chapter V). Such massive conditions are, however, very much in the minority, and they stand from a psychiatric point of view on the boundary-line where the more subtle schizophrenic symptomatology goes over into simple dysglandular weak-mindedness and gross idiocy. Among the circulars, on the other hand, somatic events which may be regarded as analogous to the activities of the endocrine glands in the narrower sense, have so far not been met with, but only clear connections with the general bodily condition, particularly with the weight of the body and the process of fat-metabolism. It is possible that here, on the assumption of secretional etiology, we have to do with other components of the blood-chemistry, such as, *e.g.*, the great intestinal glands, and not primarily with the endocrine glands in the narrower sense.

In this connection it is also significant that all the psychic effects of individual endocrine glands which we know up to the present are primarily operative in the psychæsthetic scale, while they are far less determinate in their diathetic action. Castration, for example, in the vast number of experiments which have been performed on domestic animals, has not an influence of an euphoric nature, so much as a very clear influence on the psychæsthetic conditions, in the direction of a certain phlegmatic dulling of the temperament. The psychic lives of eunuchoids have many qualities which are closely analogous to those of certain schizoid groups.[1] In the same way in gross thyroid disturbances in human beings —in cretinism and myxœdema—the psychæsthetic dulling is the most marked characteristic. And vice versa, abnormal production on the part of the thyroid gland in Basedow's disease produces an exquisite hyper-

[1] Cf. Fischer (Giessen), *loc. cit.*

æsthetic nervousness ; moreover the moods of puberty, which go with the decisive coming into play of the generative glands, and particularly the typical pubertial affective conditions, storminess and sentimentality, with their exclusive and exaggerated character, correspond qualitatively to definite schizothymic proportions.

Of course there is no lack of connections between the narrow endocrine system and the diathetic emotions (involution melancholia, Basedow's disease), but the latter are far less pervasive, and it is far harder to judge as to their direct correlations, because the more acute psych-æsthetic displacements are often secondarily accompanied by intense pleasure or pain sensations. But be that as it may.

In any case we can imagine provisionally that the temperament of a man, apart from the condition of his brain, is dependent on two great chemical hormone groups, of which the one corresponds to the diathetic, and the other to the psychæsthetic affective scale, or, more generally, the one corresponds to the cyclothymic type of temperament, and the other to the schizothymic. With the majority of average men these two groups of hormones are present in varying relations, while pronounced cyclothymes or schizothymes with their one-sided accentuation of one group of hormones, result either from isolated inherited variations, or some process of out-breeding in their family.

In the present incomplete state of our knowledge one must not lay any great weight on these theoretical suggestions. But it is necessary and profitable to think out such complicated theories in detail, and to make practical, if only provisionary, use of such conceptual possibilities as may be inferred from our knowledge up to date, because we can always retrace our steps. For every investigator is eventually driven to making some sort of hypothesis, however vague, about the way things hang together, and anyone who, as an empiricist, tried to get on without reflexion, will fall a victim to the grossest brain-mythology, as has, alas, been the case so often in past decades. For this reason we shall carefully avoid any one-sidedness or dogmatic assertion, and in our conception we shall always leave room for direct causal

factors of a cerebral nature acting on the temperament as
well as on the physique, even if according to the present
conditions of scientific research an explanation in terms
of secretions is altogether more plausible.

Far more important than the theory is the grasping
of the direct empirical results of our investigations, of
which we give a few of the more important in the following
table :

TABLE XV

THE TEMPERAMENTS

	Cyclothymes	Schizothymes
Psychæsthesia and mood.	Diathetic proportion : between raised (gay) and depressed (sad).	Psychæsthetic proportion : between hyperæsthetic (sensitive) and anæsthetic (cold).
Psychic tempo.	Wavy temperamental curve : between mobile and comfortable.	Jerky temperamental curve : between unstable and tenacious, alternative mode of thought and feeling.
Psychomotility.	Adequate to stimulus, rounded, natural, smooth.	Often inadequate to stimulus : restrained, lame, inhibited, stiff, etc.
Physical affinities.	Pyknic.	Asthenic, athletic, dysplastic, and their mixtures.

The temperaments, then, separate off into the two
great constitutional groups, the cyclothymes and the
schizothymes. Inside the two main groups there is a
further dual division, according as the cyclothymic temperament is habitually more on the gay or the sad side,
and according as the schizothymic temperament tends
towards the sensitive or the cold pole. An indefinite
number of individual temperamental shades emerge from
the psychæsthetic and diathetic proportions, i.e., from the
manner in which in the same type of temperament, the
polar opponents displace one another, overlay one another,
or relieve one another in alternation. Besides asking
about the proportions of any given temperament, we
must at the same time ask about its admixture, i.e.,
about the tone which the particular type of temperament
which dominates has got from inherited ingredients of
other types.

This wealth of shades is further enlarged by variations
in the psychic tempo. Here, at any rate as far as cyclo-

thymes are concerned, we have the empirical fact that the more gay are usually the more mobile, while those who belong to the moderate class with an inclination to depression, are usually more phlegmatic and slow. This we should expect from long clinical experience of the close connection between bright excitability, swift flights of ideas, and psychomotor facility, as manic symptoms, and in melancholic symptomatology the connection of depression with inhibition of thought and will. Among healthy cyclothymic temperaments also a certain mood-disposition usually goes with a certain psychic tempo, so that gayness and mobility are often bound up with the hypomanic type of temperament, and a tendency to depression and slowness with the melancholic type.

But on the other hand such fixed relations between psychæsthesia and definite psychic rhythms are not to be recognized in the schizothyme, so that with the tender hyperæsthetics we often find astonishing tenacity of feeling and will, and, vice versa, capricious instability in people of pronouncedly cold indolence. So that in the schizothymic circle we often meet with all four combinations : sensitive as well as cold tenacity, and jerky sensitivity as well as capricious indolence.

Individual differentiations of the schizothymic temperaments we have already described in detail. The hyperæsthetic qualities manifest themselves empirically chiefly as tender sensibility, sensitivity to nature and art, tact and taste in personal style, sentimental affection for certain individuals, hypersensitivity and vulnerability with regard to the daily irritations of life, and finally, in the coarsened types, and particularly in post-psychotics and their equivalents, we find it in the shape of violence working in combination with ' complexes '. The anæsthetic qualities of schizothymes are manifested in the form of cutting, active coldness, or passive insensitivity, as a canalization of interest into well-defined autistic directions, as indifference, or as unshakable equilibrium. Their jerkiness is now rather indolent instability, and now active caprice ; their tenacity takes on the most varied shapes : steely energy, stubborn wilfulness, pedantry, fanaticism, logical systematism in thought and action.

The variations of the diathetic temperament are far
fewer, if we leave out the strongly alloyed dispositions
(the querulous, the quarrelsome, the anxious, and the
dry hypochondriacs).   The hypomanic type, besides the
ordinary gay mood-disposition, is also manifested in
quick-tempered jollity.   It varies between the quickly
flaring-up fiery temperament, the energetic, sweeping and
practical, the ever multifariously occupied, and the equable,
sunny, and bright.

Cyclothymic psychomotility is distinguished by the
natural quality of reaction and bodily movement, which
is now quick, now slow, but (apart from severe pathological inhibitions) always rounded and adequate to the
stimulus.   While among schizothymes we often meet with
psychomotor peculiarities, particularly in the lack of
adequate direct connection between psychic stimulus and
motor reaction, in the form of aristocratic reserve, extreme
restraint, or affective-lameness, or finally occasionally
inhibited, stiff or timid motility.

In their complex attitudes and reactions to environment
the cyclothymics are in the main men with a tendency
to throw themselves into the world about them and the
present, of open, sociable, spirited, kind-hearted, and
' naturally-immediate ' natures, whether they seem at
one time more jolly, or at another cautious, phlegmatic,
and melancholic.   There emerges from them, among
others, the everyday type of energetic practical man,
and the sensual enjoyer of life.   Among the more gifted
members of the class, we find the broad expansive realists
and the good-natured, hearty humorists, when we come
to artistic style ; the type of observant, describing, and
fingering empiricist, and the man who wants to popularize
science for the laity, when we come to scientific mode of
thought ; and in practical life the well-meaning, understanding conciliator, the energetic organizer on a large
scale, and the tough, strong-minded whole-hogger.

The attitude towards life of the schizoid temperament,
on the other hand, has a tendency to autism, to a life
inside oneself, to the construction of a narrowly-defined
individual zone, of an inner world of dreams and principles
which is set up against things as they really are, to an
acute opposition of ' I ' and ' the world ', a tendency to

an indifferent or sensitive withdrawal from the mass of one's fellow-men, or a cold flitting about among them with regard to them and without *rapport* with them. Among them we find, in the first place, an enormous number of defective types, or sulky eccentrics, egoists, unstable idlers, and criminals ; among the socially valuable types we have the sensitive enthusiast, the world-hostile idealist, the simultaneously tender and cold, formal aristocrat. In art and poetry we find them as stylistically pure, formal artists and classicists, as romanticists fleeing the world, as sentimental idyllists, as tragic 'pathetics', and so on to the extremes of expressionism and pessimistic naturalism, and finally as witty ironists and sarcastics. In their scientific method of thought we find a preference for academic formalism or philosophical reflexion, for mystical metaphysics, and exact schematism. And, lastly, of the types which are suitable for active life, the schizothymes seem to produce in particular the tenacious energetics, the inflexible devotees of principle and logic, the masterful natures, the heroic moralists, the pure idealists, the fanatics and despots, and the diplomatic, supple, cold calculators.

Let us group these special dispositions, which have been dealt with in more detail in Chapter III, according to the group to which our investigations have shown them to belong biologically, into a table, but with the proviso that the table only includes the plus-variants of social value, and only the most important of these, so that it only contains a part of the total temperamental group.

TABLE XVI

SPECIAL DISPOSITIONS

	Cyclothymes	*Schizothymes*
Poets.	Realists. Humorists.	Pathetics. Romantics. Formalists.
Experimenters.	Observers. Describers. Empiricists.	Exact logicians. Systematists. Metaphysicians.
Leaders.	Tough whole-hoggers. Dashing organizers. Understanding conciliators.	Pure idealists. Despots and fanatics. Cold calculators.

Our task is concluded. If at many points we have only been able to give glimpses and suppositions, and not satisfactory conclusions, it is due to the size of the problem, which presses on indefinitely into the depths of biology and psychological science. Here and there, when the material was not sufficient for ultimate proof, we have had to sketch in suggestions between the facts of which we were certain. We did not do this in order to arrive at a premature conclusion, but to get co-operation, to offer a starting-point for possible trains of thought and investigations in the various sciences involved. Through such sympathetic correction and co-operation on the part of technical investigators many new points of view may be obtained not only for medical and anthropological purposes, but in particular for general psychology, and for the answering of certain æsthetic, literary, and historical questions. If we are successful in the application of this scientific and, more specifically, biological mode of thought to provinces of the psychic life which were hitherto foreign to it, and if on the other hand it is here made possible for clinicists and biologists to get a broad view over the questions of psychology from a well-grounded point of vantage, so that they can see problems which must hitherto have appeared too subjective, vague, and misty, then along these lines we shall have helped in the advance towards the firm synthetic articulation of the entire field of modern thought.

APPENDIX

ON RECENT CONTRIBUTIONS TO THE STUDY OF PHYSIQUE AND CHARACTER

By E. MILLER, M.A., M.R.C.S., L.R.C.P., D.P.M.

Psychiatrist, West End Hospital for Nervous Diseases

Author of *Types of Mind and Body*, etc.

THE study of temperamental differences goes to the very heart of the problem of Types, for inasmuch as physique is a function of psycho-physical inheritance, human reactions manifest in the normal and in the psycho-pathological can only be understood in terms of process, rather than in terms of bare structure. In dealing with Experimental Psychology in relation to Types, Kretschmer has linked his researches to those inquiries which have attempted to show how the reaction types are exhibited in various forms of psychological activity. The experimental study of Form and Colour appreciation, of Psychical Splitting and Perseveration has been pursued in various countries and some have regarded the peculiarities of reaction, noted in these processes, as indications of type distinction. Perseveration has in particular been studied by Stevenson and Pinard in this country on psychotic subjects, and some promising work has also been done by Vernon and Miss Kerr indicating that here, too, type distinctions emerge which may have some relationship with the Eidetic and Non-Eidetic subjects of Jaensch. The typology of this last observer has yielded considerable results with which complete agreement is hardly yet possible. In his most recent work Fricke, following in the Marburg school of Jaensch, has carried out experimental work on personality types and tissue function, he claims to have established a relationship between the direct electric current resistance of the skin and the Integrated and Disintegrated types of Jaensch.

While there are few who will accept his findings and march with him to what he calls the most fundamental processes of life, any research which attempts to establish psycho-somatic unity is to be welcomed, even if we are not prepared to agree that Jaensch has discovered in the " Integration " type the fundamental form of human existence. But German science, which at the moment is governed by political motives, is bound to seek the perfect type which they already know exists in the Nordic race. Many of these speculative conclusions from preliminary experimental work, must be accepted with reservation when so much special pleading is involved.

Since the last edition of Kretschmer's *Physique and Character* a considerable literature has grown up which has been concerned largely with statistical studies of the physical types, which had not up till then been carefully carried out with scrupulous accuracy. While there are variations in the index figures given by a large number of observers, the graphic representations published, for example, by Westphal and his co-workers, show that fairly clearly delineated types are thrown up, corresponding to the main clinical forms of Kretschmer's classification. Most recent researches have introduced a note of sobriety into the discussion, and some time ago Kolle, for example, gave a cold douche to earlier enthusiasm by his discovery not only of a large number of mixed types but of the existence of many cases with leptosomic physique who suffered from cyclothymia in one form or another.

The vast amount of statistical work and experiments with various indexes has shown how complex must be the processes which underlie the variations of physique, which are sometimes quite minor in character, but none the less, significant.

Regarded biologically, there seems to be a clear case for regarding certain morphological characters as more important than others. For example, it seems at first strange that the Cephalic index should be so little related to the major morphological bodily indexes, and this rather shows that inasmuch as the Cephalic index is a delineating mark of racial type, the factors making for clinical distinction in the Psychoses are connected with processes which are more plastic in nature than those making for race distinction. As far as the Psychoses are concerned, no race appears to possess an overwhelming number of Pyknic, Athletic and Leptosome forms, corresponding with the clinical types with which these have been associated.

Some races are on the whole given to a Pyknic physique

and others to an Athletic-Leptosome physique, but there are no satisfactory indications that Manic Depressive Psychosis and Schizophrenia predominate in these respective races. In fact, as will be noted in this edition, Kretschmer has so far failed to discover any correlation between race and his theory of types. The only reasonably constant racial index appears to be the Cephalic index, and the present writer has found in two racial groups no correlations whatsoever between the Cephalic index and the Kretschmer types estimated by Werthem and Hesketh's index.

That there is no racial factor involved is shown by the frequency of Dementia Præcox amongst Jewish types, and the high correlation in this race between Dementia Præcox and the Leptosome Physique. The Jewish type is morphologically most variable ; for example, the Cephalic index varies amongst Jews from the Brachy-cephalic Slavonic and Mid-European Jewish type to the relatively Dolicho-cephalic type found predominantly in the Hispano Jewish and the Arabic Jewish communities.

The general bodily index of the Jewish type seems to show no relationship to long or short headedness. It has long been observed that long-headed Jewish types occur most frequently in communities which are long-headed, and round-headed types amongst round-headed communities. The leptosomic physique is most usually found in Jewries all the world over, and my own figures show that in male and female cases the Morphological index of Werthem and Hesketh tends towards the Leptosomic value in both Manic Depressive and Dementia Præcox (schizophrenic) cases. Nor are the distinctions between Pyknic and Leptosomic forms so clearly marked off as in other racial groups. Yet there is no evidence to show that the Jews as a race are more mixed than the average population, say of middle Europe. Furthermore, I have noticed the frequency with which Jewish cases, particularly of the hospital type, starting off their clinical career with Manic Depressive characteristics, appear to change with the passage of years or to degenerate into Dementia with clear schizophrenic features. Other observers, too, have noticed how physique in chronic cases tends to change. The relentless endocrinic changes which develop with chronicity must surely be responsible for the dysplastic changes which supervene particularly in ageing psychotic women.

S

It is interesting to note that the tendency to schizophrenic-leptosomic constitution and to Manic Depressive Leptosomic constitution is most frequently found amongst Jewish types who have lived for generations a Ghetto life with its associated privations and persecutions. In the so-called emancipated groups the appearance of Athletic types is significant. This has been particularly so in Western Europe and in America. Anthropometrists who had opportunity for studying the recent settlers in Palestine have noted the appearance of Athletic Pyknic types in children and young adolescents.[1]

It was stated above that certain morphological features might be expected to show a closer association with certain clinical types than do others. For example, hand forms should reflect psychological endowment in many more ways than such morphological features as the trunk volume or ratios of diameters to one another. Furthermore, facial configurations, while betraying racial differences, have from time immemorial been regarded by physiognomists as the mirror of character. Kretschmer has not failed to recognize the fact, but there are still many characters of the face which should call for further investigation. At present, there is a certain tendency seen in all the work of Kretschmer's followers, to define morphological types in terms of indexes which are based upon ratios of length to breadth, of bodily diameters and lengths, and of the diameters and lengths of facial features. Whether the analysis of the human face will continue to reveal type distinctions on this basis remains to be seen, but the interest in the human face lies not only in its static quality but more in its dynamic qualities, in the play and mobility of muscles. Some of Kretschmer's followers have certainly been interested in the subject of motor responsiveness or motoricity. Ewald, Klages and others have described character in terms of certain psychological functions such as Retentiveness, Intra-Psychic Life, Impressionability, Rhythm, Dexterity or Motoricity and Impulse. Some of these functions should be capable of analysis in terms of physiological psychology, and in that respect these functions, or at least some of them, may be indirectly related to morphological endowment. These would yield, or rather reveal, the dynamic aspects of the organism which are crystallized out, as it were, in bodily form,

[1] The writer is publishing a statistical and clinical study of Psychosis amongst the Jews.

and inasmuch as such inquiries would be descriptive of differences in functional activity, they would serve the purpose of link concepts with psychological endowment, that is to say, with psychological and clinical types. To return to the difficulties or shortcomings inherent in the search for morphological indexes, it has been found that circumferential measurements, for example, are clinically very variable in individual cases, but they should not be entirely neglected because such variations, due to changes in body weight, and to the vagaries of endocrine balance which lead to changing distribution of fat, reflect metabolic peculiarities. Our knowledge of the endocrine glands demonstrates something of the psychophysics of personality. It would appear, therefore, desirable, if we are more accurately to describe the dynamics of physique, to consider the variations in index values in any given individual alongside the variations in the progress of a given psychosis. Many observers have noted, for example, how index values vary with age, a study that has not been sufficiently attended to. In addition, these variations are related to the oncoming of dysplastic changes.

Before leaving the subject of morphological indexes and their value in establishing the ultimate truth of the physical types which Kretschmer's researches have defined, it is necessary that all general body indexes should be subject to correlation with more specialized ratios, such as trunk lengths, body height ; arm length, body height ; shoulder breadth, pelvic breadth ; etc. These inter-correlations will determine whether the proportion of length to breadth is the true basis for morphological type distinction. This has, of course, been done very thoroughly in the work of Walter Plattner. Westphal and Strauss have attempted to show how a series of bodily indexes have a high degree of correspondence.

It has been generally found by most observers that dysplastic physical features occur almost exclusively in those with leptosomic physique, and with schizoid clinical features. As far as German observers are concerned, the reason for this has not been sufficiently emphasized. French and Italian students such as Pende and MacAuliffe, however, have stressed the importance of endocrine studies, and it is surely in this field that the whole subject of morphological types will be profitably explored. For, inasmuch as endocrine balance is the basis of temperament, insofar will the clinical types receive their most illuminating explanation. The fact that amongst the schizophrenic types dysplastic features are so frequently found, prompts the speculation that schizophrenia, as against cyclothymia, is the result of a much more fundamental degenerative process. Over and above these dysplastic characteristics are many somatic anomalies which Nolan Lewis has drawn attention to, such as poverty in the development of the walls of the blood vessels and in the dimensions of the heart. It has been shown from X-Ray Examination of the chest that many persons with leptosomic physique have what one might call leptosomic heart shapes. To sum up this topic, the Kretschmer classification opens up deeper layers of human morphology and prompts to research into the functions which underlie morphological distinctions.

While we owe so much to Kretschmer for his classification of the main physical and clinical types, we must not neglect those type distinctions which have been made clear to us by the study of the psycho-genesis of mental disorders. It is true that Manic Depressive Psychosis and Schizophrenia have clearly defined clinical boundaries, even admitting the existence of so-called mixed types. But it would be idle to neglect the psycho-analytic explanation of the development of the psychoses. Freud and his followers have laboured to show that the major psychoses are due to regressions to certain levels of pre-genital development of the Libido. In this account, one cannot enter into detailed analysis of the psycho-analytic point of view. But what is necessary to ask is, what determines the fixation of the Libido at these various levels of instinctual development and organization? Is it possible that the constitutional tendency towards degenerative growth in schizophrenia is responsible? It may well be that, inasmuch as schizophrenia tends statistically to emerge in full flower at adolescence, it is at this point of endocrine organization and stabilization that the leptosomic and dysplastic types are inadequate to face the demands of reality, and that in consequence, regression to the psycho-analytic fixation point tends to occur.

The fact that in psycho-analytic theory the regression point in Manic Depressive Psychosis is not at such a primitive level as is the Schizophrenic regression point, is in conformity with the comparative benign character of Manic Depressive

Psychosis. It is, however, very important, particularly with regard to Schizophrenia, that we should realize the various forms in which Schizophrenia appears. The classical form of Schizophrenia tends towards a considerable degree of mental degeneration, but there are other forms in which this degenerative character is. not nearly so marked. Most clinicians will agree, however, that it is amongst the dysplastic types that the most profound clinical disorders occur. The writer's experience has been that physical dilapidation and mental dilapidation appear to go hand in hand.

Kretschmer is inclined towards the belief that both the main types of psychosis appear in a larval form, as it were, in a pre-psychotic personality. That is to say, that in the general community, schizoid and cycloid characteristics can be detected. This is to some extent true of adult persons. The evenly balanced or syntonic person inclines towards a harmonious physique, whereas persons inclined to introversion, to solitariness and mysticall eanings, betray leptosomic characteristics in faceand physique. It might be supposed that, since schizophrenia is associated with profound constitutional anomalies, a so-called pre-psychotic character and physique should be recognizable in children. Ossipowa and Suscherewa in working amongst feeble-minded children have noticed that the Kretschmer typology holds good. In actual fact, however, few observers of psycho-neurotic children have been able to notice any clear indications of the three types of physique in children—although Schizoid characters are found in children with Asthenic Neuroses and Cycloid characters in children with Sthenic Neuroses, or, broadly speaking, Disorders of Behaviour.

The writer's own observations on Neurotic children have shown him that the Werthem Hesketh index when used does not disclose clearly marked physical types corresponding with the clinical features of cases.

In his interesting work on *Men of Genius* Kretschmer has found striking corroboration of his theory of types. But inasmuch as he has limited his observation to the broad characteristics of the careers of genius, he has not devoted much attention to the intimate peculiarities of Men of Genius in their choice of medium, and the various incentives and obstructions that have entered into their lives. He has not been sufficiently concerned with the deep psychical processes which act as determinants not only to the choice of vocation but to the intensity of the drive, and the devotion to a particular medium of expression and to special ways of expression. Most artists betray an almost obsessive interest in some subject matter and in the mode of using it. Michael Angelo, for example, is particularly preoccupied with muscular forms in attitudes of stress and strain. There is in his work a dynamic, rather than a static quality, which is peculiar to only certain kinds of Schizoid characters. On the other hand, a pyknic cyclothymic type such as William Blake, constructed a mystical vision in both poetry and art which would be called Schizoid in character. It is interesting to note that Kretschmer stresses the fact that, as far as European culture is concerned, Men of Genius have been born on the frontiers where physical types or racial types have intermingled. He brings out the fact that the musical genius of Germany has occurred where Alpine and Nordic mixture has taken place. He asserts, however, that military and political genius has flowered particularly amongst the purely Nordic peoples of Leptosomic physique. His theory does not take into account historical, social, or environmental factors which Lange-Eichbeaum regards as important factors in the recognition and production of so-called men of genius.

The latter writer is of the opinion that men of genius are talented "value carriers", and that genius is not an intrinsic quality of certain personalities. This observation is of great value, not only in the interpretation of culture, but in bringing home to us the importance of environmental factors in the production of reaction types. We therefore have to conclude from all the evidence that Kretschmer's classification is not only of great value in itself, but has given us indications for further researches into personality differences. For it is clear to us that, while constitution is the primary determinant of form and function, the vicissitudes of life are still responsible for those nuances which make for the most interesting differences between one personality and another.

INDEX